Doing Business
in the New China

Doing Business
in the New China

A Handbook and Guide

BIRGIT ZINZIUS

Westport, Connecticut
London

Library of Congress Cataloging-in-Publication Data

Zinzius, Birgit.
   Doing business in the new China : a handbook and guide / Birgit Zinzius.
      p.   cm.
   Includes bibliographical references and index.
   ISBN 0–275–98031–6 (alk. paper)
      1. Investments, Foreign—China—Handbooks, manuals, etc.   2. Corporations,
   Foreign—China—Management—Handbooks, manuals, etc.   3. Business
   enterprises—China—Handbooks, manuals, etc.   4. Corporate culture—China—Handbooks,
   manuals, etc.   5. China—Commerce—Handbooks, manuals, etc.   6. China—Economic
   conditions—2000—Handbooks, manuals, etc.   7. China—Social conditions—2000–.   I. Title.
   HG5784.Z56   2004
   330.951—dc22   2003057986

British Library Cataloguing in Publication Data is available.

Library of Congress Catalog Card Number: 2003057986
ISBN: 0–275–98031–6

First published in 2004

Praeger Publishers, 88 Post Road West, Westport, CT 06881
An imprint of Greenwood Publishing Group, Inc.
www.praeger.com

Printed in the United States of America

The paper used in this book complies with the
Permanent Paper Standard issued by the National
Information Standards Organization (Z39.48-1984).

10   9   8   7   6   5   4   3   2

Hun shui mo yu

Catching a Fish in Troubled Waters

Chinese Proverb

Contents

Figures and Tables   xi

Preface   xiii

1. Going China   1

   Unparalleled Economic Growth   2

      Development Without Parallels in the Global Economy   5
      Bright Future   5
      Development of the Hinterland   6
      Market Segmentation   7
      The Internet: Controlling Customers, Markets, and Minds   8
      Brands Make the Race   11
      Market Success: Not Only a Question of Money and Time   13
      Effort and Success Are Related   14

   China Business in the Twenty-First Century   16

      WTO Membership—a Two-Sided Decision   19
      China's IT Boom: Motor for Dramatic Change   23
      Broad Choice of Investment Opportunities   24
      Future Growth Markets: IT, Biotech, and Services   27
      China—the Export Giant   37

   China Business and Intercultural Communication   42

      Confucianism—More Than a Philosophy   42
      The Teachings of Confucius   42
      Confucianism and Economic Growth   43

Communication Plus Understanding   44
Different—but Not "a Book with Seven Seals"   46
Situation and Perspective—the Intercultural Aspect   48

To Do's and Taboos in China   50

Names and Forms of Salutation   50
Professional Titles and Positions   53
Leisure Titles: *Xiao* and *Lao*   54
Mr., Mrs., Ms., Miss   55
Greeting   55
Topics of Conversation   57
Language—Ignore Negatives   58
Body Language   61
Gifts   63

Ways of Negotiation   66

Bureaucracy   66
Hierarchy   66
Kaihui (Endless Meetings) and Negotiations   67
Discussion Styles   68
Prior to the Negotiations   71
The Contract   72
Recommendations for Contract Drafts   73
Negotiations   73
Protocol   75
Translator   76
The Christmas Strategy   76

2. The Chinese Company—Getting Started   83

Strategies to Access the Market   83

Special Strategies for a Particular Market   83
Costs and Benefits; Risk and Profit   86
What China Needs   88
Preventing the Investment Site from Becoming a Trap   89
Finding a Partner   92
Selecting a Site and a Partner   95
The Example of Smart Investors   97

Founding a Company   99

The Socioeconomic and Legal Background   99
The Way to Approval: A Marathon with Hurdles   103
Don't Overlook the Differences   105
Tips for Contacts with Local Authorities   106

Qualified Employees: Foundation for Success   106

Finding Employees—the Chinese Labor Market   106

Chinese Labor Costs   108
Chinese Industrial Law and Foreign Companies   110
The Calendar and Holidays   111
Management: Everything Chinese?   112
Integration of Expatriates   114
Overseas Chinese: The Best of Both Worlds?   115
The New Generation   118
The "Old Guard"   119

The Face: An Essential Concept   121

The Chinese Picture of Humankind   121
Keeping, Giving, and Losing Face   122
Personal and Social Face   124
Motivating Employees: Keeping and Giving Face   124
Western–Chinese Face Problems   126
Morals, Taboos, and Social Values   127

Money and Foreign Currency   129

Restructuring the Banking System   129
Financial and Monetary Policies   131

3. The Chinese Company—Keeping It Running   135

Management Problems—Preprogrammed?   135

Efficient Company Operation—Mission Impossible?   137
Pushing Productivity—Without Losing Face   138
Implementing Vision and Mission   140
Employee Education: Essential for Success   141
IT—Setting Up the Company Backbone   143
Quality Management and the New Chinese Standard   147

Legal Regulations   152

Trade Laws: Changing Jurisdiction   153
Intellectual Property Laws (TRIPS)   155
Taxes and Customs   157
Law and *Guanxi*   159
Financial Control Mechanisms   160

The Market and Marketing   164

Market Research in China   166
Value-Added Marketing: Think "Chinese," Act "Western" 167
Company Names in Chinese   172
Advertising in China   174
Chinese Branding and Marketing   176
Polite but Merciless—Competition in China   178
Problem Areas: Distribution and Logistics   179

A Better Understanding of the Chinese   180

    Increased Individualism—and a Higher Standard of
        Living   180
    Harmony, the Moral Code of the Chinese   181
    Guanxi—the Universal Lubricant   182
    Money Above Everything   184
    Managing in China—Learn from Experience   185

4. Cross-cultural Management   189

    China's History: Cultural Knowledge as a Management Tool   189

        First Contact with the West (Nineteenth Century)   190
        Opium Wars—Fighting for the Chinese Market   191
        Years of Chaos (1911–1949)   193
        Victory of the Communists (1949–1966)   193
        Great Proletarian Cultural Revolution (1966–1976)   194
        First Normalization   195
        Reforms and Opening to the West (since 1976)   195
        Massacre in the "Square of Heavenly Peace"   196
        The New China   196

    Education   197

    Leisure Time   200

    Chinese Food   202

    Banquets—Seating Arrangements—Toasts—Delegations   203

        Eating and Drinking   204
        A Chinese Banquet   205
        Table Manners   206
        Seating Arrangements   207

    Feng Shui   209

The Expatriate Package   213

Conclusion   217

Appendix 1: Recommended Web Sites   219

Appendix 2: Abbreviations   223

Recommended Readings   225

Index   227

Figures and Tables

Figure 1.1   Economic growth rates and gross domestic product
of China 1980 and projected through 2020   2

Figure 1.2   Annual and cumulated foreign direct investment in
China, 1983 to 2003   3

Figure 1.3   Percentage of U.S. imports by country, 1989 to 2004
(estimates)   22

Figure 1.4   Foreign investment in China by country of origin
and by sector, until 2002   25

Figure 2.1   Key parameters of doing business in the new China   85

Figure 4.1   Seating arrangements at Chinese dinner tables   208

Figure 5.1   Home based net salary approach for expatriate
salaries   215

Table 1.1   Worldwide telecommunications statistics,
September 2003   9

Table 2.1   Company forms for foreign investments in China
(foreign investment enterprises—FIEs)   102

Table 2.2   Characteristics of Western and Chinese mentality   113

Table 2.3   Ethnic overseas Chinese by country of residence,
2003   117

Table 3.1   Chinese and Western cultural values   169

Table 3.2   Ranking of Chinese industrial and consumer
             brands, 2003   177

Preface

Within three decades after the start of the economic reform in 1978, China has burst onto the world's economic stage with a force and speed that has never been seen before. It has become a pillar of the world economy, as some exemplary figures show: In 1978, China ranked number 32 in world economic trade; in 2003 it was already the fifth-largest trading nation, and the second-largest economy based on purchasing power parity; since 1980 China's economy has grown annually by more than seven percent, the highest growth period ever seen in history. China is the world's largest producer of more than one hundred product categories, such as cellular phones, cement, cotton apparels, motherboards, steel, televisions, and toys; a consumer base of more than four hundred million middle-class Chinese results in exploding domestic markets. These data exemplify the rapid growth that is changing China and, thus, the world economy. The development seems to be déjà vu of the Japanese, Korean, and Taiwanese economic miracles in the 1980s and 1990s, but on a far greater scale.

A major contributor to China's development is the inflow of foreign capital and technology. China is one of the world's largest recipients of foreign direct investment. Thousands of international companies are active in China, and hundreds of thousands of foreign managers and specialists work in joint ventures and foreign-owned enterprises. Westerners, however, must be adequately prepared for the challenges of doing business in the new China.

In this book, I provide a detailed picture of today's China as it actually is, based on fact and experience. It shows why going into the Chinese market is not only an important, but a success-oriented move. And it explains why one should not wait for political or humanitarian changes, which may not occur in the way that the West is expecting. This book does not confine itself only to the reasons for and ways of doing business in China. Based on fact, the chances as well as the risks of economic engagement in China are detailed.

It is a handbook for investors, managers, entrepreneurs, consultants, and specialists, who want to obtain in-depth and praxis-oriented information about the opportunities and risks of a professional or commercial engagement in China. Former President Bill Clinton stated during his presidency, "If China's economy continues to grow at a similar pace as it does today, it will become the largest economic nation of the twenty-first century." The West has a unique opportunity to be a part of this development.

More knowledge about China means more success in China. I wish this to all readers of my book!

Dr. Birgit Zinzius
Beijing, July 2004

CHAPTER 1

Going China

One investor feels compelled to follow customers and permanently intensify commercial relations with Chinese partners. Another simply wants to use the advantages of low labor costs. But the most frequent reason for "going China" is the conviction that it is important, even necessary, to be present in one of the world's most successful and promising economic growth regions—the gigantic Chinese market, a market that attracts not only large-scale enterprise but also midrange investors and entrepreneurs.

In a recent interview, 68 percent of midscale investors in China described the "attractivity of the market" as their primary investment motive. A second reason investors gave, was that China is a "starting point for the Southeast Asian markets." Almost 20 percent mentioned China's comparatively low wage costs. Whatever the motive, all China investors agree on one point: A successful opening up of the Chinese market presupposes their direct presence in China. Presence in China: a categorical imperative for successful business in China.

More than 465,000 foreign enterprises have followed that imperative. Together they employ more than 20 million Chinese people. In 2003 alone, over 41,000 foreign investment projects were approved in China, the majority coming from Asia. The major part of the international engagement in China has been related to heavy industry, such as construction, chemicals, electrical engineering, or automobile manufacturing. Since the mid-1990s, investment increased most strongly in chemicals, pharmaceuticals, services, and consumer products such as electronics, telecommunications, textiles, and toys. Also, medium-sized enterprises have increasingly committed themselves in China.

UNPARALLELED ECONOMIC GROWTH

China's economy is growing strongly, although not as dynamically as in the years prior to the 1998 Asian crisis. Since the start of Deng Xiaoping's reforms in 1978, more than 200 million Chinese have emerged from poverty—encouraged by his famous saying, "To get rich is glorious." That number equals almost the total American population at the beginning of the reforms in 1978, an impressive figure. China's economy grew annually by an average of 9 percent between 1978 and 2000. Already today the change from an agricultural to an industrial society can be seen clearly. The percentage of the country's total population who work in agriculture dropped from 71 percent in 1978 to less than 50 percent in 2000; by 2020, the State Development Planning Commission expects the percentage of agricultural workers to drop to 30 percent. Urbanization is expected to grow from 35 percent in 2000 to 50 percent in 2020.[1]

However, this enormous economic growth is not evenly distributed throughout China, as income levels vary significantly between rural and urban areas, as well as between different regions. In 2003, the nationwide yearly per capita income was US$1,090; it exceeded US$4,500 in Guangzhou and Shanghai, which is contrasted with a yearly income of from US$175 to US$350 in the western Chinese provinces. The World Bank predicts an annual income of US$13,500 for China in 2020.[2]

This continuing economic growth is often attributed to the historic trip Deng Xiaoping made in 1992 to the southern area of Shenzhen. The then 87-year-old statesman challenged local politicians to double their efforts to attract foreign capital. Deng's comments led to double-digit economic growth that lasted a decade. Foreign investment has led to immense

Figure 1.1
Economic Growth Rates and Gross Domestic Product of China 1980 and Projected through 2020

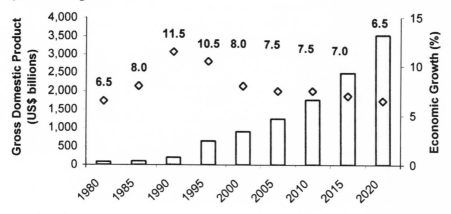

growth rates, especially between 1992 and 1994, when the economy grew by 14.2 percent, 13.5 percent and 12.7 percent respectively. The accumulated capital influx developed from US$5 billion in 1979 to more than US$500 billion in 2003 (see figure 1.2). In 2003, economic growth was 9.1 percent, and foreign direct investment US$53.5 billion, 1.4 percent growth— despite the SARS epidemic.[3]

It was Zhu Rongji, at that time head of the Chinese Central Bank, who in 1995 applied the breaks to slow the economy and prevent hyperinflation. Even then, growth slowed to "only" 10.5 percent in 1995, and continued at about 8 percent thereafter. The World Bank predicts average annual growth rates for the Chinese economy of about 6.6 percent until 2020.[4] These figures are more impressive considering China is the most populous country in the world.

How far can we trust the official statistics? Local bureaucrats are judged according to economic growth within their area of responsibility, how many jobs they create, and how much money is flowing into the country. The political imperative to achieve the plan figures is still in place. And since the Asian financial crisis, it seems that China's economic growth has never fallen below seven percent, a growth rate that is much higher than that of its neighbors.

It has to be mentioned, therefore, that official Chinese figures have been questioned in various quarters. Several Western economists and journalists claim, using catchy language such as "Why China Cooks the Books," that China's real economic growth is much less than official governmental figures imply. In 1998 and 1999, they say, China's economy receded at minus 2.2 percent and minus 2.5 percent, and in 2002, they estimate China grew at about 3 percent. A similar pattern exists for unemployment fig-

Figure 1.2
Annual and Cumulated Foreign Direct Investment in China, 1983 to 2003[5]

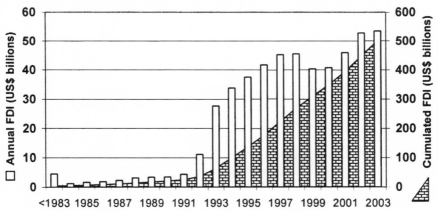

ures, which the critics see at 8.5 percent instead of the official 3.6 percent for 2002.[6] Increasing protests by newly laid off Chinese workers support such claims. The Statistical Bureau of China and especially its vice director, Qiu Xiaohua, vehemently rejects such claims and insists that China's figures are calculated based on international standards. This is done by increasing the number of private and third-party polls in order to reduce the incidence of political or governmental palliation. In 2003, some analysts even suggested that China was understating its economic growth figures, so that, in case of economic turmoil, it would still have hidden reserves.

Which data are correct? At what rate is China's economy really growing? One thing is for certain: In the last 30 years, China's economy has changed drastically—it has exploded. The average annual economic growth between 1978 and 2000 was 9 percent, higher than the record rates of South Korea or Taiwan. Yet China has a population 20 times that of both of those countries combined. Historical growth rates of European nations also look small by comparison. In the height of the industrial revolution between 1870 and 1913, the French economy grew by 2.4 percent annually, the German by 5.5 percent, and the United Kingdom's by 3.0 percent; only the United States had a higher annual economic growth rate of 10.1 percent.[7] China's economic growth rates are far higher, and no matter where they are exactly, they are unique in today's global society. However, they are also at a level which necessitates that China restructure its agricultural and industrial sectors, and put unemployed farmers and workers, laid off from unprofitable state owned enterprises, back to work.

The World Bank has acknowledged that China achieved in the past two decades what other countries needed centuries to do. China today is the third-largest economic nation and the second largest in Asia after Japan; based on purchasing power parity, an internal measure used by many analysts, China is already the second-largest economy. In 2020, presuming the World Bank's optimistic prediction is accurate and China's economy grows by 7 percent annually, China's portion of worldwide production output will increase from 1 percent in 1992 to 8 percent in 2020, and it will contribute 10 percent to the total worldwide trade, only surpassed by the United States.

Even if a multinational company, manufacturer, trading house, or service provider not yet present in China dismisses the opportunity to be in the largest market in the world, China will nonetheless be the most important market and definitely the most important production and export platform of the twenty-first century. China is furthermore the ideal springboard into Southeast and East Asia; with a population of more than three billion people, Asia is home to more than 50 percent of the world's people. In this way, China offers an ideal marketing stage for Asia, as in culture and mentality the Chinese are much closer to Asian customers than any-one could be in Europe or the United States.

Development Without Parallels in the Global Economy

According to statistics of the World Trade Organization, in 1978, China ranked 32nd among the world's trading powers; in 1997, it ranked 10th, and in 2003, it became 5th largest trading nation with growth rates of more than 35 percent. China's export volume has tripled since the beginning of the 1990s, and grown 40 times since 1978. Foreign-Chinese enterprises, mainly joint ventures, are strongly involved—they account for more than 40 percent of China's export business. Between 1978 and 1995, China's gross domestic product has quadrupled and continues to grow at more than 7 percent annually since, making it one of the main engines of the world economy.

Because of economic, especially financial crises in neighboring Asian countries, the Chinese government fears a deceleration of economic growth. It has therefore launched governmental programs and economic stimulus packages to maintain economic growth throughout the Asian crisis. A persistent or continuous slowdown of the Chinese economy is therefore currently not expected.

China's economy is in the fortunate situation of being much less dependent on exports than its Asian neighbors, particularly Japan. The Chinese domestic market has been and will remain the engine of economic growth. It is true that China pushes exports, but nevertheless essential future potential lies in the domestic Chinese market. The quantitative dimension of the consumer segment of the Chinese market is immense. Four hundred million wealthy Chinese are consumers with a high social status and, thus, making growing demands on product image, quality, and value. These status-oriented Chinese often purchase branded products to reflect social status.

It is certain: Those able to establish themselves in China, either now or during the coming years, will take part in a market development that is without precedent. Successful participation depends on correctly judging the market, being able to adapt to its peculiarities, and not being too easily disillusioned by the difficulties of doing business in China, which undoubtedly exist.

Bright Future

Expanding Chinese industry with capital goods manufactured in China promises a bright market in the future. With the development of infrastructure and growth in the housing market, as well as the buildup of industry, rapid growth can be predicted.

And the consumer market? Everything indicates that it will grow enormously in the coming years. Nevertheless, one should see the situation realistically and not be carried away by the population figures of 1.3 billion. Chinese consumers generated a retail sales volume of US$544 billion in 2003, growing by about 10 percent, compared to 2002.[8]

The Chinese market offers foreign investors a great deal. Nevertheless, it should be seen clearly that this market must not be skimmed off to the sole advantage of the investor. One must understand from the outset that "foreign enterprises" in China are Chinese enterprises and thus a part of the Chinese economy. That economy is developing visibly and becoming an export-oriented, globally active economy. One might be surprised about current developments. In 1978, total foreign trade volume was US$20 billion, and in 1998, it was already more than US$320 billion. In 2003, total foreign trade surpassed US$840 billion—US$410 billion imports and US$430 billion exports; the trade deficit with the United States reached US$124 billion.[9]

China increasingly exports engines and electronic products, finished goods and industrial parts. The export of low-tech products, which dominated in the past, is stagnating. This reflects strong technological orientation and rapid modernization. What does this mean for foreign investors? China is not only the fifth-largest market in the world, it is also a strong, progressive economy. One is not investing in a third-world country.

The Chinese expect investors, especially European and U.S., to bring with them technological know-how and the highest standards of quality. Those who want to go to China only to manufacture and sell low-cost products will rarely succeed; they will probably not be allowed to manufacture to begin with. It is true that the Chinese market offers a pleasant and enticing picture, particularly with a view to its development potential. The Chinese know this and are therefore demanding in their requirements of foreign investors. Important for the Chinese are their own expectations—they need useful and successful partners if they are to become global players.

It is important for China to become a global economic power following the United States, Europe, and Japan. Foreign companies operating in China must take this clearly into account: They must work and invest for China, in China.

Development of the Hinterland

It would be a mistake in investment strategy to regard China as a single, large, and rather uniform growth market comprising 1.3 billion consumers. One needs to examine the market potential carefully, considering the product or service, target customer, and consumer power. The purchasing power parity differences between rich and poor regions are significant. To successfully target the 1.3 billion-strong Chinese market, investors must extrapolate current market potential for "their product." Yet they must not overlook the long-term opportunities of the Chinese market.

More than 70 percent of the Chinese population, that is, more than 800 million people, live away from the economic centers in the "economic miracle hinterland." But this is where future potential for growth lies. China is set to drive development forward in these areas. It has approved massive investments in numerous infrastructure projects. The course for industrial growth has been set, and foreign investors are starting to become more engaged in the hinterland.

Currently, while most investment is in production, there is also investment in services, transport, communication, and civil projects. This creates workplaces and income and generates increased consumption, which in turn promotes the influx of investment. It is an upward spiral that is just starting to take off.

Market Segmentation

For marketing activities in the West, market segmentation means the crucial question of "Which customer group shall we target"? Is this also the key to the Chinese market?

Those offering consumer products and following the usual marketing consultations must look for their respective target customers in groups such as "average wage earners," "rich," or "superrich," depending on need and prices of products. It is clear that Chinese conditions must be applied to the standards for this customer segment of the society.

People with an annual income of more than US$5,000 are regarded as superrich. The rich are people with an annual income of between US$3,000 and US$5,000, whereas normal wage earners are not considered poor in the Chinese sense. They have an annual income of US$1,500. These groups are regarded as "solvent consumers." In 1995, approximately 15 percent of the population was accounted for under these groups. In 2003, almost 30 percent (i.e., 400 million people) emerged as rich due to their spending power.[10] This is a coarse and probably understated estimate, as it does not take the family-oriented Chinese social structure into account. It also excludes the earnings of grandparents and other members of the extended family. Such people must be included if we are to calculate the actual family income.

Those offering capital goods or services will find that their customers are the decision makers in state enterprises and the authorities. The way to this target group is as laborious as it is in the West, even longer and full of traps. Establishing and cementing relationships with contacts can shorten the time it takes to complete the deal. For the marketing of capital goods or corresponding services, careful attention to relationships is needed, as networking is a fundamental part of Chinese culture.

Another target group comprises candidates for investment services. Here the most influential network has to be found, providing access to the authoritative decision makers; in some cases they might only be contacted through this network. In addition, for Chinese partners, it is almost imperative that the offered products or services are excellent, including their technological features and cost-benefit ratio.

One must also take into account that many Chinese have additional income from second or even third jobs that is not taxed or statistically accounted for. To select target groups for consumer products according to income, therefore, is as problematic and statistically blurred as selecting them according to profession or place of residence. Naturally the super-rich and rich are to be found in cities or their surrounding areas rather than in the hinterland. Therefore, it is advisable to concentrate, for example, on a strategy of outdoor advertisements in the large cities and megacities, thus showing a strong presence.

However, that does not ensure effective targeting of all potential customer groups. With the exception of a few less-developed provinces, China is steeped in a consumer revolution that reaches all layers of the population. Everyone is trying to earn more. In short, there is one common theme among the Chinese population: making money. This makes target group determination difficult, especially with respect to income.

It would be risky in principle to segment the target groups for sales and marketing campaigns purely by age. That would lead to the younger generation being the main target group according to traditional Western principles. Old and young generations are very close in China. Youth has neither particular virtue nor privilege for the Chinese. Being old is no disgrace; rather, it is a distinction of high social value. All social layers share this opinion, including the youth. A strict targeting of young consumers, especially advertising that implies that the Chinese population consists mainly of teenagers and young adults will likely fail.

Are target group segmentations and segment-oriented product ranges that follow Western marketing practices advisable in China? Or are they ill advised? Should all Chinese be looked at as a distinct but unique target group? These questions shall remain unanswered for the time being, although they are important for foreign consumer products. They will be discussed in more detail in the section "The Market and Marketing" in chapter 3. One comment: Chinese and Western consumers are similar in ways that might render sociodemographic target group segmentations superfluous, such as an extremely distinctive brand orientation.

The Internet: Controlling Customers, Markets, and Minds

The Internet is denoted by *huo liang wang* in Chinese, which literally translates as "connect" "all others" "network." This is what is happening in China at present. Communications and media are increasing exponentially, and so is the volume of exchange of information. The following statistics about the Internet in Asia and China—compared to other regions—demonstrate this development. The Internet will influence or even change China in crucial areas as the number of Internet users increases exponentially. In addition, the use of mobile phones, PDAs, and even MP3 music players will influence China's modes of communication, even its culture.

Here are some figures about telecommunications and the Internet in China. In 2001, the United States had the largest number of mobile telephone users, 110 million. In 2003, China surpassed the United States and became the largest mobile phone market in the world with 238 million mobile subscribers—although this may include 50 million double counts of users with two or more cards; about 150,000 users are added every day. Figures for Internet use are similar. During his presidency, Bill Clinton predicted that China would have one million Internet users in 2000; in fact, it had more than 20 million.[11]

The Internet rating agency Nielsen/NetRatings announced in early 2003 that China had surpassed Japan in its number of Internet connections with 68 million (9.8 million broadband connections); Japan had only 59 million. Only the United States had more with 184 million. At present 54 percent of American households and 36 percent of Japanese households have Internet access; in China this figure is still less than 6 percent. It is assumed that by 2008, 300 million households in China will be connected to the Internet, and up to 50 percent will be connected via broadband cable. In 2002, a full page advertisement in the *New York Times* and the *Asian Wall Street Journal* proclaimed "Chinese to become the number 1 Web language by 2007," and the Chinese e-commerce market is expected to surpass US$110 billion by then.

The competitive market for Internet portals and Internet service providers (ISPs) has potential for enormous growth. Sina.com, Netease.com, and Sohu.com are the three major Chinese players; they compete against heavyweights such as Hotmail and Yahoo!. All three are listed on NASDAQ and offer a variety of services, such as mobile phone support and online

Table 1.1
Worldwide Telecommunications Statistics, September 2003

	Asia	China	Japan	Europe	U.S.
Fixed phone lines (millions)	403	236	74	269	192
Mobile phone lines (millions)	480	238	80	323	141
Internet connections (millions)	210	68	59	199	184
Inhabitants (millions)	3,590	1,312	128	723	292

Source: www.internetwoldstats.com; governmental sources. Arranged by B. Zinzius

games that have helped increase their market share to 54 percent. After years of losing money, Sohu had its first profitable year in 2003, with revenues of US$22 million, and a profit of 12.1 percent in the third quarter alone.[12] The Chinese model of Internet portals seems therefore to vary from that of the United States where mobile phone services don't bring additional revenue and profit. In China, ISPs can generate up to 45 percent of their income from mobile phone customers. This is an interesting example of how in many cases Western business models cannot be transferred to China. A failure in the West may be quite successful in the East, and vice versa. Even as the world becomes more globalized, local peculiarities in customer behavior, especially in China, will still prevail.

E-commerce will certainly play a dominant role in China. Despite the low acceptance rate for credit cards and the small number of credit cards in use, the purchase of products via the Internet is becoming more and more widespread in China. The payments are usually handled via cash-on-delivery (COD) systems, which are collected by mail courier. Business-to-business applications will also increase strongly, due to the drive to cut costs and reduce inter-company transactions. The government will play an important role in the how people in China use the Internet. Chinese authorities already try to control and regulate the Internet at different levels, as the following examples show.

- In recent years the Chinese government has tried to control the admission of Chinese Internet domain names. The Chinese Internet Network Information Center (CINIC) sees itself as the official organ in charge of assigning Chinese Internet domains (e.g., .cn). In 2001, CINIC accused VeriSign, the worldwide agency that controls Internet domain names, of infringing on the sovereignty of China. In 2003, the number of international sites in Chinese (e.g., .com.cn) nevertheless surpassed the number of Chinese sites.[13]

- The Ministry for Public Security has developed software to control certain information on the Internet. This includes sexual, violent, and religious content (for example the Falun Gong movement). All Internet communications from and to China and all Chinese Internet service providers are routed via eight state-owned and -controlled servers. Even nonlisted servers can be monitored. The editor of one Web site was sentenced to prison in 2001 after posting subversive information. In 2003, the government announced new efforts to monitor all users of the more than 110,000 Internet cafés. The Internet café technology management system will allow the collection of personal data on users, including sites visited.[14]

While on the one hand there are restrictions and controls on Internet use in China, on the other, the Chinese government sees the Internet as an essential engine for future business development. The government's tough stand on certain aspects of the Internet is contrasted by a very dynamic encouragement of its use. The government has started various large projects on the Internet. Their purpose ranges from fighting crime and smuggling to speeding up tax and customs payments. China has already started implementing its electronic government. The government supports the latest technologies, and it has issued various laws and decrees to spread the use of the Internet and its hardware and software components.

The at times ambivalent and pragmatic handling of the Internet by Chinese authorities reflects the general political situation in China. The prevailing conservative, Communist attitude that complete control must be exerted seems in stark contrast to the increased growth and focus on a market economy and consumerism. China is a country caught between two systems; an archaic, political system that is bent on staying in power and a new economic system driven by foreign investment and technology, and poised to make China the largest economy in the world.

Despite the tremendous growth of the Internet, the figures have to be looked at with some caution. The number of Chinese Internet users is very high, but this number is also influenced by household structure. More people live in a typical Chinese household than in the West. The number of business-related Internet connections is also important when determining growth rates for this sector. Therefore, figures for China cannot be directly compared with those of the West, and have to be analyzed based on the specific Chinese situation.

In any case, the development and rapid growth of communications technology, especially the Internet, in China will possibly change the country more than the resolutions of the twentieth century were able to. The social structure of the Chinese, built on Confucianism with its strict and patriarchal communication structures, is changing. For millennia, China had strict hierachical communication structures. Parents did not explain to their children the reasons for rules and regulations; they simply had to be obeyed. Emperors told the people what to do, and the Communistic Party simply distributed the plans that had to be adhered to. Bosses told their subordinates which jobs to do. All of this was done without giving reasons or explanations.

The dramatic economic changes that began in the 1980s have begun to break up the ancient communication structures. The use of the Internet, e-mail, mobile phones, and satellite television is changing old structures and patriarchal ways of communication. Communication in China is increasing exponentially and independent of one's status. Subordinates are questioning their bosses, and ideas and proposals are being discussed based on their innovation and merit and not because of the high rank of the person proposing them. Thus, China is becoming more mature and starting to exploit the real potential of its people.

Brands Make the Race

"No-name" products are bound to lose in China. Foreign and Chinese brands govern the market. Foreign brands even dominate some market segments, but that does not mean that they are imported products. They can well be products made in China under foreign brands. The detergent business, for example, is largely occupied by foreign brands of the enterprises Procter & Gamble and Henkel. The car and commercial vehicle market, which had annual growth rates of more than 40 percent between 2000 and 2003, is also dominated by foreign brands. In 1998, joint ventures of Volkswagen had reached a market share of almost 60 percent of the total car market. This market share has, however, fallen to 33 percent in 2004 due to strong competition. Most of these foreign brands, including VW, are produced by joint ventures with Chinese majority partners.[15]

Chinese brands, however, dominate the foreign competition in markets such as the electric and home appliance market. Market leaders for color television sets are the brands Changhong, TCL, and Konka. For refrigerators and other electric household appliances, Haier is the leading brand, possessing a market share of over 30 percent. The Chinese washing machine brands Little Swan, Rongshida, Haier, and Little Duck have a combined market share of almost 60 percent. Even these strong Chinese brand leaders must fight hard for their positions in the market. The competitive situation in the Chinese consumer market can be described as the "War of the Brands."

Purely Chinese enterprises are in competition with Chinese-foreign joint ventures, among themselves, and against foreign competitors. Chinese brands are advancing in all consumer areas. This fact is shown by the top positions Chinese brands occupy in various market sectors, which are generating billions of dollars in turnover. Further details are discussed later, but here are some examples of top domestic Chinese brands, some of which are also major suppliers for Western markets:

Television: TCL (TCL International Holdings), Changhong (Sichuan Changhong Electronic), Caihong (Caihong Electronic Group), and Konka (Konka Electronic Group).

Home appliances: Haier (Haier Group) Little Swan (BSW Household Appliances), and Rongshida (Rongshida Group Co. Ltd.).

Air conditioners: Chunlan (Jiangsu Chunlan Refrigerating Equipment) and MD (Guangdong MD Holdings).

Textiles: Erdos (Inner Mongolia Erdos Textiles).

Automobile: Chery (Shanghai Automobile Group), Hong Qi (First Automobile Works Group), and DFM (Dongfeng Automobile Group).

Motorcycles: Jialiing (China Jialiing Industrial Group).

Biotechnology/pharmaceuticals: 999 (Yanjin Enterprise), Tong Ren Tang (Beijing Tong Ren Tang), Tai Ji (Tai Ji Group), and NCPC Orchid (NCPC Orchid Pharmaceuticals Company).

Beer/alcohol/beverages: Tsingtao (Tsingtao Brewery), Yanjing (Beijing Yanjing Brewery), Gujing (Haozhou Gujing Brewery), Wahaha (Hongzhou Wahaha Group) and Apollo (Guangdong Apollo).

Computers: Lenovo (Legend Group).

Tobacco: Hongtashan (Yuxi Cigarette Factory) and Yunyan (Kunming Cigarette Factory).

The success of these and many other Chinese companies, including the "Chinese" brands of joint-venture companies, can be attributed to four major factors:

- Chinese consumers have become more quality conscious and safety oriented. Branded products offer far higher guarantees than no-name products, and the new Chinese safety mark—Chinese Compulsory Certificate (CCC)—will further increase quality and safety standards. China's consumers are putting reliable quality above price.

- Chinese buyers are rather status oriented. They would like to "keep face" (this Chinese concept is discussed later), including in their consumer behavior. Social adjustment is more important than self-willed individuality. Chinese tend to emulate others—brand names to them, ensure safety.

- The Chinese are increasingly less convinced about the superiority of imported foreign products. They believe in the equality or even superiority of Chinese-branded articles. There are still product areas where foreign brands are regarded as superior and of higher value. This is the case for cars, personal computers, mobile phones, perfumes, cosmetic items, and other luxury goods.

- Chinese companies have learned quickly how to reengineer, build-up and market brands. They use Western experience without emulating the West slavishly. They apply the West's brand policy under Chinese conditions and on Chinese consumers. It is time for foreign suppliers to say to themselves, "The Chinese have learned from us; we must now learn from them."

Market Success: Not Only a Question of Money and Time

Those going to China to make a profit with the least possible effort and investment and in the shortest time will certainly fail. One must be willing and able to invest money and time and be patient to achieve success and profit.

The market volume is smaller and there are more competitors than one might think. Labor costs are not as low as assumed. There is no guarantee of finding reliable partners and capable employees. Without building up and maintaining interpersonal relationships one will soon face problems. Concerning invested capital: It might take years until invested money generates a profit. And although all of this has nothing to do with market success, it is a precondition at least.

To attain market success, one must first establish oneself in China. Even if one's product appeals to consumers and is of excellent quality, it must still be offered and sold. A comment about advertisements: Advertisements alone, even the widespread and almost naively used television advertising, will not by itself create a lasting demand. Providing good service is also necessary; customer service is widely and very skillfully used as a promotional tool by private Chinese companies and state-owned enterprises, particularly those still operated by the army today. Advertising, primarily television advertising, is important but also quite expensive. Customer service is even more important and almost certainly more expensive. But those who want to achieve success cannot omit service excellence. Reaching the markets of China cannot be done by "selling cheap" and skimping on services.

Since distribution is also part of selling, one must reckon with special Chinese peculiarities as well as their problems. It is extremely difficult to build a regional, let alone a nationwide, distribution network in China. There are basically no large, supraregional chains of retail stores, but countless retail companies that are partly privately owned, partly under state or municipal control. This scattered distribution network requires complex logistics, which must cope with additional problems. China's traffic infrastructure has only improved to satisfactory levels in some provinces. Is it nevertheless worthwhile to invest in China, to commit oneself to China business? The answer is clear: It is worthwhile, not for everybody, but for many.

Effort and Success Are Related

Despite negative reports, the consumer product market is in neither a stagnating nor a consolidating phase, nor even in a recession. Positive development is reflected by the continued economic growth (9.1 percent in 2003). The consumer retail sales grew by 10.3 percent, foreign trade by more than 35 percent. Forecasts and trends point toward further growth in income and spending power. This is most important because the real measure lies not in per capita income but in per household income and related data on spending power expressed in *purchasing power parity*.

Approximately four hundred million urban Chinese have a per-capita income of US$4,300, and an average household income of US$13,760; both figures are expressed as *purchasing power parity*.[16] The spending power of these households corresponds directly to a yearly per-household income in the United States of US$42,400. Four hundred million Chinese in about one hundred million households with more than one-third of the American spending power: this exceeds many markets the world can offer!

A crisis-safe market sector with enormous sales potential is pharmaceuticals. Chinese spend enormous effort and large amounts of money on their health and to prolong life. Currently almost 2,000 joint-venture enterprises produce Western pharmaceuticals in China. This market is steadily rising with a turnover of US$11.5 billion for the year 2003 and over US$14 billion are expected for 2005, and US$24 billion for 2010.[17] A large part of the turnover is achieved from products produced in China. The sales volume for Chinese pharmaceutical products was about US$8 billion in 2003, accounting for 70 percent of the market. The annual growth rate for 2002 was 15 percent, and is estimated at 6 to 8 percent for the next 10 years. Growth everywhere! Here are further significant examples (figures are in U.S. dollars):

Chemical industry: In 2003, more than 21,000 chemical companies were active in the Chinese market. The market size is estimated at $32.5 billion, estimated annual growth rate for future years: 8 to 9 percent. The polymer sector grows by more than 15 percent annually, and China will be the world's largest manufacturer by 2012. Overcapacity is, however, threatening profits.

Building and construction: 22,000 related companies employ 53 million people in this sector. Market size in 2003 was more than $400 billion, estimated annual growth rate beyond the year 2008: 8 to 9 percent.

Textile: Market size in 2003 was $144 billion, 18 percent up against 2002. Without international trade restrictions, China's textile market may grow to $250 billion as early as 2008, representing 50 percent of the world clothing and textile exports (2000: 21.6 percent world market share).

Environment protection: Market size $6.6 billion, 15 percent growth (2001). The industry is expected to reach $24 billion by 2005.

Communication equipment: Market size $35 billion, −1.5 percent growth (2002). Unit growth is estimated at 10 to 15 percent per annum.

Logistics: Market size $230 billion, growth rates are above 20 percent (2002). Logistic accounts for 20 percent of the Chinese GDP.

Retail business: Market size $544 billion, 10 percent growth (2003).

Investment in construction in all segments such as power plants, railroads, roads, bridges, waterways and airports, is reflected in governmental figures: In the Tenth Five-Year Plan, between 2001 and 2005, the People's Republic of China continued to invest gigantic sums of money in infrastructure, especially in the western provinces. This includes $60 billion in the energy sector; $42 billion for the expansion of the railroad network; $120 billion for the expansion and new construction of roads; $4 billion for bridges, and so on.[18]

Of the required capital, 8.5 percent is coming from foreign sources.[19] Whether the government will completely be able to realize all of its plans is not certain. However, it is clear that a number of colossal projects are currently realized and that Western investors are involved via capital, via direct joint-ventures, or via wholly foreign-owned enterprises, of construction and engineering companies, and increasingly since China's accession to the WTO.

CHINA BUSINESS IN THE TWENTY-FIRST CENTURY

Since the collapse of the Chinese empire, the West predominantly believes that communist systems, and particularly a socialist, planned economy, cannot survive in the long term. Worldwide, the present and future belong to the free-market economy, which by definition requires a democratic, freedom-oriented, and basically liberal "social order."

It seems almost a paradox that the "capitalistic economy" has for years invested billions in Communist China. However, this is consistent with the capitalist principle of profit maximization: One cannot disregard a market like China, despite its communist political and social order! Being part of China's economic development therefore makes economic sense. What other reason would have induced foreign investors to invest more than US$500 billion in China since 1978?[20] Moreover, it is a common Western belief that investing in China can be deemed "politically correct." Investments help to widen the free-market economy and as soon as the roots of such a marketplace are seeded, nothing can hold back the development of more personal and political freedom.

It was more than 20 years ago that the People's Republic of China opened itself to foreign investors and the free-market economy of the West. At the same time, with the Sino-foreign investment law enacted in 1979, the PRC began allowing limited private property, including means of production. It also has allowed a profit-oriented, limited private trade. In the years since, China has experienced unprecedented economic growth and technological development and an unparalleled increase in national and individual wealth. This "Chinese economic miracle" definitely has certain capitalist aspects. Nevertheless, the question must be asked, "Can a China ruled by Communists be called a 'socialist people's republic?'" Or from a different perspective: "What can investors expect politically and socially in today's China?"

It is clear that China's Communism has not been "defeated" by capitalism, as was the case for communism in the Soviet Union. Communism in China has not only survived the opening toward a market economy, but even seems to have been strengthened by it! The Communist Party of China (CPC) is ruling and steering the country unchallenged, both politically and economically. The CPC has undoubtedly become more flexible ideologically and with respect to the exercise of power. For years now, concepts and phrases such as "dictatorship of the proletariat" or "world revolution" have been absent from the vocabulary of Chinese Communists.

The Chinese Communist ideology has changed to a Confucian pragmatism, a change that is so profound it is basically a change of the Communist paradigm. The CPC sees itself as the "guardian" of morality and order, the harmonizer of political and social forces. To fulfill these functions, the party utilizes a totalitarian bureaucratic system, which basically controls every area of life, especially the economy. The state exerts influence on the economy, influence that apply to state-owned as well as to private economic enterprises.

State control is carried out on three levels, namely the central, regional, and local levels. Directives are given from the top down that is from the central government in Beijing down to the city and village administrations. The central government and the Politburo, as the topmost party organs, are practically identical. Both decided in the 1980s that as a target the Chinese economy should be placed on a solid political basis, allowing a long-term, dynamic growth and considerable advances in living conditions for the population. Nevertheless, all of these changes should be done in the context of a *socialist market economy.*

This directive has led to the foundation of private Chinese enterprises, foreign enterprise, and joint ventures, which operate according to the principles of a free-market economy. One of the results of the directive was and still is, the reform of state-owned enterprises (SOEs) that are under the direct influence of central, regional, or local administrations. These were partially opened to foreign investors and partly restructured. State-owned enterprises, which comprise about 70 to 80 percent of all enterprises, were and are meant to become more competitive and more profitable.

It is nevertheless difficult to accomplish this goal for different reasons. The main reason is that until now most SOEs were virtually forced to work inefficiently. They were subject to administrative plans that forced them to operate in a plan-oriented manner, rather than in accordance with the economy. In addition, as a state-owned enterprise, the *danwei,* or work unit, acted not only as employer but also as the social support unit for its employees. This forced very costly and burdensome tasks upon the investing companies. In 2003, however, only about 20 percent of all Chinese depended on the *danwei* system.

The problems of the danweis are a major obstacle to the streamlining and restructuring of state-owned enterprises. However, freeing enterprises from their social responsibilities would bring about social problems for a large part of the Chinese population. After all, more than 60 percent of Chinese people are employed in SOEs and thus integrated into their respective danwei. That fact at least limits a rigorous privatization of SOEs, as private companies do not have comparable social obligations. Today, however, about 30 million private companies with approximately 70 million employees already generate more than half of the total economic output of China. These companies are largely responsible for the economic expansion, particularly in areas such as consumer goods and the service sector. Free of state orders and standard production plans, they produce and sell according to demand. And they do this in a manner that is as rational, efficient, and profit oriented as the domestic and export markets allow.

The economic reorganization of the SOE's and the large-scale urban migration demand a new type of social security network. In the 1980s, the government had introduced so-called *shequ*—community organizations— as a volunteer organization for social functions. Since the 1990s, with the diminishing importance of the danwei, new responsibilities in areas such as education, health, and unemployment, were given to shequ in selected districts throughout the country. The model is currently developing positively as a link between the local governments and their constituents, and may contribute to China's development of a civil society.

The success and profit-oriented operation also applies to the so-called autonomous collectives, the *township* and *village enterprises,* privatized small and medium-sized former state-enterprises, mostly in rural areas. Today, they are the property of communes as well as private capital investors. And this certainly applies to enterprises with foreign participation, the joint-venture enterprises.

Cooperation with foreign investors in joint ventures as well as direct foreign capital investment in state-owned enterprises are sure ways to restructure the country toward a *free-market economy.* This is a way steered by the state and thus in principle, a planned economy. Foreign companies looking for a local or regional joint-venture partner therefore have to decide in favor of the SOE. The "planned target" is the modernization and restructuring of the state economy!

In most cases, both cooperative partners have benefited or will be able to benefit, and as parts of a joint venture, both will no longer be subject to central government control. Joint ventures are free to plan production and sales and can decide on how to use their profits. Principally, this policy has been issued by the state, however, is not always and everywhere ensured. The decentralization of economic planning ordered by Beijing only partly handed economic responsibility to the enterprises, bringing economic planning closer to markets and consumers. This decentralization still occurs mainly within the administrative hierarchy and to the present the government has not managed to fully reform this hierarchy. Regional and local administrative organs, which are occupied almost 100 percent by Communist cadres, have taken over the controlling and planning functions.

State-owned enterprises are fully subject to this far-reaching dictation of the bureaucracy. This includes product, employment and financial matters. However, to a lesser degree, regional and local authorities also influence Chinese and foreign private economic enterprises. The bureaucracy keeps such enterprises dependent, for example, by exercising control over the granting of import or export licenses, the supply of raw materials and workers, financing, and so on. In addition, joint ventures and foreign corporations must submit their production and sales plans when applying for their approval at the respective authority. In almost all cases such applications are approved, although sometimes approval is granted more quickly than others. If bureaucratic influence is one of the characteristics of a socialist system, the market economy in China can be described as a *socialist market economy*. The Chinese themselves regard their system as a socialist market economy that is practically embedded in a politically and ideologically planned economy.

Those not paying close attention could well confuse the Chinese system with the Western *social market economy*. The differences are enormous. To explain briefly: In the Western *social market economy*, the state sets the economic boundary conditions, which carry social obligations without fundamentally limiting freedom. In the *socialist market economy*, it is an important aim of the state to subject the economy to medium or long-term planning. The political and economic transformation of China's society as a socialist market economy will continue in its Chinese way. It will make China one of the leading global economies. China will, however, remain a unique society different from the West—a society that requires a profound know how and distinct approaches for everyone active in China—investors, managers, consultants, politicians, technical specialists, or purchasers.

In October 2003, 25 years after the start of economic reforms, the Chinese Communist Party leaders set a timetable for the country to complete its economic reforms by 2010. The policies involve financial reforms, social security, and the money-losing state sector. Major issues are the amendment of the constitution to allow private business, and the protection of private property, which was a taboo-theme during the twentieth century. Communist Party Chief Hu Jintao has also introduced an annual report of the Politburo to the Central Committee. For the first time, such a democratic measure will allow people to hold politicians accountable.[21]

WTO Membership—a Two-Sided Decision

In Geneva on September 17, 2001, China was admitted to the World Trade Organization (WTO) after 15 years of difficult, sometimes combative negotiation. More important than the acceptance itself was the strong commitment of the Chinese government to continue the deep economic, legal, and administrative reforms already initiated. Entry into the WTO confirms China's basic agreement to respect international trade regulations and laws and to restructure its impenetrable and weblike administration.

What will membership in the WTO mean for China and Asia as a whole? Will it lead to the creation of new jobs or the closing down of more unprofitable companies? How will it affect China's unemployment? Will foreign investment increase or decrease? How will membership influence the political landscape? What will it mean for human rights?

Already today it is clear that economic and political change in China in the coming years will be difficult. Tough decisions will have to be made about large, rundown SOEs, which make up a large part of the Chinese economy. Deng Xiaoping described the problem as the contradiction between socialism and capitalism, which has to be solved. The result will be millions of newly unemployed farmers and workers. Unrest will increase, as is happening today in several provinces. The continued reduction of import restrictions will further increase the pressure on Chinese companies and the agricultural sector. In 1992, average import duties were 42.9 percent, in 2001 they were already down to 15 percent. With China's admission to the WTO, a further reduction to 9.4 percent is expected by 2005.[22] That will lead to increased imports and increased economic pressure on China.

On the other hand, many arguments allow a very optimistic outlook for China's economy. Low wages combined with government subsidies and benefits will attract additional foreign investment. The very large yet often untouched inner Chinese market is a further argument for why economic growth will continue. Already today about 400 million better-earning Chinese help China to equal or exceed the purchasing power parity of Europe or the United States. Trade barriers are being reduced, technological transfer is being enhanced, and the opportunities for foreign investment are continuously multiplying. In this regard, the West should be worried about Asian investors from Hong Kong, Taiwan, Japan, or South Korea walking off with the best and most attractive pieces. And the WTO-membership will provide a more competitive stage for private Chinese companies, as they will be able to compete better against ailing SOEs whose financial support has to be reduced as a condition of China's entry. Here are some examples of changes one can expect:

- China's share of the world's exports will increase from 4 percent in 2001 to 6.5 percent in 2005. Without admission to the WTO, China's share of the world's exports would be only 4.5 percent in 2005. The U.S. is the second-largest importer of Chinese goods, behind Asia.

- Average import duties were 15.3 percent 2001, 11 percent in 2003, and will decrease to 9.4 percent in 2005. In 1992 they were 42.9 percent. The import duties in Information Technology are especially targeted by the WTO, the current 13.3 percent (as of 2001) will be completely eliminated until 2005.[23]

- Massive reforms will decrease local trade barriers and create a legal framework for importers, local producers, and service providers. This will further increase the pressure on the rundown SOEs, but it also favors local entrepreneurs. Reforms have started in all relevant business sectors, especially in agriculture, banking, telecommunications, and the automobile industry.

- Foreign companies can increase their local shares to between 50 and 100 percent, depending on the sector. Foreign companies with 33 percent or more can trade their shares in the stock market.

- Foreign companies are allowed to set up a distribution system for their own products to improve their logistical processes. This includes maintenance, repair, stock management, and transportation.

A 2003 survey of foreign managers in Asia supports the mixed picture. Whereas 26 percent of all expatriates expected the situation to worsen, 55 percent saw the admission of China to the WTO as positive for the economy and the political situation in China as well as in the whole region. The growth of Chinese exports to the world and especially to Asia is already rapid and will continue as such. Since 2000, Chinese trade with the United States is also growing strongly, and in 2003 China became the largest exporter of products to the United States.

How do companies in Asia cope with this shift to China? For several years, Uniqlo has been a shooting star in the rundown Japanese textile industry, surpassing such companies as GAP in Japan. Uniqlo can offer its fashion products at reasonable prices as they are produced in China. There have been serious protests by several of its Japanese competitors but none of them is able to produce competitive products on an international level. Despite a strong local lobby, the Japanese government is not willing to increase import taxes on these Chinese-made garments, especially as Uniqlo is a Japanese company. Several other textile companies have already followed Uniqlo and are now producing their fabrics in China.

Japanese companies' products—made in China? That was unthinkable just several years ago. Where is the Japanese production efficiency, the highly praised automation, or *kaizen*? The example of Uniqlo is no exception; rather, it represents the tip of the iceberg and another step in Japan's steep recession. The best-selling book *Japan as Number One* has been replaced by a new title, *Arthritic Japan,* an indicator of the state of the Japanese economy and China's strong position as successor.

The table of contents of the April 2002 issue of the *Asian Wall Street Journal* contained the following: "Flight to China: Japan's Industry Fights Back." The journal detailed the economic situation in Japan, where a large number of companies are breaking the unwritten rules and shifting their production to China. This is especially the case in the automobile and telecommunications industries. Isuzu is producing its trucks in China; in 2002, Nissan acquired 30 percent of its Chinese joint-venture partner. Nissan aims to produce one million cars annually at Zhengzhou Nissan within three years. Other manufacturers such as Toyota, Suzuki, and Honda are looking for partners in China. Thus, the Japanese manufacturers are following the footsteps of Europeans, especially Volkswagen, who

Figure 1.3
Percentage of U.S. Imports by Country, 1989 to 2004 (estimates)

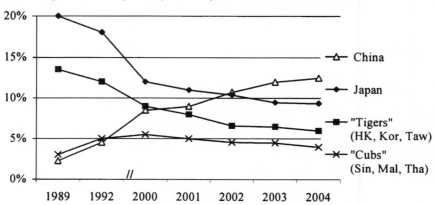

holds about 33 percent market share in the Chinese car passenger market. Nissan expanded its investment with Dongfeng Motor Corp. into a US$2 billion venture in November 2003.[24]

The Japanese producers, on the other side, have their strength in the compact car segment, where they can manufacture cars very efficiently. This is the reason companies such as Honda are able to earn three times as much profit per car sold in China, despite very low prices, when compared to the United States. United States manufacturers try to emulate the European and Japanese success. In 2002, General Motors invested US$1.5 billion in a new factory outside Shanghai and launched its first minicar, called Spark, in November 2003 with a retail value of about US$6,000.[25] Another example for international investors is Motorola, one of the largest telecommunication and chip manufacturers worldwide. Motorola has eliminated 40,000 jobs in Japan, while at the same time it has invested US$3.4 billion in China. This makes Motorola the largest foreign investor in China. But even Motorola has profitability problems in China because of the rapid price decrease of cellular phones. More than 50 percent of all large Japanese companies are currently indicating that they want to shift their production at least partially to China, despite the low local price level. More than 73 percent of them mentioned high Japanese manufacturing cost as the reason for this shift.[26]

China and the WTO—for the Chinese this will bring further dramatic changes in the economy, politics, and society. China's economic growth will within a few years make it the second-largest economy in the world, just behind the United States. And that development will bring more problems for China's neighbors than for China itself, as China's growing export business will be felt in all of Asia and beyond. "Made in China" will be seen worldwide—from Berlin to Bangkok and Boston, from Stockholm to Sydney and Seattle—in ever increasing quantities and strongly improved quality.

China's IT Boom: Motor for Dramatic Change

The politically driven economic development of China is one important driver of general change in the country. There is another factor that is changing the people and the economy: rapid development in the area of communication such as the Internet and communications technology and its influence on society. *Internet* was *the* term of the 1990s in Western as well as Asian nations. What will the Internet bring for China? To answer this question, first some statistics. In 2001, there were more than 22 million Internet connections in China, which had grown to 68 million in 2003. More than 120 million Chinese Internet users are predicted by the end of 2004. This would give China the highest number of Internet connections in the world. As of 2000, more than 100,000 domains were registered under *.cn* which grew to more than 300,000 in 2003. Chinese is supposed to be the most widely used language on the Internet in 2007.[27]

Electronic commerce—that is, business-to-business (B2B) and business-to-consumer (B2C) commerce will strongly gain in importance, and the role of B2B commerce will be more significant than it is in the West at present. The United Nations Conference on Trade and Development predicts that electronic commerce in China will grow from US$15.6 billion (B2B: 57 percent) in 2002 to US$98.8 billion (B2B: 77 percent) in 2006.[28] Current developments show that this may be even understated as online auctions in many business fields see Chinese competitors flooding the world's markets. The Chinese government sees e-commerce as a strategic pillar of the country's economic and social development. As then President Jiang Zemin mentioned during the opening of an international computer conference, "The melding of the traditional economy and information technology will provide the engine for the development of the economy and society in the 21st century. We should deeply recognize the tremendous power of information technology and vigorously promote its development."[29]

Jiang's words reflect not only the opinion of the Chinese government but also the state of the economy and society. China's government strongly supports development of the Internet and its use by the economy and society, although not uncontrolled. As in the West where the Internet has a strong influence on daily life, the Internet is beginning to change China and is growing exponentially. Under its growing influence, not only the economy but also Chinese society is changing. What had been unthinkable some years ago is now reality—free and seemingly uncontrolled communication via the Internet and mobile phones. Chinese communicate with Chinese, but also with the rest of the world. Information, news, services, and products—the Internet connects China with the world.

The world is becoming a global village, information is no longer a privilege but a commodity, and the problem is less one of how to get information than one of being selective. The phenomenon is changing China. China's economy, its political structures, its social system, even human rights will be influenced.

Change may not come as rapidly as the West might wish, especially in regard to human rights problems, abuses of the judicial system, and corruption. But China is on its way to becoming a member of the global village and thus there is increasing pressure for it to adhere to international standards.

With its 1.3 billion people, China has tremendous potential, and it is building up a very strong technology-based economy. Based on this background and the economic data of the past decade, it becomes obvious that China will play a pivotal role in the twenty-first century. China will be a central part of the global village and a dominating economy as well.

Broad Choice of Investment Opportunities

The amount foreigners have invested in China since the beginning of the 1980s is so immense, and the enterprises founded by those foreign investments so numerous, that one can basically speak of an unprecedented capital flood. However, as a flood is something irregular and potentially disastrous that might not be a good comparison. The investment boom in China is a side effect of a carefully planned and successfully proceeding economic reform strategy. The "investment flood" is planned and controlled; call it "canalized." China investors should be clear about that. From the viewpoint of the Chinese government, and thus the CPC, these investments have been and continue to be a means toward the realization of a planned process—that is, the development of the gigantic economic potential of the People's Republic of China! Potential China investors should and will bring both capital and know-how to a country that offers more efficient production and increased productivity.

Foreign investment is invited to and allowed to stay in China for three reasons:

- First, to help drive the financial recovery and to restructure and increase the efficiency of lame, inefficient, and loss-generating industrial state-owned enterprises.
- Second, to help drive export and thus bring in foreign currency.
- Third, to be a catalyst for technological development and a vehicle for the transfer of know-how from the West to the East.

Figure 1.4
Foreign Investment in China by Country of Origin and by Sector, until 2002

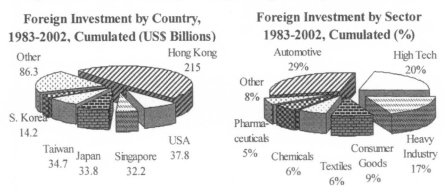

Foreign Investment by Country,
1983-2002, Cumulated (US$ Billions)

Other
86.3

Hong Kong
215

S. Korea
14.2

Taiwan
34.7

Japan
33.8

Singapore
32.2

USA
37.8

Foreign Investment by Sector
1983-2002, Cumulated (%)

Automotive
29%

High Tech
20%

Other
8%

Pharma-
ceuticals
5%

Chemicals
6%

Textiles
6%

Consumer
Goods
9%

Heavy
Industry
17%

Source: MOFCOM, China. Arranged by B. Zinzius

It might well be that Beijing does not intend to oversee a gradual, let alone complete, liberalization as the West is hoping for. Nor might the government intend to globalize the Chinese economy according to Western liberal capitalist standards. Certainly, however, the Chinese government plans to develop the economic potential and increase the productivity of the economy, especially in the sector of national and municipal SOEs.

This helps one understand China's efforts to restrict foreign investment to specific forms and steer them to certain economic sectors. China provides a framework for investors in which relatively free economic development can take place—geared toward effectiveness and efficiency. Foreign investment is not subject to regulations that direct operational decisions in accordance with certain plans. Investors are free to decide how to use their profits. They even participate in China's growth by earning profits.

There are several ways in which investors can access and be present in the Chinese market. The presence that affords the investor the least opportunity is called a *representative office*. A license for such an office is not attained easily. Usually it is assigned only for three years, and must be renewed annually. A representative office without a Chinese business partner is often subject to restrictions. For example, it cannot trade or invoice. Business activities are restricted to observing the market, establishing relationships, and initiating business.

Investment in *capital shares* of existing Chinese enterprises is a possibility for those interested in capital investment. This form of direct investment is promoted intensely by Chinese authorities because they hope for increased capital funding of state-owned enterprises. A prerequisite is the transformation of such operations or operation complexes into stock companies. This investment is possibly not yet of great importance. It is still the rule that the participation in an existing Chinese enterprise can only be in the form of a joint venture, not as an acquisition. The book later goes into detail about the conditions to be found in a joint-venture enterprise; therefore, only basic facts are listed here. For 20 years, the *equity joint venture* (EJV) has been the most common form of foreign capital investment in China. Equity joint ventures are mutual companies that can be compared to a limited liability company. At least one Chinese and one foreign partner contribute money, assets, or other resources to such a company. The company must have a clear strategy and goals, which have to be approved by the administration.

Besides the long-term partnership of a mutual enterprise that binds the invested capital, there is the option of contractual cooperation—that is, a cooperative enterprise described as a *contractual joint venture* (CJV). The legal framework for this venture is not as narrow as for the equity joint venture. A contractual joint venture does not necessarily have to be a legal entity. The organizational form is not stipulated as mandatory as it is for equity joint ventures. Foreign and Chinese contract partners cooperate toward the realization of exactly defined projects in a specific time frame.

Foreign Business Forms in China

- Trade or production via third parties
- Representative office (RO)
- Branch in restricted industries (banking, insurance)
- Foreign investment enterprise (FIE):
  - Contractual joint venture (CJV)
  - Equity joint venture (EJV)
  - Wholly foreign-owned enterprise (WFOE)

A general rule for joint ventures is that those investing in the founding, buildup, or expansion of an equity joint venture in China want to be present in the Chinese market. This means long-term binding of capital. Those investing in contractual joint ventures want to be involved in the realization of definite projects and in general do not want to commit themselves for the long term. In general, all joint ventures require a relatively large investment, close ties with Chinese partners of the government-run economy, and dependence on the reliability and competence of Chinese management.

Wholly foreign-owned enterprises (WFOEs) offer foreign investors less capital expenditure and more independence. These are 100-percent-foreign-owned companies. They are Chinese legal entities that are founded according to Chinese law. Admittance is granted only if the enterprise offers technical innovation and is willing and able to produce for export. Since the late 1990s, WFOEs are the preferred investment, and in 2003, about 60 percent of all foreign investments were WFOEs, although many investors maintain a second company form in order to have flexibility in the market. It has to be pointed out that often the authorities only reluctantly allow the foundation of a wholly foreign-owned enterprise. Admittance is often granted only under the condition that the local municipality or local "industrial area" can invest up to 10 percent in the foreign enterprise. This basically leads to the status of an equity joint venture.

Generally, foreign companies and their representative offices (RO), are not permitted trade—that is, to sell and purchase in China. However, a good market representation can be obtained by cooperating with an authorized Chinese trading company. In 1997, the Ministry of Internal Trade (MIT) issued the first Chinese franchise law (Regulation on Commercial Franchise Business, November 14, 1997). Until August 2003, about 3,000 franchise rights have been granted, especially in the fast food and real estate sector. The law suffered, however, from numerous problems especially corruption by the administrating authorities. The State Council has therefore launched massive reforms, and a new law with simplified procedures and less government influence took effect in 2004. Franchises such as McDonald's, Kentucky Fried Chicken, Pizza Hut, and Starbucks have strong expectations for this business model in China's US$48 billion fast-food market, and hope to open hundreds of outlets every year.[30] Until 2003, most foreign companies manage their retail operations themselves with Chinese partners, often with different partners in different territories or cities. E-commerce is still fairly immature as regulations; efficient authentication systems, secure and reliable online systems, and efficient delivery chains do not exist. Moreover, the current battle about assigning Chinese domain names makes the situation even more difficult.

Future Growth Markets: IT, Biotech, and Services

The Chinese Government is strongly focused on sustaining China's economic growth. In 2001, Chinese spending in research and development reached nearly US$60 billion, and was only surpassed by Japan and the United States.[31] Besides the fast-growing and well-known industrial sectors (e.g., automobile, chemicals, construction, energy, textile) that already have attracted many foreign investors, several new and promising industries offer additional potential in China. Those sectors will grow consistently in the future supported by China's research and development efforts thus enlarging the base of Chinese business. Information technology (IT), software, electronic equipment, telecommunications, services, and biotechnology are some noteworthy areas. The enormous potential and importance of IT is evident from the words of Wu Jichuan, Minister of Information Industry: "In comparison with 1999, the proportion of China's information industry out of total national GDP has increased to 7.6 percent from 3.3 percent and the information industry's direct contribution to GDP growth is expected to rise to around 40 percent from 10.5 percent."[32]

Information Technology, Computers, and Software

The Chinese IT market is the largest in the world; the number of computer owners and Internet connections is estimated to grow to more than 300 million in 2010. One reason for this is the so-called one-child family which leads to a 4-2-1 family demography. One child has two parents and four grandparents, and therefore the child has practically unlimited spending power. The Chinese also believe in offering the best possible education to their children which makes computers an essential part of the household. Over 410 million Chinese consumers are today under 20 years old, making China the largest potential market in the world.

Chinese companies dominate the domestic computer market today and local competition is growing. Legend, which has changed its brand name in 2003 to Lenovo, is the market leader with a market share of about 30 percent. Legend offers low-budget personal computers of a good quality below US$500, and is the dominant market player with about 30 percent market share. New customers are automatically guided to Legend's popular Web portal fm365.com. International companies have difficulty competing with their Chinese competitors. Therefore, America Online signed an agreement with the Legend Group in 2001 to enter the Internet service provider (ISP) market together. But to date both partners have had difficulty attracting a significant number of subscribers despite a US$200 million investment. The launch of their new site remains on hold. Sina, the largest Internet portal has about 60 million subscribed customers, followed by Sohu and NetEase. Yahoo, which is in the top 10, has about 25 million, while Microsoft and AOL do not reveal their number of Internet service users.

Chinese companies have recently also begun to shift their focus to the laptop market. Until 2006, manufacturers such as Jing Dong Fang aim to surpass Japanese competition and make China to the second-largest laptop producer in the world behind Taiwan. Another very attractive, growing market is in digital cameras. The case of Kodak is discussed in detail later, and several other companies, such as Canon, Olympus, Minolta and Sony, have established large production plants for digital equipment.

Since 1990, several Chinese companies have successfully developed computer hardware and software for the Chinese market. Years before Microsoft brought the first Chinese versions of its Windows software to the market, Chinese developers released RichWin. Soon RichWin had gained a 90 percent market share of the Chinese personal computer software market. All Chinese software developers, such as RichWin and KingSoft, had funding problems throughout the 1990s, which enabled international companies such as Microsoft to fight back. Microsoft has developed complete Windows and Office software programmed by Chinese programmers. This was a necessary step to appeal to Chinese customers but it entails immense cost and effort to make the product a real "Chinese" one.

Microsoft invested in several other joint-venture companies in 2002 to further its market position. Microsoft acquired 50 percent of Shanghai Wicresoft, a software service provider. Together with Beijing Centergate Technologies and the Stone Group, Microsoft formed the joint company Zhongguancun Software, a software service provider for company and government services. Other companies that invested recently in the Chinese software market are Oracle and BEA. Both are setting up their own development centers in China and have employed hundreds of engineers. In June 2002, Microsoft signed a US$750 million investment plan with the State Department Planning Commission. The investment aims to develop the Chinese software industry, particularly for export.[33]

Despite the initial success of Microsoft's strategy, it is not certain whether its efforts are sufficient to dominate the Chinese market. In 2003, the Chinese government made KingSoft office software the standard for various government branches. The decision in favor of KingSoft, who had held a market share of 90 percent in the office software market in the early 1990s, demonstrates the government's preference for local companies, in spite of large investment by foreign companies.

A serious problem area for software manufacturers is piracy. It is estimated that about 90 percent of all software in China is copied illegally, and the American Ministry of Trade estimates annual losses for American companies to be about US$2 billion. With China's entry into the WTO the government has increased efforts to fight against illegal copies, but this will take a long time. As soon as one hole is plugged three others seem to open up. Software companies such as Microsoft try to prevent counterfeiting by cooperating with personal computer manufacturers and installing the licensed software in the factory. It is also advisable to have strict internal controls in order to prevent piracy. It is mandatory to patent all software developments as early as possible, although this does not prevent piracy. One of the more important protections against illegal copying is to make it impossible for a would-be copier to put the complete software on one CD. Oracle and IBM, for example, keep their source code on central servers which are highly protected. Thus, nobody can walk out of the office with a CD containing the complete product. Further details are discussed in the section on intellectual property laws in chapter 3.

Telecommunications

China today is the largest mobile phone market in the world with over 200 million mobile phones; it overtook the U.S. in 2003, when over 43 million phones were sold in the first six month alone. In 1999, the Ministry of Information Industry (MII) mandated that all telecommunications equipment sold in China have a licence. Such regulations benefit local companies that are trying to establish themselves in the Chinese market supporting companies like Haier, Ningbo, and TCL, which strongly challenge established international phone companies like Motorola, Nokia, and Siemens. Several joint ventures between foreign and Chinese companies exist, and the MII is trying to pressure the foreign partner to transfer sufficient technical know-how to China. Within six years after China's admission to the WTO the restrictions will be reduced. By then, foreign investors will be able to hold up to 50 percent shares of Chinese telecommunication companies, in the hardware as well as service sectors.

Chinese state firms currently dominate the telecommunications service sector; those firms include China Telecom, China Netcom, China Mobile Communications, China Unicom, and Jitong Communications. For several years, the Chinese government has been restructuring this sector and as of 2002, various companies had been split, privatized, and brought into the stock market to increase the sector's competitiveness. As in many other areas, the intense market competition currently is leading to higher-quality services at lower prices. In 2001, the telecommunication market was estimated at about US$16 billion. Despite the large market size and growth potential, the general development should give investors a break. The price pressure and fight for market share is enormous and many companies are just breaking even. In 2003, the government decided not to set a G3 mobile phone standard, including the locally developed TD-SCDMA, in order to stimulate competition. It issued, however, standards for wireless applications (Wi-Fi), which are incompatible to international ones, favoring Chinese companies. China also announced in 2004 that it would develop the next generation Internet protocol (Ipv6) mutually with Japan and Korea. The Chinese government is, thus, shaping the economy with a fine balance between free competition and technology influx on the one hand, and the protection of strategic industrial sectors on the other.

The Semiconductor Industry

In 2001, the Chinese semiconductor market amounted to about US$10 billion, about 7 percent of the world market. By 2005, the Chinese market is expected to double to US$14 billion. The biggest producer of chips today is Taiwan, a territory that China regards as a renegade province. New factories are planned in Europe and the United States, but the largest investments are currently in Asia, especially in Taiwan and China. Intel, one of many examples to be mentioned, announced in 2003 the construction of a new semiconductor-chip factory in Chengdu, an investment of US$200 million in China's hinterland.

Despite China's admission to the WTO, import duties in this area are not expected to decrease soon, which is one reason for continued investment in Chinese joint ventures. Leading chip manufacturers from Taiwan, such as Taiwan Semiconductor Manufacturing and United Microelectronics Corporation, are presently establishing production facilities on the Chinese mainland; others are in concrete negotiations. These negotiations started several years ago but the Taiwanese government only recently, in 2001, issued a law to allow and make official such negotiations. Investments prior to this law are investigated, and some are even nullified. However, the Taiwanese government has sent a clear signal that it is willing to allow such investment in the Chinese market as of today, allowing world-leading Taiwanese companies to secure parts of the largest market of the future.

A wealth of investment capital, sharing the same language and mentality as the Chinese, and being located only one flight-hour away from the mainland are the immense advantages the Taiwanese enjoy compared to the Western competition. However, these investments will not include support from the West for the latest state-of-the-art products. The 300-millimeter wafer technology with 0.13-micrometer lanes is prohibited from being exported from the United States and Taiwan so that it remains a technological and military advantage. However, the production of 200-millimeter wafers with 0.25-micrometer lanes has already been exported to China and will reduce costs by 30 percent. Nevertheless, besides the export restriction, there are already two wafer factories with 0.13-micrometer technology existing in China: Semiconductor Manufacturing International and Grace Semiconductor Manufacturing, the latter started production of ultramodern 300-millimeter wafers in 2003. Both companies are backed by Taiwanese and Chinese American investors, and the technology comes from Japan and Europe. Because of strict local export regulations, not only are the American and Taiwanese companies losing direct business, but China is developing into their strongest competitor. Therefore Taiwanese companies follow a wise proverb: "If you can't beat 'em, join 'em."

United Microelectronics Corporation is supposed to have close connections to a planned chip factory in Suzhou, near Shanghai, with a cost of US$1 billion. Advanced Semiconductor Manufacturing plans investments of up to US$300 million over the coming years. In addition, Taiwanese chip design companies already have subsidiaries in Beijing and Shanghai.

The brain drain, in addition to the technology drain, is a problem, especially for Taiwan. The continuous flow of foreign capital into China and the resulting construction of large industrial businesses attract large numbers of well-trained professionals to China. The geographical proximity and similar cultural background make going to China easy for Taiwanese professionals, despite legal restrictions. In 2003, over 300,000 Taiwanese professionals worked in mainland China, transferring skills and technological know how. The Taiwanese government is now drafting laws to curb the brain drain—that is, efflux of "sensitive" professionals to China.

China will not become the leading semiconductor producer within the next few years; it is only beginning in this industry. But already, given the proximity of Taiwan and China and their increasing efforts to collaborate, one can easily imagine that the two countries will be a dominating force in the production of semiconductors in the future.

Biotechnology, Nanotechnology

The advantages, tax reductions, and benefits the Chinese government offers to foreign companies that are willing to invest in China are not restricted to labor-intensive consumer products. Besides the semiconductor industry, several other high-tech industries are emerging, such as biotechnology.

Japanese companies began over a decade ago to transfer their production to China. One example of such an investment is TaKaRa, a leading beverage manufacturer that diversified into biotechnology. TaKaRa Biotech is the leading Japanese biotech company and the second-largest genome-sequencing firm after the U.S. giant Celera, the company that sequenced the human genome. TaKaRa's molecular biology product lines (annual revenues of US$100 million) are manufactured in Dalian, a Chinese coastal city just one flight-hour away from Japan. Other Japanese biotech companies are following suit. Another is the biotech-investment of a German manufacturer of diagnostic products, which formed a joint venture with Shanghai Electro in the 1990s. The joint venture is a rather unusual diversification for the energy giant, but because it is developing well and is Shanghai Electro's only profitable joint venture after several other investments in areas such as real estate failed, this biotech cooperation is a positive experience for the Chinese energy company and the small-sized German manufacturer.

China actively supports basic research in biotechnology, something that may not be known to many abroad. A Chinese research team published the DNA sequence of the rice genome in April 2002, at the same time as a Swiss company. Thus, the Chinese were able to surpass a Japanese-led international scientific consortium that had worked for years on the project. It was a milestone for the Chinese biotech research industry, especially because rice not only is the main source of food for Asia, but also is the ancestor of all cereals. The genetic sequence of rice contains a huge potential for new agricultural products and food.

The Chinese government newly regulated this market in early 2002 and allowed imports of several genetically modified organisms (GMOs), such as soybeans, from the United States. This opened up a multibillion-dollar market for American and European companies. In 2003, 19 foreign companies were allowed to export GMOs to China, and 7 Chinese trading companies were able to market GMO products, including rice, potatoes, and cotton.

This liberalization of import restrictions shows the government's support for so-called "green" biotechnology, the most prospective biotech sector in the near and medium term. The relevant Chinese laws concerning genetic research are far less restrictive than in European countries, except for the new legislation on human cloning, which was issued in 2003 and is even more restrictive than that of the United States. Consumer acceptance for GMO-food is also far less critical in Asia than in the West. Therefore, immense growth in biotechnology and food technology is predicted for the coming years, a prediction that is supported by China's own research investment, which has grown from US$17 million to US$112 million between 1985 and 2000. In 2002, 141 genetically modified crops had been developed in China, 65 of which were already in field trials, the largest number outside North America. Chinese companies are thus well-placed to compete in this highly important biotechnology market.[34]

To protect Chinese research and development, the government issued new guidelines in 2002 for foreign investment in several industries, including biotechnology. These guidelines are supposed to prevent foreign companies from investing in the profitable business of GMOs, especially in the agricultural sector. On the one hand, the legislation is supposed to regulate the handling of such products but it also protects Chinese developments. If the Chinese are able to develop their own GMOs, this will be a large commercial success. If foreign products prove more attractive, the seeds may be imported illegally and the market would be lost for both sides. A risky approach for the Chinese as they are betting on their own research capabilities. Foreign companies are voicing their protests against the restrictions, especially as they believe these restrictions are not in the spirit of the WTO.

For several years, nanotechnology has been a field strongly supported by the Chinese government. In 2002, the nanotechnology budget for the Chinese Academy of Science equaled the biotechnology with US$90 million. The programs include more than 60 individual projects in areas like nano-electronics, nano-biotechnology, nano-functional materials, and nano-detection. Centers have been established in Beijing, Tianjin, Nanjing, and Shanghai, among others. The results of these governmental efforts can be seen in the number of publications and patents in Nanotechnology, where China has grown rapidly over the past years and is in the world's third place following the United States and Japan. Between 2001 and 2003 alone,

Chinese scientists applied for more than 1,400 nanotechnology-related patents, 12 percent of the world's total, following the United States and Japan.[35] A number of international companies have realized the attractiveness of China as a partner in Nanotechnology, including technology and venture companies from Europe and the United States, especially in nano-electronics and -biotechnology.

Logistic Services, Transportation

One of the bottlenecks of the Chinese economy is logistics. China is a vast country with an underdeveloped transportation network. Roads, railways, airports, rivers—in general, millions of kilometers of transportation routes—have to be built or upgraded in order to establish a viable economy throughout China, especially in the central and western regions. There are already various large projects under way, and since 1996 more than US$100 billion has been invested in the construction of roads, railways, and bridges. Plans for the construction of a railway to Tibet were decided on in 2001; this project will become the worlds highest train system. Many harbors have been constructed, deepened, or enlarged, such as the harbor of Shanghai, which was completed in 2001. The Three Gorges Dam project on the Yangtze River is the largest engineering project in the world since the building of the Great Wall. And the government has just decided to spend US$200 billion over the next 10 years on the infrastructure in Chongqing, China's largest city in the southern province of Sichuan.[36] Especially in the hinterland, however, China's transportation system is still at an early stage, despite all these efforts. One of the major obstacles for integrated supply chain companies is also that until recently foreign companies are not allowed to offer local transportation services. They are therefore forced to utilize the three million local transport companies, which offer only limited electronic integration and no nationwide coverage. When the manager of a French retail chain came to China in 2003, as one example, he discovered that 17,000 logistic companies were registered in the company's local database.

Another problem that should not be neglected is the fact that until recently foreign companies were not allowed to take care of their own transportation—that is, they lacked control over their supply chain. This situation is changing with China's admission to the WTO and the passage of corresponding legislation. This presents new and attractive opportunities for logistic service providers, such as in warehousing, transportation, or other services in this area. The cargo expert DHL was acquired by Deutsche Post in early 2002. This was a strategic move, especially for the Chinese market, as DHL already had a strong logistic network in place for China under the name *China first*. DHL dominates the Chinese market with a market share of 37 percent, followed by Federal Express with 11 percent and United Parcel Service with 9 percent. A major reason for the market share is the cooperation with Sinotrans, China's leading logistic service provider. In 2003, DHL increased its stake in Sinotrans by 5 percent; DHL also holds a 30 percent stake in the Cathay Pacific Airways subsidiary Air Hong Kong. The DHL package offers a complete service from customs clearance to intermediate storage to end-user delivery—a 24-hour service that is equivalent to international standards.[37] Thus, Deutsche Post was able to acquire a well-placed partner and market share in a strongly growing market. The air cargo volume in China is currently estimated at US$300 million per year, and annual growth rates are expected to be above 25 percent. Currently, the Chinese government and Deutsche Post are negotiating a deal in the conventional letter and parcel mail market. The German partner plans to invest more than US$1.5 billion in locations, warehouses, and sorting equipment. Deutsche Post recently stated that its goal is to "become the premier logistic provider in the Asian-Pacific area."

In 2002, the Chinese government announced the purchase of 20 airplanes from the European Airbus Industries, an investment of more than US$1 billion. Up to 50 additional planes are supposed to follow in the coming years. The government knows that logistical capabilities are the backbone of the continued development of the economy, and it is therefore dedicated to building up and modernizing the country's infrastructure.

Another attractive market in the transportation sector is transportation systems. Two of the more prominent systems are the magnetic levitation train, or Maglev, and high-speed railroad systems; both systems are for the expansion of the air cargo and passenger transportation. In 2001, the German companies Siemens and Thyssen started to construct the Maglev between the Shanghai airport and the city center, a train system capable of running at 250 miles per hour. This first commercial magnetic levitation train, a US$950 million project, had its test run on New Year in 2003. The Chinese State Council decided in early 2004 against the wide-scale use of the Maglev technology; simultaneously, German, French, Japanese, and Chinese consortia are currently placing offers for an even bigger project, a conventional high-speed train connection between Beijing and Shanghai.

The Chinese automotive market has been the most promising in the world for several years. Many renowned international manufacturers have invested heavily in production facilities, and some critics see an overcapacity building up. Until 2003, the annual growth rates were at a staggering 40 percent or higher. The annual production of cars and trucks jumped from 1.8 million in 2000 to 3.9 million in 2003—compared with 12 million in the United States, 10 million in Japan, and 4.8 million in Germany.[38] China is expected to produce 5.2 million cars in 2004, making it the third-largest car producer worldwide. Tens of thousands of supply companies are following this development, from tire manufacturers to electric wire factories and paint producers. Prices for cars are tumbling with increased capacities and growing competition; the list price for a new Honda Accord, for example, was US$50,000 in 1999, and just US$27,000 in 2003. As a consequence of continuous investment, China is expected to produce the highest number of vehicles worldwide within a decade, and to dominate many export markets. China's strongly increasing raw material demand in the construction and automotive industry has resulted in worldwide supply shortages and soaring prices. To overcome supply shortages, Chinese wire manufacturers are even importing old European currency copper coins as raw material for their wires.

Banking, Consulting, Services

China's banking system is one of the most sensitive sectors of its economy; it is closely controlled by the Communist Party, who for decades, allowed loans without proper guarantees. The volume of non-performing credits in China is estimated at US$500 billion, or 40 percent of the annual GDP. The government started therefore in the 1990s to overhaul the Chinese banking system to prevent a looming financial crisis. This includes the establishment of a supervising authority, the China Banking Regulatory Commission, and limited market access for foreign banks. Various foreign investors have started to open Chinese subsidiaries to capture the growing middle-class. In 2003, Citigroup purchased a 5 percent minority stake in the Shanghai Pudong Development Bank; since 2002, the U.S. based Newbridge Capital holds about 20 percent shares in the Shenzhen Development Bank; and U.K. giant HSBC Holdings is the most aggressive foreign buyer, with 8 percent shares in the Bank of Shanghai, 10 percent in Ping An Insurance, and it is also in talks with several other commercial banks.[39] Other European banks have established similar joint ventures, including Deutsche Bank and Dresdner Bank. In 2004, the Chinese Government initiated a new round of restructuring and injected US$45 billion into the Bank of China and the China Construction Bank to cover their non-performing loans, and to improve their books to attract more foreign investors. Free market access is expected for 2007, just in time for the Olympic Games one year later. International insurance companies, including American International Group, Allianz, and the Munich Re, have also established local offices and alliances.

A number of international and national companies are active in consulting services. International consulting firms such as Accenture, A. T. Kearney, Bain & Company, Boston Consulting Group, Deloitte, and McKinsey are currently increasing their staff in China, and many companies are transferring employees from other Asian countries. The current business volume is estimated at US$100 million, with expected annual growth rates of 25 percent. There is strong competition in the market, which is attractive for clients but rather difficult for the consulting companies. The prices are far below those of the international market, yet the customer demands are much higher. Often, several companies are asked to make two to three rounds of presentations until a partner is chosen. This gives clients various ideas and proposals from which the best parts can be selected.

The market is, nevertheless, attractive enough for many international players to invest in the Chinese consulting business; at the least they do so to secure a good market position. The Chinese government is currently pushing many SOEs to use consulting agencies to get a neutral and qualified opinion about the details of restructuring and joint ventures. It is the declared goal of the government to stop its financial support and turn loss-making SOEs into profitable companies. This generates plenty of opportunities for consulting services, despite high demands and low margins. This segment is a good representative example of the competitive Chinese market of today.

Another area recently emerging is call centers: Since 2000, Chinese companies are establishing call centers for the domestic market, but also for East Asian markets, especially Japan, Korea, and Taiwan. These call centers are a market segment that is not available for Indian or Western companies because of language barriers; they are located on the east coast, especially in Shanghai, Guangzhou, and Dalian. Major clients are international banks, insurance companies, telecommunication and software firms, and retail industries such as telemarketers. The industry is expected to grow to US$27 billion by 2007.[40]

China—the Export Giant

The financial benefits to be had in China continue to attract foreign investment. The government has two main motives in attracting foreign companies. For one, China's industry needs to be remodeled and improved to be able to compete in the twenty-first century. Second, China wants to expand its role in world trade and become the world's largest economy, which can only be achieved via export. And although that goal is still far away, China's export business is booming and is currently a major motor for worldwide economic growth. In 2003, China was already the world leading supplier of more than one hundred product categories, including motherboards, televisions, cell phones, toys, and textiles.[41]

Reasons abound for China's export success; it is not due only to restructured state enterprises and low manufacturing costs. For centuries, Chinese have emigrated from China. Southeast Asia, especially Indonesia, Japan, Malaysia, Singapore, Thailand, and Vietnam, has been a favorite destination, and since the middle of the eighteenth century, the Chinese have also gone to the United States and Europe. Although many of these overseas Chinese emigrated generations ago, their culture and family ties are still deeply rooted in China. The Chinese are widely spread throughout South-East Asia; see Table 2.3 for further details.[42] And even if the Chinese percentage of the local population is rather small, as in Indonesia where Chinese represent just 4 percent of the population, they control a major part of the business, in some areas more than 90 percent.

The spread of the Chinese through Southeast Asia has two important implications. First, it offers a cultural and language base for Chinese exports. The overseas Chinese have existing contacts in China and thus have easy access to Chinese products. Many international American and European companies note that this export pressure from China is growing continuously, especially in Asia. Price decreases and competition from China have already forced mergers and restructuring in the world's chemical, food, and pharmaceutical raw materials industries. In other areas, a similar picture can be seen.

Second, in addition to the growing Chinese exports, the overseas Chinese serve as major investors in China, which may surprise westerners. The large investors in China are not coming from the United States or Europe, but from Asian countries with a large Chinese population. Less than 30 percent of all investment in China is coming from the United States or Europe. Hong Kong, Singapore, and Japan are the leading investors; even Taiwanese businesses invest large amounts in China; unofficial figures indicate that cumulated Taiwanese foreign direct investment is three-times as large as that of the United States. And the U.S. figures include investments made by U.S.-based overseas Chinese, such as those in San Francisco, where 30 percent of the population has Chinese roots. Asia accounts for more than 60 percent of the world's population, and China is securing a major part of this market for itself—in addition to the European and American markets.

As one rides from the international airports of Bangkok, Hanoi, Jakarta, or Manila to the inner city, the picture one sees is often the same. Large billboards stand alongside the streets, and often international brands alternate with Asian and especially Chinese ones. Already today Lenovo/Legend, Tsingtao, and especially Haier are prominent brands all over Asia. Do you know Haier? Haier is one of the world's largest manufacturers of household appliances, and the largest manufacturer of refrigerators worldwide. It has a manufacturing plant in Camden, South Carolina, where it produces Wal-Mart's top line Magic Chef. Other customers of Haier include, among others, Lowe's, Best Buy, Home Depot, Office Depot, Target, Fry's, ABC, and BrandsMart.[43] More about Haier later. Tsingtao Brewery is China's largest beer producer; it has a market share far above that of all local and imported brands. Tsingtao is already exporting to more than 40 countries worldwide and aims to be among the world's top three beer producers within 10 years. In 2003, Anheuser-Busch bought

9.9 percent of Tsingtao to get a stronghold in the vast Chinese market, with a further option to buy up to 27 percent for a total of US$182 million.[44] The second-largest Chinese beer brewer, Yanjing Brewery, is investing strongly in Yao Ming, the new NBA-superstar, to promote Yanjing Beer in the United States. The list of world-class Chinese export companies is long, and their contribution to China's economy is very strong. In 2000, Chinese exports grew by 25 percent and reached US$249 billion; between 2001 and 2003, annual growth exceeded 35 percent, and China's exports generated US$430 billion in 2003, more than many Western countries.

Among the many reasons for the focus of Chinese companies on the export business is local competition. The large number of local manufacturers that have built state-of-the-art production facilities has led inevitably to massive competition, and increasingly to overcapacities in many industrial sectors. To gain market share, many Chinese and international companies have lowered their prices to attract more customers—a vicious cycle. This is especially the case in the electronics and telecommunications market, but it can also be seen in sectors such as consumer products and automobiles. Several companies have recently offered new compact cars for about US$3,000. To evade or subsidize this price erosion, companies turn to export as an interesting alternative. Export also helps to fill existing production capacities, and many large Chinese companies have therefore opted to strongly enhance their exposure in Asia.

Chinese companies have strong advantages compared with their European or American competitors. Besides short transportation routes and low manufacturing costs, the Chinese culture is deeply rooted in Asia. From Vietnam to Thailand and Singapore, from Indonesia to Korea and Japan, Chinese are present all over Asia, often controlling the business. And although there is no general Asian mentality or a single Asian culture, their social behavior, networking, and relationships, their *guanxi*, is very common practice. Therefore, the differences among the Asians are less than those between the Asians and the Europeans or Americans, and the basic hurdle a company must negotiate to enter another Asian country is much lower for the Chinese company than for the company in the West, as the example of the rising number of call centers shows.

The Chinese are able to transfer product lines or marketing and sales strategies relatively easily to other Asian countries. Where the Europeans are forced to consult language specialists, these jobs are done automatically by the Chinese. Where the Americans are still discussing color combinations or shapes or feng shui, for the Chinese this is a part of their daily life. With appealing products and professional local marketing, *Made in China* is now conquering the world, after decades of relative calm and focus on its home market. The Western nations must be careful not to lose their markets completely to China.

- Haier is probably the best-known and most successful example of restructuring a Chinese company. The Qingdao Refrigerator Company had a cooperative venture with the German company Liebherr (Chinese–Libohaier), a manufacturer of household appliances and construction equipment. The German-Chinese joint venture did not do very well; the Chinese-built refrigerators were often of such bad quality that they were scrapped right from the production line. In 1984, the company Haier was founded under its present president, Zhang Ruimin. Since that time, Haier has been a pure model of success. The company was built in three basic steps. First, the brand was established; then the quality was systematically improved; and since 1998 the company has expanded abroad. Haier grew from 800 employees to more than 30,000; every year it sells more than 2.5 million refrigerators and more than 2 million air conditioners in 160 countries. Haier is the fifth largest household appliance maker worldwide, the largest refrigerator maker worldwide, and the first Chinese company to be listed in the Fortune 500. Haier was the fastest growing company in the United States in 1997, ahead of General Electric and Siemens, and in 2002, Haier opened a flagship showroom in a landmark-building on New York's Broadway, called the Haier Building. In recent years Haier has been able to successfully expand its cooperative ventures abroad. It possesses manufacturing plants in America, Asia (including Japan), Europe, and Australia. Sampo is its partner in Taiwan, and Sanyo Electro in Japan. Its present export volume is about US$280 million, which is supposed to increase to US$1 billion in 2005. Haier's example has been discussed internationally for years, and in 2000 Zhang Ruimin was ranked 26th by the *Financial Times* on its list of the most successful managers in the world. Haier's story is an outstanding example of the restructuring of a Chinese company, but investors should also take heed of the mistakes made by the original German investor.

- Tsingtao Brewery produces more than three billion liters of beer a year and has the largest market share in the Chinese brewing industry with annual growth rates of 30 percent. Tsingtao was able to increase its market share within six years from 2 percent to 11 percent by various acquisitions in China. By 1997, Tsingtao had purchased more than 40 Chinese breweries; it is now expanding in the Taiwanese market, where it founded Taiwan Tsing Beer Corporation. Within five years, Tsingtao aims to have 20 to 25 percent of the Taiwanese market. Tsingtao is taking on importers such as Kirin of Japan and Heineken of the Netherlands. To succeed in its bid for the Taiwanese market, Taiwan Tsing Beer will invest US$85 million to build production facilities.

- Yanjing Brewery, China's second-largest beer brewer, started promotion in 2002 in the United States, where it is building up brand awareness with the Houston's NBA-superstar Yao Ming as a Chinese icon.

- Giordano was actually founded in the former British crown colony Hong Kong, which since 1997 has belonged as a special administrative region to China. After several years of expansion in China, Giordano started in 2002 to invest US$3 million in the Chinese market and open from 50 to 100 new megastores. The flagship store will be its Shanghai showroom, for which Giordano paid US$10 million for 20 years' rent in a prime location.

- Jialing Industries is China's leading manufacturer of motorcycles. It sold over 11 million motorcycles, and is with 20 percent market share the largest Chinese producer. In 2001 Jialing exported more than 400,000 motorcycles to Vietnam alone, bearing prices that were 60 percent below those of the Japanese competition. Vietnamese import tariffs were a set-back for Jialing. The expansion in Asia, however, continues in countries such as Hong Kong.

- In 2002, PetroChina, the largest gas and oil producer in China, paid more than US$200 million for the offshore rights of the Indonesian company Devon Energy. At the same time, PetroChina announced that this will be only the first of many foreign investments to support the rapidly growing demand for energy in China. In the coming years, it expects to invest billions of dollars in gas and oil pipelines to supply sufficient energy to the densely populated area of eastern China. PetroChina is on a massive buying spree in Asia.

The list of equally successful companies could be continued much further, and it will be interesting to see who finally gains the upper hand in the competition between the West and China. Not much imagination is needed to predict the outcome today; the conditions are set. Excellent production costs, new production equipment, continued investments and technology transfer from the West, and an increasingly professional marketing approach give China the clear edge, especially in Asia. For more than a decade, the Japanese economy has been declining despite massive tax breaks, financial support, and extremely low interest rates. At the same time, China's export volume increased annually by more than 30 percent, far above the already impressive domestic growth. China already has large market shares in adjacent countries. It will soon be Vietnam's third-largest supplier with imports of more than US$2 billion; in Indonesia, it has already improved from number seven to number five; in Malaysia, it has grown from number seven on the list of supplying countries to number six. In Thailand, 30 to 40 percent of all videodisc players are imported from China, and Huawei Technologies just received a multimillion-dollar order from Thailand for telecommunications equipment, a first for a Chinese company.

China is currently repeating Japan's successes that began in the 1970s and Taiwan's successes since the 1980s. Both of those nations first established a reputation as a low-cost manufacturer and thereafter improved product quality significantly. However, until some years ago, even Asian consumers would have commented about the cheap quality of Chinese products. Using immense foreign investment and the transfer of know-how, the Chinese are bringing their products very close to Western and Japanese quality standards; but those products are far less expensive.

Former Malaysian prime minister, Mahatir Mohamad, summarized this recently: "We have to live with the fact that China exists and it will be very successful, very big and economically very strong." Comments by his colleagues from Thailand and Singapore have a similar tone; Singapore's former prime minister, Lee Kuan Yew, said that China will challenge the United States as the largest economy in the world in 2050.

CHINA BUSINESS AND INTERCULTURAL COMMUNICATION

Confucianism—More Than a Philosophy

How did the Chinese economy become so strong—after almost two centuries of political, social, and economic struggle? Is there a basic factor for the success of Asian economies like Japan, Korea, Taiwan, and China? To answer these questions, we should look at Chinese philosophy—that is, Confucianism.

Confucianism was a national doctrine of China for more than 2,000 years, from the Han dynasty (206 B.C. to A.D. 220) until the end of the empire in 1911. Probably no society has had such a continuation. Confucianism invaded all areas of social life. Even today, with the economic growth of the "socialist market economy," the Confucian ethical teachings influence deeply the actions of the Chinese. What does Confucianism mean? What significance has it held and does it have now for Chinese society? What are the differences between it and Western philosophies and ethics? Finally, to what extent is the current social and cultural life of the People's Republic of China influenced by Confucianism?

The Teachings of Confucius

The teachings of Confucius are lessons in ethics without religious content. Confucius (Kongfuzi) was a scholar of modest descent who lived circa 500 B.C. in China. He was not the founder of a religion but was a philosopher. Confucianism as it is practiced today is nothing but a series of pragmatic rules for everyday life, which are deduced from what Confucius thought were the teachings of the Chinese history. The most important lesson of Confucianism concerns the unequal relationships between men, whereupon the stability of the society is founded. According to the teachings of Confucius, the society can therefore be nothing other than a strong hierarchical and patriarchal system, if it wants to maintain stability. According to Confucius, there are five basic human principles, called *wulun:* between emperor and subordinate, father and son, older and younger brother, older and younger friend, and man and woman. It is important that these are never relations between two equal persons, but are strongly hierarchical relations. The younger partner owes respect and obedience to the older, and the older partner owes protection and care.

The role of the family is also important, as it resembles the germ cell in the Confucian view of life. The smallest unit therefore is not the individual but the family. The consequences for the person are that a man is not an individual but a member of a family. The highest rule is therefore not self-realization and the development of one's own personality—but rather the adaptation and overcoming of one's own individuality to preserve the harmony of the family. In accordance, harmony shows that everyone keeps face (*mianzi* or *lian*). This means that values such as dignity, self-respect, and prestige are central factors in a relationship. In the Chinese tradition, loss of dignity is identical with the loss of eyes, nose, and mouth. Social relations should be designed so that everybody has the opportunity to keep face (*weihu mianzi*). Showing respect equals giving face (*gei mianzi*); being compromised means losing face (*diu mianzi*). For more details, see "The Face: An Essential Concept" in chapter 2.

A key element of the Confucian ethic is order in human relations and in the relationship between the state and the people. Nothing is more detested than disorder (*luan*). Order can be reached only by obedience to the hierarchical basic relations between men. Refuge from these relations means chaos, disorder, and a disturbance of harmony. Harmony is a further key element of Confucianism. According to these ideas, the golden middle way should always be taken, which means the harmonization of contrasts. Thinking in the extreme, that is, pushing for one's own claim— as is very typical in Western societies—is unknown and strange to the Chinese. Harmonious cooperation, not contest, is important. Willingness to compromise, rather than readiness for conflict, is typical of Asians.

Another important value in the Confucian worldview is virtue. The Confucian ethic differentiates between behavior toward one's fellow man and oneself. Virtue means to treat one's fellow man in the way one would like to be treated. In general, one should be kind toward one's fellow man; however, this kindness does not extend as far as the Christian command to love one's enemies. Confucius could have argued: "If you love your enemies, what is left for your friends?" According to Confucius, everyone must live an orderly life in a way one can justify for him- or herself. The one who tries to use his or her abilities and expands them lives a virtuous life. Importance is given to hard labor, thrift, perseverance, and persistence. In contrast, excessive consumption, boundlessness, and lack of self-control are taboo. Moderation in every aspect is taught.

Confucianism and Economic Growth

To what extent does Confucianism influence the cultural and social life of the People's Republic of China today? The economic success of East Asian countries such as China, Hong Kong, Singapore, South Korea, Thailand, and Taiwan over the past decades has been phenomenal. Thus the West asks, "Where does their success come from?" Scientists and economists recently reached a conclusion that the economic boom of various East Asian countries can be attributed mainly to one point: common cultural roots—in other words, Confucianism, which has influenced the values of all these societies.

The recent economic developments in Asia lead to the conclusion that Asian countries have a competitive advantage compared with Western cultures—due to their Confucian ethics. This thesis has been confirmed by recent social, anthropological, and cultural studies.

Confucian Values

- Perseverance and persistence
- Classification of a relationship according to status
- Adherence to the order
- Thrift
- Protection of face

For businessmen, characteristics such as perseverance and persistence are clearly advantageous. Classification according to status as well as obedience to the order reflects the Confucian ethic of the unequal relations between men (*wulun*). Especially in large companies, a harmonious and stable hierarchy as well as complementing roles can only be an advantage. The positive value of thrift is also to be mentioned: In China it is common to offer one's savings and manpower, for example, to a company of a relative, as long as that assistance is necessary. Only those who operate economically and thriftily will be able to save money for further investments.

The extreme importance face assumes for the Chinese is indicative of the sensibility of the Chinese in their social contacts. This can only be a positive in business relations. Chinese place great importance on complying with etiquette, and they are always aware of their duties and obligations toward their business partners.

Communication Plus Understanding

A Western businessman has negotiated with a potential Chinese business partner for hours. It has been good conversation, and the parties could close the gaps between their positions and gain a mutual understanding. What might the Chinese say at the end of the talk? He says, "I feel embarrassed that you had to spend so much of your valuable time with me." The westerner might well be shocked if he fails to understand what the Chinese means by that. Such an expression is intended as a polite phrase without any relevant connection to the negotiations. Thus, it should not be taken literally.

It might confuse Western businesspeople that during a first meeting Chinese people already start asking personal questions—for example about one's age, whether one is married or has children, or how much one's monthly salary is (although divorce, illness, bereavement, or family problems are absolutely taboo topics to start a conversation). Chinese avoid negative, especially embarrassing, topics. A foreigner deems even positive questions as impolite or indiscreet. For the Chinese, however, they represent nothing further than polite phrases. A Chinese businessman does not expect any concrete answer or information; he seeks only to signal that his opposite is important to him and worth taking an interest in. This behavior, meant to express politeness, seems to displease us. For the westerner, Chinese politeness is too stereotypical, too personal, and too paraphrased.

Paraphrased? It is absolutely correct that in their welcoming the Chinese display a wealth of ideas that seems exaggerated to the Western foreigner. During negotiations they use strategies and tactics that are inappropriate according to our standards. Chinese seem to especially enjoy a game of cat and mouse with their negotiating partner. It is a kind of fighting game, an intellectual tournament, that nevertheless is aimed toward a mutual agreement. In short, negotiating with Chinese businesspeople follows different rules.

Those who want to communicate successfully and get along well must observe and accept the different rules and behaviors. To be able to do so, one has to realize that the strategic tricks and tactical refinements of the Chinese are rooted in their culture. This is exactly what makes business in China complicated and difficult: It is not the type of business relations or communication to which we are accustomed in Western business circles. It is communication with partners who belong to a completely different culture.

It has to be realized that the Chinese economy is not autonomous, but is a cultural phenomenon that only fully makes sense in the context of the complete culture. Economic relations between two different cultures have to be viewed and arranged under the aspects of cross-cultural communication. In this context, culture has to be defined as the mutual behavior and perception of the members of that culture. Culture is formed by common ground and is acquired by learning. Culture also has a historical aspect—it evolves, and it is helpful to know about the historical development.

Cross-, or intercultural communication is communication between members of different cultures. Each not only perceives the other's differences but takes them into consideration, accepts them. As does every communication, intercultural communication has a purpose. However, it is exactly the purpose that causes problems. Communication is fulfilling its purpose only partially if it is used to understand, or more precisely, used as a tool to understand—that is, to exchange more wisely, efficiently, and successfully with members of a different cultural circle. Such "use" of communication is certainly necessary, but it remains superficial and is not much use in understanding a different culture and its phenomena. Intercultural communication, in addition, teaches to read between the lines, to analyze motivations and cultural backgrounds, a task which is especially important in China.

Only those who are willing to go beyond pure perception in language and to consider and accept different behavioral patterns will make full use of cross-cultural communication. They will possess the key to China. There is, without doubt, the purely pragmatic interpretation and use of intercultural communication. Intercultural communication provides the behavioristic framework and etiquette for communicating with the Chinese. Consequently, the aim is to soften the cultural differences and to smooth cooperation.

Different—but Not "a Book with Seven Seals"

The psychologist Hofstede defines several cultural dimensions to characterize different cultures, such as power distance, individualism, uncertainty avoidance, and long-term orientation. According to Hofstede, China possesses the highest power distance and the lowest individualism among all Asian nations; in contrast, its long-term orientation is the highest. These sociocultural values cannot only be attributed to a long authoritarian rule, but also to a high level of inequality of power and wealth within China.

One Chinese behavior that can be most shocking is the seemingly baseless, sudden unreliability of Chinese partners and employees. Maybe one has learned in a cross-cultural seminar about the importance for the Chinese of "keeping face." Therefore, one takes care to avoid anything that could lead to a loss of face for the Chinese. However, later, in day-to-day work, one discovers that there are Chinese who do not stick to agreements. Questioned about their wrongdoing, it seems that they do not care about losing face. Such behavior occurs—and the question is "Why don't these Chinese perceive this as a loss of face?" The explanation is simple but painful to learn for the foreigner: There have been and are two categories of people around whom the Chinese don't care about keeping "face," that is don't care about their moral reputation—foreigners who do not belong to their circle or who did not build up a network, and enemies!

Those who are strangers or enemies of the Chinese, more because of their behavior than of their foreign origin, morally don't exist. The stranger has no face, and one doesn't need to keep one's own face with respect to a stranger. Those who know this fact will strive not to remain a faceless stranger but to build up a personal relationship, to become a friend of their Chinese partners. Relationships have to be initiated and nurtured.

It would be completely ineffective to use common Western management methods or pressure with Chinese coworkers or employees in order to "keep them on track." The Western concept that conflicts can be solved with a "stormy dispute" is not shared by the Chinese. Those who confront a Chinese employee about a mistake or sloppiness, who offend him or her, will not excite contrition or even guilt. Doing this in front of colleagues will make the Chinese feel ashamed—but because of the colleagues only. He or she will certainly not improve, at least not immediately. But his or her colleagues will most certainly be in solidarity with him or her. The cultural background of this behavior is as follows: The Chinese perception follows the idea that foreigners and enemies do not exist morally and are therefore irrelevant. Therefore, in contrast to what might be the case in Western cultures, foreigners and enemies don't cause Chinese to feel guilty. The sense of shame they may feel for the social environment is, however, important; it is perhaps the most essential moral factor for Chinese.

Obviously conflicts in China must not be solved according to Western rules of "dispute." One doesn't get far in China with the aggressiveness that is frequently practiced and even appreciated in Western companies. A sharp voice, even a sharp look, may evolve into a lack of understanding and disapproval. Such behavior will brand the "dynamic manager" as a foreigner and an enemy. Chinese are exceptionally sensitive with regard to respect and face. A deliberate violation of a Chinese worker's sensitivity can lead to an immense stubbornness, even rebelliousness and boldness, especially if the incident is not straightened out. It is therefore advisable to take this sensitivity into account. One should know well the Chinese cultural background. Americans find it normal to make eye contact with each other. Chinese see this as aggressive, imperious, even denoting a lack of respect. They feel it is impolite and disrespectful to look directly at a superior or elderly person. Avoiding the gaze of a respected person does not mean one wants to hide something or has a bad conscience. It is for a totally different reason—to maintain respect, which is directed by the strict hierarchical setup of Chinese society, especially toward a senior or older person.

Whether a Chinese person does or does not make eye contact, then, represents an inadequate criterion by which to judge his or her honesty or credibility. The forms of Chinese communication are indeed "a book with seven seals" for those who don't understand China's cultural background. Once one is familiar with the context—for example, the strong social relationships and hierarchies—many strange facts are no longer inexplicable. It is obvious and natural that there will be friction during contact with the Chinese. This is especially the case where the flat Western company hierarchy meets the hierarchical Chinese corporate and social culture.

For example, usually in China important topics are discussed only between persons of like rank. People with no rank or title have no competence, and thus have no decision-making power. What such people discuss can only be a prelude to negotiations. Based on experience, we can say that negotiations European and American companies undertake with their Chinese partners often take a long time. The business cards of Western negotiators often do not show important titles. A further difficulty is the fact that Western negotiators seem too young to their Chinese counterparts. As a rule, Chinese negotiators are in the sedate age of over 50. Their Western counterparts should ideally be only a few years younger; otherwise it is difficult for the Chinese to regard them as competent and to take them seriously. Both factors are important—a corporate denoting decision-making power and an adequate age.

Are these peculiarities minor points that may be overlooked? That would be a detrimental self-deception. In contacts with Chinese there are no minor points. It might seem that the Chinese show no reaction to cultural mishaps or impolite or even irreverent behavior. But be assured— they have watched closely and noticed everything. The Chinese will "hear" even those points that have not been discussed, in accordance with a basic principle of Chinese communication:

> Don't listen to what you are told, but listen to the gaps
> in between, to what you are not told.

Situation and Perspective—the Intercultural Aspect

If futurologists are correct, two phenomena will primarily define the twenty-first century: the internationalization of the economy, popularly described as globalization, and a polycentrism with both political and social consequences. There will be several "world centers," determined primarily by their economic power. "Greater China," which means mainland China and the approximately 25,000 to 30,000 networks of foreign Chinese, also called overseas Chinese, will play a dominant role in a new, polycentric world system. Dominance will mean something other than it has meant since the seventeenth and eighteenth centuries and during the time of complete world dominance by the West. Geopolitical dominance will be replaced by geo-economic power politics.

The question remains of whether Asia will be one or even the main geo-economic center of power. In any case, the People's Republic of China will be a core region of the Asian-Pacific area. A number of facts justify that statement: The economy of China is growing at a rate far above the rates of all other industrial countries. The gap between mainland Chinese and overseas Chinese is narrowing. Within the last several years, more and more enterprises in the PRC have taken up relations with networks of foreign Chinese in other countries. And with the return to China of the British crown colony Hong Kong, a central junction between Southeast Asian and foreign Chinese networks became integrated into China's economy, or at the least became available for use by China.

The PRC is appealing to a wide variety of Western investors. Billions of dollars in foreign investment have been and are being used for the modernization of the economy and for the restructuring of the Chinese export and trade industry. China is using foreign investment to increase the effectiveness and efficiency of its economy. It was possible for the experiment of a socialist market economy to be carried out until the present without grave political or social friction or disruption. The coexistence of a privately organized market economy and an increasingly market-oriented governmentally planned economy is not only possible but has been successful in terms of China's overall economic development. An understandable question comes up regarding the perception and acceptance of cultural differences a question of great interest for intercultural communication: Why is something a reality in China thought to be impossible anywhere else? How can the Chinese be implementing the economic strategies of the West but ignoring the political and social values of the West?

Some westerners seem never to tire of asking the whole world to take on their democratic and legal values. China, however, doesn't seem to be listening! Sometimes, though, we see signs of liberalization. For example, such was the case in summer of 1998 when the Chinese government asked those responsible for state family planning to refrain from coercive measures of birth control and to no longer imprison women unwilling to undergo abortions, that is, to adhere to the strict one-child policy of the government. From time to time, also, outspoken members of the democracy movement are allowed to leave the country. But at the same time, some political activists and monks are imprisoned and the Falun Gong movement is strongly suppressed because of its potential threat to destabilize the government. Besides the ability to earn and spend as much money as possible, freedom for the Chinese is rather limited in the Western sense. And as amazing as it may seem at first, actually it is not difficult to understand how the vast majority of Chinese people can accept such a situation.

The freedom to earn money, become rich, and consume seems fulfilling for the moment. Just using that freedom keeps them fully occupied. The Chinese recognize that freedom of the individual is of absolute importance in the West. They are aware that almost all Western social and legal systems are based on individual rights, but that concept does not find full acceptance in their society. The idea of individual rights and freedoms, a basic value of the Western culture, goes against the basic tenets of Confucianism and Chinese Communism. It is the task of intercultural communication to clarify these basic differences. Clarifying differences will bring answers to the questions posed earlier this section. Fundamental differences between the West and China are rooted in developments extending over millennia. Such differences are much older than either communism or capitalism. They continue today and are determining influences in Chinese culture.

In Chinese culture, the group assumes a higher priority than the individual. Social cohesive strength and recognition in one's associated social environment are still more important than individual self-fulfillment. There is still the concept of common discipline, where discipline is integrated into the structured hierarchy of the community. The community order is controlled by a strong central power, which has a wide network of regional and local subcenters. It is one of the functions of this power complex to oversee and keep the social order.

Through the millennia and still today, the social order, geared toward community, is the Chinese ethos that determines behavior. It is the moral duty of each individual, each group, to remain in line with this ethos. Fulfilling this duty means saving face, preserving social reputation. In principle, this is neither a democratic nor liberal social order. It is also not necessarily a result of Communist education. Even under Mao, Communism could not remodel the characteristics of Chinese Confucianism. One could say that the Confucianism characteristic of the nature of China has survived Maoism and is changing Chinese Communism today. Continuity of Chinese culture has only at times been interrupted and even then, only partially. Chinese "Confucian harmony" was not even jeopardized by Mao. At that time, one just had to be in harmony with the party.

Living in harmony with a dictatorial political power? A puzzle for us! But only until the different cultural definitions of harmony become clear. Harmony for the Chinese is not pure agreement but excellent integration or subordination to the sense of the community. A good part of the phenomenal Chinese success is based on this "virtue." It has a double floor and a very strong safety net: the floor of the community and the floor of a strong state, backed up by a dense network of relations. These are the structural elements of Chinese society and the Chinese economy.

TO DO'S AND TABOOS IN CHINA

Names and Forms of Salutation

In regard to the conventions of addressing and titles, what is valid in Europe, the United States, or other parts of the Western Hemisphere might have no validity in China. For the American or European, this means that

he or she is confronted with mundane things such as the formality of
addressing a person in uncertain terrain. A discussion of Asian traditions
of titles and salutations is necessary. Following an American or European
manner or model of contact will cause tremendous problems. Mistakes
with Chinese names cause both contradictions and precarious social situations. Many faux pas occur in salutations. According to Western form,
one would greet a gentleman named Wang Aidang as "Mr. Aidang"—
taking for granted that the rules that apply to Americans or Europeans
also apply to the Chinese.

Order of Names		
• *Chinese:*	Wang	Aidang
	Surname	First Name
• *Western:*	Jane	Smith
	First Name	Surname

The opposite, however, is the case: Whereas in the United States, or
Europe the first-mentioned name stands for the first, or given name and
the second mentioned stands for the surname, in Chinese exactly the opposite is true: Here, the first name stands for the family name, and the
second name corresponds to the first, or given name in the West. This may
result in an unintentionally odd situation after a first greeting between a
Chinese and a Western business partner. Erroneously, Mr. Wang would
be greeted by his given name—he himself is too polite to make the stranger aware of the mistake. He draws his conclusion about the visitor's lack
of manners. On the other side, especially a European may feel strange if
the Chinese partner addresses him or her with his first name.

The American way of using the first name ("Please, call me Jane"),
should also be transferred with caution. The Chinese use their first name
not as an expression of familiarity. It is the best choice to address the
Chinese counterpart with the surname, even if he uses the American's
first name. One should, however, not take offense if a Chinese does not
address you by your first name—even though you have repeatedly offered it to him.

The increased Western influence over the past years has softened these
rules, and some Chinese appear to be more interested in assimilation than
their sometimes unintentionally impolite guests. There are those Chinese
whose dealings with westerners cause them to rearrange their names in
the hopes of making it easier for foreigners. Thus, with great foresight a
letter of Mr. Wang's to a Western business partner would be signed with
"Aidang Wang." Now, Mr. Wang is not counting on a business partner

who knows the Chinese rules of address so he is surprised to receive a letter with the greeting "Dear Mr. Aidang."

Or listen to the Chinese news: Reports about the former German chancellor, Helmut Kohl, referred to him as chancellor Helmut. Given names carry much more significance for the Chinese than for the Europeans. It is for them an expression of personality and portrays the individuality of a person. Here is a Chinese virtue in which the people remain inconspicuous; they do not want to call attention to themselves or make their presence felt through individual emphasis. Moreover, the myth is widespread in China that if one draws excessive attention to oneself, disaster approaches.

These examples show that Chinese conventions of naming can cause great confusion. Complications of this kind cannot be avoided. Thus, only one thing remains to be done—get oriented to Chinese rules and regulations. A very important rule: Over 95 percent of the Chinese family names are monosyllabic. In Chinese, there are 350 to 400 family names; Wang ("King") and Li ("Plum") are the Chinese Millers and Smiths. The given name, on the other hand, consists in Chinese mostly of a double word; for instance Aidang ("Party Lover")—a typical man's name—or Fangfang ("Nice Smelling"). With the first name, everything is permitted. The parents gladly give their children a name that either symbolizes good luck or directly implies it: "Become a Doctor," "Long Life," "Clear Away Sickness." In the 1950s and 1960s the names were political. Names such as "State Founder," "Bridge Building," "Combat USA," "Red Army," and "New China" were popular. English and German names are popular as nicknames. One finds names such as Karl, Gustav, John, and Paul stylish; popular girls names are Erika, Marlies, Jenny, and Connie. In contrast to Chinese given names, which one should not mention because they represent a bad omen, these "Western" names are acceptable.

More and more young Chinese have monosyllabic first names—as, for example, in the names Chen Quin or Zhao Zhe. Westerners and also the Chinese will ask themselves which of the two names is the given name and which is the surname. In this case Chen and Zhao are the family names. They are lucky, however, in that this generation is still stuck in its infancy and still are not yet business partners. A new trend exists: giving children a particularly unusual name. Many parents go especially to the library and look for extravagant names for which no characters exist in modern Chinese. Often these characters are not registered in the registration authority's computer, so the characters have to be devised. The name should set apart the offspring of the proud parents from the masses. These children who are symbolized by their names are considered quite special.

Some Chinese like to name children after foreign currency. A name, such as Yen, or Dollar, is popular. In the meantime, there are youths who carry the name Three Thousand Yuan, Four Thousand Yuan, or Ten Thousand

Yuan. A man who had two sons really made news: When he announced the birth of his second son, he had to pay 3,000 yuan (US$360) as a penalty, because he had not heeded the one-child policy of the government. As a result, he named his son 3,000 yuan. Others have followed his example. And since the penalty has increased, the names have changed: Now, one calls his son Ten Thousand Yuan. With a certain pride, a man will present such a son—is he not proof that one is rich enough to pay a penalty of 10,000 yuan (US$1,200).

Professional Titles and Positions

The Chinese love to use titles for salutations. They use both terms of relationship and job-related titles. In the family circle, one uses salutations such as "older brother," "daughter-in-law," or "first uncle." One cannot address older family members by their given names. The older family members, however, should call the younger ones in the family by their given names. It is widespread in China to use expressions of relationship such as uncle, aunt, brother, grandfather, and grandmother. This also extends to those who are not related. It is also important to keep a distance and show necessary respect to the older generation.

Professional Titles (Preceding)	
Minister	*Bu zhang*
Governor	*Sheng zhang*
Mayor	*Shi zhang*
Chairman	*Zhu xi*
Director	*Zhu ren*
General Manager	*Gong jing li*
Factory Manager	*Chang zhang*
Department Manager	*Bu men jing li*
Manager	*Jing li*
Chief Editor	*Zhu bian*
Teacher	*Lao shi*
Foreman	*Zhu zhang*
Accountant	*Kua ji*
Chief Engineer	*Zong gong cheng shi*
Engineer	*Gong cheng shi*

If one has a monosyllabic first name, one would be addressed with first and last names. For Kang Wei, it feels too intimate, in fact quite unpleasant, when his family or friends address him with a monosyllabic given name. These examples illustrate clearly the major roles the hierarchical thinking of the Chinese family's inner selves plays. Pay attention to professional salutations: In Europe, it is a sign of special attention to use the name of the business partner, whereas in Asia it is disturbing. Even regarding surnames, one recommends caution. It is better to use professional titles for addressing: "Department Manager," "Teacher," "General Manager," or "Leading Engineer" is consequently politer than "Mr. Li" or "Ms. Chen."

It may be a bit surprising to a westerner that the Chinese use, in addition to their customary salutations, those also used customarily in Europe, such as Doctor, Consul, Lieutenant, Professor, and so on. It is quite normal in Chinese to use job titles for address where a Westerner would not normally use them. These job titles are usually put before the family name— Manager, Department Manager, Chief Engineer, Foreman, Office Manager, Bookkeeper, Superintendent, Editor-in-Chief, and so on. These titles are used as formal addresses. They have become so popular in Chinese that they can be placed on the same level with the titles Doctor, Professor, and so on.

Leisure Titles: *Xiao* and *Lao*

Even for the very formal Chinese, there are situations in which a less formal address appears more appropriate. A friendly form of address for all those who belong neither to the family nor to the closest circle of friends is *xiao* or *lao*—prefixes that are placed in front of the family name. The young coworker Li Weiguo will in this case be addressed *xiao* Li and not Li *xiao*. *Xiao* as well as *lao* can be used regardless of gender; however, *lao* is usually used with the male gender. Both titles are associated with the relative age: One could translate *xiao* as a reference to "young" or "junior"; *lao* could be translated as "old" or "senior." In general, it is permitted to address someone who is younger than oneself with the title *xiao;* on the other hand, one calls someone older than oneself *lao*. One uses this even with a slight age difference. So it would be absolutely correct for someone in his late twenties to address a friend who is merely a few years younger as *lao*.

Although *lao* is normally placed before the surname, one can express one's special respect for an older person by putting *lao* after the surname. *Lao* is used in such a case to express honor for a wise and dignified person. Pay attention to how the Chinese address a person. For example, the Chinese in your group should address the translator as *xiao* Gao. Regardless of the age difference between yourself and the translator, you should also follow the Chinese example and address the translator as *xiao Gao*. Both the Chinese business partner as well as the translator would consider it a breach of tact if you were to address the translator as *lao Gao*. If one is not certain about the use of *xiao* and *lao,* which are mainly used in cases of familiarity, it is preferable to use the professional title, or the courtesy title for Mr., Mrs., Miss, or Ms.

Mr., Mrs., Ms., Miss

In the 1980s, influenced by the opening to the West, some Chinese began to use Western standards of address. Equivalents to the English Mr., Mrs., Ms., and Miss were introduced. Westerners should pay attention though: Just as the first name normally stands after the last name in Chinese, the title will be placed after the last name, as, for instance, in the forms of address Mr. (*ni hao* Chen, *xian sheng!*), Mrs. (*ni hao* Li, *tai tai,* or, *ni hao* Li, *fu ren!*), Ms. (*ni hao* Wang, *nu shi!*), and Miss (*ni hao* Chang, *xiao jie!*). A Chinese man with the name Mr. Li would therefore in Chinese be addressed as Li *xian sheng* (literally translated as "Li Mr."). A Chinese woman with the name Miss Chang would be addressed in China as Chang *xiao jie* ("Chang Miss").

Courtesy Titles (Following)

- Mr.   *Xian sheng* (Chen *xian sheng*)
- Mrs.   *Tai tai* (Li *tai tai,* general), or *fu ren* (Li *fu ren,* formal)
- Ms.   *Nu shi* (Wang *nu shi*)
- Miss   *Xiao jie* (Chang *xiao jie*)

A noteworthy peculiarity is that women don't take on their husband's names, but rather keep that of their fathers. A married woman in China receives the title *tai tai,* or more formal, *fu ren.* Both forms of address refer to the marital status—comparable with the English Madam, which is fitting in responsibilities. In contrast, equivalent to the English Ms. is *nu shi,* which does not refer to the marital status, and is less formal than *tai tai* or even *fu ren.* Unmarried girls and young-looking married women, on the other hand, should be addressed as *xiao jie.* Miss Zhao will be correspondingly Zhao *xiao jie.*

Greeting

The Chinese greet each other customarily with *ni hao.* This greeting is generally translated as "Hello." The literal translation, however, goes, "You are well." Formulated as a question, *ni hao ma?,* the greeting goes, "Are you well?" As an answer, one usually receives a *ni hao.* Both forms of greeting can be used interchangeably and regardless of the time of day or the position of the person who is being greeted. Don't hesitate to use these greetings, even if you usually speak no Chinese. You will make a positive impression, and they will regard you as a courteous person. A socially highly posed personality or a venerable gentleman is greeted one with *nin hao* or *nin hao ma? Nin* is a polite form of "you," and is used predominantly in northern China.

The most conventional method of greeting, for which there is no corresponding expression in English, is to use the name of the person and to add to this a word that signifies respect. A man named Li, for instance, will be called "Li *xian sheng*." The English translation for this expression is "Li Mr." Westerners may answer this with a "Yes?" However, in Chinese, it would be proper to greet the person back using his or her name plus the polite form, like "Wang *nu shi*," ("Wang Ms."). Furthermore, in Chinese there is no equivalent to the Western set phrases: "Good morning," "Good day," "Good evening," or "Good night." True, one hears frequently on television the greeting form *zao shang* and *wan shang hao*. These are, however, word-for-word translations of English, and thus inspired Western neologisms. The traditional Chinese greetings *nar qu ya?* and *ni qu nar?* both have the meaning, "Where are you going?" For the most part, they are used if one meets someone on the street or in a building. A precise answer is, however, usually not expected. It may appear a bit strange to be addressed in such a way by an acquaintance on the street, but this should not cause you to worry. By no means are you expected to give detailed information about your intentions. It is sufficient to answer, "I go there," and at the same time give vague directions with the head or hands.

Another traditional Chinese greeting is the question *chi le ma?*, which means nothing more than, "Have you eaten?" Usually one puts this question to someone at noontime or in the evening. It frequently causes confusion when an American or European is greeted by a Chinese, "Have you already eaten?" at 11 A.M. The westerner expects a meal invitation or at least a meal together with such a question, while the question is purely rhetorical for the Chinese. Actually one is not seriously interested in whether you have already eaten or not. The question portrays in general no invitation to a joint lunch or dinner. The adequate answer to this greeting is a simple, "I have already eaten" or "I will soon eat." The answer "No, I haven't eaten yet" signals that one has no time or is not interested in a discussion, which may lead to an early end of the meeting.

A customary form of greeting with which a westerner is not familiar is a rhetorical question having to do with one's activity. An example: You are writing a letter and a friend visits you. A typical Chinese greeting in this case would be, "Oh, you write a letter" or "Did you write a letter to your family?" Chinese people frequently encounter this kind remark. They want to show their interest in the other person. A really general answer will suffice. Under no circumstances does the greeter expect a comprehensive explanation of what you have just written.

To westerners who are used to general greetings such as "Good morning" or "How are you?" the Chinese type of greeting may appear too personal. The personal greetings of the Chinese result from their living conditions, such as the restricted housing circumstances, and the distinctive networking of the Chinese society. The increasing Western influence can't be overlooked. As can be seen, one often encounters the European type of greeting—handshaking. Especially in big cities and coastal regions, this "imported" greeting is widespread. Here one can greet Chinese entirely with handshakes; one should be gentle, however. One should wait for a woman to offer her hand first.

Whereas in the West a welcoming kiss or embrace upon greeting is quite popular, that is still taboo for the Chinese. Bodily contact between the sexes is not morally acceptable. Thus, to avoid any misunderstandings, greetings should only be followed by a handshake.

Topics of Conversation

Westerners talk with each other willingly, especially if they are acquaintances, about harmless things such as the weather or sports. Chinese, on the other hand, talk only about the weather if it is unusually bad or if they really have no interest in the counterpart. Perhaps on an extraordinarily nice day, if need be, they might get carried away with "A nice day today, don't you think so, too?" In general, however, the Chinese begin a conversation with far more personal questions. Typical formulations are "Where do you work?" or "What is your occupation?" If already acquainted, the Chinese might inquire as to the health of the family. Say something about your husband or your wife and children or show your family photos and a Chinese will quickly take you to heart.

You should show your interest. Do not shy away from the company of Chinese with whom you have only business dealings. Signal to them your interest in their families. Questions about the place of origin of your counterpart are harmless. Most Chinese will gladly talk about their homeland, customs, and traditions. At a banquet, for instance, it is desirable to talk about Chinese cooking and its peculiarities.

Highly awkward, however, are themes that have anything at all to do with sex. Exceptions prove the rule. If you were to pick out as a central theme sexuality and erotica, you would quickly realize from your counterpart's reaction that you have come across a topic about which one does not speak in public in China. Most Chinese start to giggle, because it is somewhat embarrassing to them.

It is a delicate matter in China to discuss political questions, especially more recent political developments in China. A lot of themes have been discussed in the West, such as, for example, the Tiananmen Square massacre, Tibet, human rights, and abortion. The Chinese will meet these themes with silence. Themes of this kind can be discussed in China only in close circles. The Chinese find it unacceptable if you make a critical remark about high-ranking politicians. Also, one who jokes about China's leading politicians or the country will quickly become unpopular with the Chinese.

During all discussions, you should show great interest in the well-being of your partners. The best discussion for the Chinese is a harmoniously running conversation. Under no circumstances should you criticize the political and economic developments or monetary policy of the country, such as the yuan valuation. Complaining, voicing disapproval, boasting, and know-it-all mannerisms are considered taboo. Also, the Chinese perceive complaints about the weather, the meals, or the hotel room as impertinent. Concentrate instead on positive things. Bragging about individual achievements or those of your children also violates the Chinese sense of modesty. Praise your Chinese interlocutor instead, and mention the recognizable assets of his children, his wife, and so on.

Language—Ignore Negatives

Chinese, that is, *putonghua* (Mandarin), is by far the most widely spoken language of the world; it is also the oldest. Chinese is a living literary language, one that continues to develop from its prototype today. Actually, no one can say with certainty when written Chinese originated; the earliest evidence, however, dates to the middle of the second century before Christ. That evidence, Chinese characters carved in bones and turtle shells, is of an already fully developed language. The great continuity Chinese shows can be seen in the comparison of its old and modern characters: The characters used today don't differ considerably from the earliest ones. The most unusual thing about Chinese is that despite the complexity of its writing, in terms of grammar it is one of the easiest languages in the world. It is hard to learn complex characters and their meaning; however, the Chinese grammar is relatively simple to master.

Chinese consists of characters that portray the graphics of an often complex content. Thus, as opposed to English or German, a Chinese syllable is a word with its own meaning. This means fundamentally that there are just as many signs as concepts. That explains why the Chinese have so many characters: Modern dictionaries contain approximately forty to sixty thousand different characters of which only about five thousand are frequently used. One requires about three thousand characters to read a newspaper. These thousands of characters must be learned by heart. Thus, it is difficult and time consuming to learn the written language; Chinese children start to learn it in kindergarten. It can take years to master the characters, especially when one sees that one character might consist of as many as 28 individual strokes. In the mid-1960s the characters were greatly simplified in mainland China. The number of strokes in a character was reduced by up to 30 percent—which often led to the loss of symbolically signed elements. So, for example, the Chinese character for love has today lost its heart. Shortened characters are used only in the PRC. In Taiwan and Singapore, the traditional long characters are still in use. This should be kept in mind when printing name cards for a trip to China: Cards for the mainland need short characters, while the one for Hong Kong, Taiwan, or Singapore need traditional characters.

Tips for Business Cards

- Carry a sufficient number of business cards
- Use double-sided cards in English and Chinese
- Prepare separate cards for mainland China (short sign), and Hong Kong, Taiwan, and Singapore (traditional long-sign characters)
- Ensure the correct translation of the name, double-check the meaning
- Choose high-quality paper
- Use a business card holder
- Don't make notes on the cards you receive or hand out
- Present the card with a slight bow while holding it with both hands
- Read the name and title of the business partner after receiving their card

---

The central characteristic of the Chinese language is its tonality. Four different tonalities are distinguishable: constant high, rising, falling, and at first falling and then rising. The meaning of a word depends on its pronunciation. On account of an extremely small amount of syllables (simply four hundred different syllables form the building blocks of Chinese, while in Romantic languages, there are at least ten thousand) the number of homophones is extremely vast. For example, the syllable *li* has more than a hundred different meanings. Which is exactly the right one? You come to the conclusion through the context and the intonation of the voice modulation. Mistakes and misunderstandings are inevitable. Foreigners especially have difficulty with the correct pronunciation.

Chinese themselves have their communication difficulties. Two Chinese converse: *"What's your name?"* *"My name is Fang."* *"Which Fang? Square or fragrant?"* *"Fragrant!"* She writes the character for "fang," means fragrant, in the palm of her hand. Choosing the right pitch can be difficult. The grammar of the spoken Chinese, however, is much easier. The Chinese are not familiar with declensions, conjugations, and articles. Thus, the word undergoes fundamentally no change in a sentence. Therefore, the context and the position in the sentence are the determiners for the meaning. A fundamental characteristic of the Chinese language, and at the same time an indication of its grammatical simplicity, is its monosyllabicity: Each syllable is portrayed by a character; each character symbolizes a concept.

Basically, even today, the formula is that a spoken syllable counts as one character and represents one word. In the meantime, neologisms of many-syllable words have been formed from the original single syllables, a development of the language required to describe new facts, subjects, and phenomena. The meaning of a one-syllable word always remains the same, and it remains in the consciousness of the speaker. In most cases multisyllable words are additions to one-syllable words.

Similar to the French, who are very proud of their cultural language and therefore consciously avoid using foreign words, the Chinese also try to describe contemporary expressions with their traditional written characters. Whereas in Japan, foreign words are gladly and frequently accepted as phonetics, the Chinese use foreign words, phonetically translated, only with very specific terms that must be used in international dealings or with expressions that have no philosophical or cultural background in China.

Western observers have long assumed that as world markets became more international, China would switch from its complex, vivid syllable language to the Latin alphabet. Far from it! Through computerization, it has become much easier to deal with the characters. Chinese text-processing programs facilitate the quick, problem-free translation of characters. Analysis of sentence patterns proves the redundancy of Western languages. The sentence "China is very big," for example, is translated in Chinese as "China very big." The verb "to be" is unnecessary in Chinese. The drawback of the grammatical easiness of the Chinese language is that it lacks precision in comparison to Western languages. In Western languages, references in the sentence are named through the grammar (gender, declensions, conjugations) and are transparent, thus allowing a precise grammatical statement. A characterization of the Chinese language, on the other hand, is its vividness and ambiguity. Thus, it is understandable, what tremendous efforts translators make and why the Chinese translators often require more time and words than in English or German. An expression of conformity to the West was the introduction of phonetic transcription, by which the Chinese sounds are represented with the Latin alphabet. In 1979, the People's Republic of China introduced *pinyin* as the official phonetic transcription system. The attempt to introduce a phonetic alphabet goes back to the nineteenth century. Sir Thomas Wade introduced the first system of romanization in 1859; in 1892, it was revised by his successor, Herbert Giles, and consequently named the "Wade-Giles" system. The Wade-Giles system was used for over a century, and is still used in several countries, including Taiwan. The phonetic *pinyin* (*Han yu pinyin fangan*, Chinese Language Transcription Proposal), was introduced by the government of the PRC in 1953, and finally implemented in 1979. Since then, China's capital, Peking, has officially become Beijing. Foreign media and governmental institutions, including the U.S. Congress, have fully adapted *pinyin*. The differences between both systems are small but clearly visible: "Mao Zedong" is the official spelling according to *pinyin*, while "Mao Tse-tung" follows the old Wade-Giles spelling. For this book, pinyin was used with the exception of few historical names and those of people living outside of the Chinese mainland, such as Chiang Kai-shek.

Body Language

The importance of the nonverbal signs in any interaction should never be underestimated. Bearing, gesture, mimicry, silence, sound of the voice, and clothing offer clues about a person's personality as well as his or her current mood. In a face- and harmony-oriented society like the Chinese, body language is used as subtle ambiguity, avoiding a clear position.

The Smile

Often irritating for the westerner is the Chinese masklike smile. It is much more than an expression of joy and happiness; it is also specifically used to keep one's feelings under control in difficult or less-than-favorable conditions. In the face- and consent-oriented Chinese society, self-discipline and control are characteristics of the highest order. The stoic expression of many Asians is used to overact and conceal. The calm and identical expression of the Asians is unfathomable to many westerners. In a society where only those able to conceal their feelings are deemed correct and proper, control over the feelings is essential.

Silence

Silence is a Chinese virtue; for that reason, long pauses in conversations are not seen as an embarrassment, but rather as the opposite. Intermissions are used to relax, think, and fathom one's counterparts as well as test their mental strength. In these situations, westerners are advised not to break the silence, but rather to endure it.

Eye Contact

Whereas in the Western world continuous eye contact is seen as faithful and earnest, in Asia it is viewed as rude and aggressive. In China, direct and offensive eye contact is avoided during conversations. Brief eye contact is usually made, and after that the eye focuses to the right or left of the counterpart. With superiors, making continuous eye contact is a sign of disrespect and provocation.

Body Contact

In the West, it is quite common for couples to stroll embraced or to hold hands and to show their affection openly. In Asia, in keeping with traditional values, such behavior is repugnant. According to Confucian teachings, contact between men and women prior to marriage is prohibited. Even after the wedding, it is improper to embrace or kiss in public. Only recently, due to Western influences—such as movies—have these traditions begun to change. Today in the cities more and more young couples can be seen strolling and holding hands. The elder generation nevertheless lives strictly according to the Confucian codes. What is more striking to a westerner is the casual intimacy between persons of the same gender. In China, it is quite common for two women to walk hand in hand. Similarly, contact between men is quite open.

During conversation, the Chinese often touch their counterpart to ensure attention. Some also place their hand on the thigh or put their arm around you. These are signs of respect and trust toward the counterpart.

Gestures

One should be careful about transferring Western standards or habits to Asia. It is an insult to beckon somebody to approach by folding an index finger or to snap one's fingers. The Asian gesture to motion somebody to approach is likewise irritating to the westerner and is similar to a child's gesturing; With the palm facing down and the thumb close to the palm, the fingers wiggle three to four times toward the inside of the palm.

Nodding is a widespread gesture, which the westerner often interprets as agreement. However, it means only that the speaker has been recognized. In case a Chinese wants to point toward himself, he touches his nose with the index finger. Unusual for westerners is the southern Chinese gesture of thanks for pouring tea, that is, tapping with the middle and index finger several times on the table.

In conversations in general and in negotiations especially, one should always keep both feet firmly on the ground, literally. It is extremely improper and a sign of disrespect to point one's shoe soles toward the counterpart. This rule of etiquette is based on the Chinese belief that the feet are the lowest body part and thus the most unclean. President George Bush, the elder, committed a faux pas of the highest order during his state visit to China: He presented Chairman Deng Xiaoping a pair of Texan cowboy boots embroidered with the Chinese and American flags. Bush did not realize that the feet are totally taboo for the Chinese. The size of this blunder was comparable to the faux-pas that happened in 2000, when the German Chancellor Gerhard Schröder presented then-President Clinton a box of Cuban cigars during his state visit. His present violated not only the American trade embargo of Cuban cigars, it also hinted at the White House scandal few years earlier.

Gestures indicating discomfort or skepticism are of special importance. They are often a substitute for the open discussions that are not possible in face-conscious China. Women, for example, signal embarrassment by holding the hand in front of the mouth. Someone scratching his or her eyebrows indicates discomfort and a mistrust of his or her counterpart. The frequent spitting of the Chinese as well as their habit of blowing the nose onto the street is disgusting to many Western people, although this habit is becoming less frequent, especially since the SARS outbreak in 2003. The Chinese see it as nothing more than a hygienic measure: the clearing of all impure body fluids. In contrast, the Chinese see the loud Western way of blowing the nose into a handkerchief as very rude and unhygienic.

Gifts

Presents are an important part of Chinese culture. Today, official policy in China forbids giving gifts, as they are considered bribery. The law distinguishes between official bribery, which involves personnel of the state, and is a criminal offense, and commercial bribery, which does not automatically constitute a legal violation but unfair competition. Rulings in 2002 indicate that gifts up to 1,500 RMB (US$180) are acceptable, whereas higher amounts, and especially cash, are seen as bribe.[45] Attitudes are beginning to relax again, as gifts are an essential element to start a relationship and to keep it going. Chinese often refer to presents as "lubricants" that help start and keep the "engine" of friendship going. An important part of giving is establishing a personal connection between two persons, the important *guanxi* (i.e. the creation of a social network). The well-established tradition of gift giving is less a matter of the exchange of commercial goods than it is the creation of a social relationship.

Presents are given at many social opportunities (e.g., within the family or on private, business, or public occasions). Nobody, for example, would go to a birthday party or visit someone in the hospital without a present. Relatives as well as good friends receive gifts during the Spring, Autumn, and New Year festivals. Also private invitations to a dinner require presents. These presents are already being influenced by fashion trends. Traditionally for a dinner invitation, food or fruits were given, whereas in Guangzhou, Shanghai, and Beijing, people have started to give Western gifts, such as colorful flowers. During a hospital visit, the Chinese present fruit or stimulating drinks to enhance the healing process. Western visitors should bring products that are also regarded as healing in the West, such as Gelee Royal. Not only the ill but also the elderly enjoy these elixirs. Traditionally, the Chinese start to celebrate their birthday from 40 onward, but only 'round' birthdays are celebrated, such as 50, 60, or 70. Lately, more and more importance is placed on children's birthdays, which are celebrated with much expense and many gifts. Well received by young and old people is money as a gift. Children receive red paper envelopes containing money at the New Year. Giving money to friends is not a sign of having no imagination but is meant to accelerate wealth. For weddings, the Chinese give extravagant money gifts or gifts for outfitting the flat. If you are invited to a wedding, Western presents always make a good impression.

When the Chinese go to Europe or America, it is essential for them to bring home souvenirs from their trip for all relatives and acquaintances. Everybody who travels must have small presents for family, friends, neighbors, superiors, and colleagues, to share one's fortune with them. You should therefore, upon undertaking a trip to China, always have small presents for your business partners as well as their friends. Popular is fine liquor for men, whereas women appreciate perfumes, cosmetics, and fashion accessories as well as household appliances. As in the West, children like sweets and toys. Please keep in mind that presents should always be adequate. If a present is too expensive, it could trouble the Chinese recipient, whereas a cheap one could offend him or her.

All over Asia, the awareness of obligations and reciprocity is much stronger than it is in Europe or the United States. Generally, giving is never without one's own interests. The present must not only fit the occasion but also fit the position of the recipient. It is important to consider the advantage one is trying to gain from the present. Because the principle of "setting off" is well established in China, a present will ensure the gratitude of the recipient. Putting your present onto the scale forces your counterpart to balance it. Balancing is a continuous process and similar to the saying "one hand washes the other"; both partners have to alternate between giving and taking. The balancing must not be materialistic, but it can be a new business relationship, a favor, or other benefits. The goal is always a harmony of the contrasts.

To westerners, the Chinese ceremony of giving and receiving presents might seem strange. The Chinese are taught modesty from an early age; therefore, it is improper to accept a present immediately. Etiquette requires the recipients to reject the present in the beginning by pretending modesty. Now, it would be very impolite if the gift giver were to withdraw the present. It is expected that he or she remain firm, insisting that the present be accepted. After a long period of hesitation and repeated insistence on the part of the guest, the host will finally accept. Nevertheless, he or she will continuously state that "this was not necessary" or even "I am sure you know somebody who needs it much more than I do."

Tips for Gifts

Appreciated presents

- Old Cognac, whisky, or other fine liquor
- Vitamins, geriatric elixirs, western-grown ginseng
- Books or framed paintings, especially about your country
- International stamps
- Beer jug or stein mug
- Chocolate, sweets
- Wristwatches (from Swatch to Rolex)
- Golf accessories (balls, clubs, putter)
- Leather items (belt, business card holder)
- Electric appliances (cellular phone, coffeemaker, children's toys)
- Branded products (sunglasses, fountain-pens, cosmetics and perfumes)
- Commemorative coins (company logo, in English and Chinese)

Presents to avoid

- Clocks (the Chinese word for clock is associated with death)
- Shoes (considered impure)
- Green porcelain (hint for adultery)
- Four of any kind (the word for "4" also means death in Chinese)

Having survived this ceremony, you should not be disappointed if the gift is put unopened in a corner, without further notice. Only after the last guest has left will it be opened. Behind this ritual is the intention to keep the face of the guest: His or her present should not be evaluated by the other guests.

Giving an unwrapped present might be done for various reasons. A delegation should receive identical company presents to ensure that nobody feels discriminated against. Another reason could be to impress the host and get him or her into a positive mood. Wrapped presents should be opened only if the giving person vehemently insists. A last hurdle might be during the farewell, where the host might try to return your present. Don't get trapped; these are mere words. The Chinese view our spontaneous unwrapping and excitement often as greedy and impatient. It might nevertheless be that a Chinese person unwraps a present in your presence. This might especially happen on the Chinese eastern coast, as the Western influence there is quite strong.

WAYS OF NEGOTIATION

Bureaucracy

The Chinese dislike of the concentration of power is expressed in the assignment of decisions to various hierarchical levels; almost every project depends on cooperation between such levels. In general, the larger the project, the more agreements are necessary. Conducting business relations with China is one of the biggest challenges of this century. Not only does an enormous consumer potential exist, but also there is a strong need for technology transfer and managerial knowledge. Another point is the vast cultural divide, which requires a different form of communication. One must be aware at all times that the Chinese business partner is not an individual person, but a representative acting as part of a large network. Nobody should expect that international standards of conducting business will become reality in China, although, with increasing globalization of China, certain international practices and ways of doing business are becoming accepted. The Chinese system is based on strict hierarchies, an almighty bureaucracy, and a well-established nepotism. Although such differences between the "old" and the "new" world could hardly be more distinct, the Chinese political and social system seems to be getting stronger more than it is changing.

Today's "New China," a China full of changes, carries many contradictions: Economic progress and political repression, capitalist development and socialist regulation, and speedy economic dynamism and inflexible bureaucratic structures exist side by side.

Hierarchy

In the traditionally structured society of China, important decisions are made at the top of the ladder. On large projects it is not uncommon to have 20 to 40 top managers who are responsible for decisions. Within this top-manager elite, the older and more experienced members have the most authority. In most cases, the younger managers have to obey the principle of seniority and must respect decisions made by the older members.

This orientation toward high-ranking officeholders often slows down processes and suppresses initiative. Lower-ranking officeholders will avoid individual decisions for various reasons. They might not be sure that the decision is in line with the basic policy of the higher functionaries, and they also want to avoid mistakes for which they could later be held accountable. "If I don't do anything, I cannot make a mistake." This frequent Chinese attitude is also based on the fact that bad decisions or bad conduct always equal a loss of face and thus bring about the contempt of the society. For the Chinese, the sanctions following a wrong decision have a much greater impact than the praise that follows from a good one. Therefore decisions for which one person could be held accountable will be avoided, and major decisions will be made as compromises within a group. Nobody wants to be noticed; everybody is seeking the "golden middle way," the common decision without individual responsibility.

The Chinese are known for discussing many things within a group and holding very long meetings (*kaihui*) to find a solution acceptable to all members of the group. This might even be extended to other departments or authorities. The larger the base for a mutually agreed-to decision, the better. It is also common practice to pass on decisions to higher levels in the hierarchy. This happens often, and the person in charge might not be able to make any decision at all because of the complexity and many layers of the problem.

Westerners over and over again are astonished at the idleness of Chinese officials, a behavior that is indicative of their hostility toward making decisions. Activity might force somebody into making decisions, which could then lead to mistakes. Thus, for a Chinese official, work means mostly *mafan*, a mixture of annoyance and disturbance. Despite all the lethargy of the officials, one should never lose one's temper. Nothing is more offensive to the Chinese or more damaging to oneself than to react uncontrollably, thus losing the respect of the official and respect of oneself.

Kaihui (Endless Meetings) and Negotiations

The Chinese principle of permanent negotiations is an expression of their moderate character—always aiming for balance. One aim of this principle is to balance the hierarchy, which itself is basically in opposition to a harmonic, balanced society. Because hierarchy might lead to very influential forces, the accumulation of power must be weakened. Thus it makes sense that many divisions, departments, or even authorities have counterparts with similar functions so as to weaken the influence of both. In addition, departments are strongly interlocked horizontally and vertically, which leads to mutual control or even competition.

Consensus—mutual agreement by all sides—is of central importance for the Chinese. Negotiations will be held until a mutual agreement is arrived at by all negotiation partners. This way of finding a mutual consensus, and especially the enormous amount of time needed to do so, is tedious and stressful for westerners. One should therefore not expect to hold Western-Chinese negotiations based on a Western time schedule. Ma-

jority decisions, as are common in the West, are taboo in China, as such a
decision would mean a loss of face for those who were vetoes. Nevertheless, this kind of consensus finding—to integrate different views and find
a minimal consensus—has an advantage, as everybody can identify him-
or herself with the decision and will therefore support it. Often Chinese
and westerners start negotiations with contrary goals. Whereas the Chinese delegation will concentrate on a consensus and emphasize points
where mutual agreement seems possible, the Western delegation will
stress those points on which differences exist. The building-up strategy of
the Chinese aims to broaden the minimal consensus base, whereas the
Western side aims to push its own goals as strongly as possible. It is common for a Western delegation to explain the facts and limits at the very
beginning, which leaves little room for maneuvering. The Chinese will
never show their cards right at the beginning but will show a much wider
base for negotiations. Thus, during the negotiations they can achieve the
goals set prior to the meeting without losing any face.

Of central importance are the differences in the Western and Chinese
ways of thinking; we can refer to those ways as analytical thinking and
synthetic thinking, respectively. The Chinese follow the strategy of "as well
as." Their art of negotiating is not to press for their own best-case goals or
to compare basic facts in search of different solutions; instead the Chinese
are interested in a synthesis of different, divergent positions into a harmonious overall concept. Harmony between the two sides as well as in
their own group, not simple facts, is important. The presentation of various options does little to speed up the decision making. It is not possible
for the Chinese to lean toward one alternative, thus denouncing another
option. Here, again, the "as well as" strategy comes into play, searching
for the best compromise. Only those who try to harmonize different opinions and positions to a harmonious, overall concept that can be mutually
accepted will have success. It is therefore strongly recommended that
Western managers not use Western-influenced thinking, such as the "either . . . or" approach or the "take it or leave it" approach.

Discussion Styles

Only the knowledge that the style and structure of a discussion is im-
parted by culture and that methods and conventions of discussion vary
according to country and cultural background enables people to have
truly cross-cultural communication. It is therefore important to envisage
the characteristics of Chinese conversation and negotiation. Especially fruit-
ful is a comparison between Western and Chinese language conventions.

The maxim of polite and modest conversation (*keqi hua*) is very valid in
China. A basic rule of any conversation or negotiation is to keep Chinese
etiquette in mind. In addition, a very modest appearance is important,

never putting one's own personality to the front. One should be especially sure to avoid open disagreements with the counterparts and not discuss negative topics. It is important to pay compliments and emphasize positive points in order to create a harmonious atmosphere. During the talks, directness should be avoided as the harmony-seeking Chinese prefer indirect conversations.

The Western style of discussion often uses concrete and direct expressions, as well as Western logical, stringent argumentation. The Chinese way of polite talking results from the centerpiece of their social world: the concept of face. In Chinese society the speaker is expected to provide an atmosphere of harmony during the talks, ensuring the balance among all parties. This aim for absolute harmony allows no open confrontation or controversy. Everybody tries to maintain balance and unity. This is so important that even minor falsehoods or white lies are accepted. Sometimes they are even necessary. A white lie might keep the harmony, whereas the unvarnished truth might upset it.

Statements such as "We have to study the case somewhat more in detail" or "We will think about it" give the Western side the impression that the Chinese are quite interested but need some more time to make a decision. Wrong! These phrases are their way of refusing a proposal. Amongst themselves, the Chinese fully understand such phrases as politely wrapped refusals. No one perceives them as impolite and no loss of face is correlated with the refusal; the message has nevertheless been delivered clearly. Terminology such as *koalue kaolue* ("We will think about it"), *yanijiu yixia* or *yanijiu yanijiu* ("We have to study the case somewhat more"), *keneng* (maybe) or sentences such as "Maybe it is presently not so suitable" or "Maybe this possibility is inconvenient for you" signal either a refusal or a disagreement, without discussing the matter in detail.

Even in the case the Chinese could answer a question clearly, they won't do so; rather, they will weaken a statement with qualifiers such as "possibly," "maybe." A too direct statement could convey the impression of a lack of modesty and too much self-display. When asking a Chinese if someone has just left the office, one will not receive the direct reply "Yes, he left already." In most cases the answer will be something like "Maybe he just left," because the speaker intends not to show off his or her knowledge.

The "maybe" (*keneng*) in this case documents the proverbial modesty of the Chinese. The huge discrepancy between styles and conventions of discussion often leads to stereotypical judgments on the part of the foreign speakers. The Chinese "language of deviations" is often regarded negatively in the West. Westerners find the style of the Chinese language imprecise, unclear, and tedious. Chinese on the other hand, describe westerners as impolite, impatient, too direct, even aggressive. Experience also shows that the Chinese often feel pushed into a corner just by the Western style of discussion. For the westerners, who are often pressed for time, it is very hard to adjust to the Chinese strategy of "coming slowly to the point" (*zhuanwan mojiao*). A wish or a request for an example cannot simply be made but must be cautiously and politely explored with all linguistic means. This method is viewed as essential in China. Talking about minor points at the beginning gives the Chinese negotiator the possibility to "check out" his counterpart and develop a relationship. Only then is it time to talk about major topics.

The most important statement will therefore always occur at the end of a discussion or speech. By then, westerners might have lost their concentration completely. Bored, because the Chinese do not come to the point, we might well miss the important main statement. In the West, it is almost the opposite, as major topics are voiced at the beginning and details are discussed later. This method is irritating and seems aggressive, as well as impolite, to the Chinese. The problem is obvious: Whereas the Western concept expects concentration right from the beginning, the Chinese will focus their concentration at the end. This conflict can be "softened" with a milder approach. For example, in the opening dialogue one could talk about American-Chinese friendship as well as respect for the country and the people.

There are nevertheless many examples of the Chinese adapting to the Western style of discussion. Chinese who have regular contact with the West often orient themselves accordingly. Sometimes they overadapt, and they surpass the Europeans and Americans in their openness and direct talk. Not knowing the border between openness and lack of tact, they express excessive requirements. By associating openness with the West, they may come to the conclusion that no boundaries exist for inquiries or requests. They have heard that to get a wish fulfilled, one has to express it; this often leads to a negative mood on the Western side. Consider this example: A German company invited a Chinese delegation to Germany. The Chinese thanked their hosts politely and asked in the same moment for an excursion to London and Paris, as they were already in Europe. The Germans were furious over the immoderate and impudent Chinese, at the way in which their invitation had been answered; they felt they had been taken advantage of.

Chinese who try to be Western do not completely understand concepts such as directness; they just use them superficially. They have no feeling for the boundaries that we learned early in the process of socialization. In the previous example, because of a cultural misunderstanding, an impression of the impudent Chinese arose. In situations of intercultural communication, the difference between the codes of the sender and those of the recipient can lead to communication problems. When parties believe that their code is the only and therefore the correct one, it leads automatically to communication problems. Such problems generate misunderstandings and prejudices that might well lead to the end of negotiations.

Prior to the Negotiations

Everyone doing business in China should automatically factor in the complex bureaucracy. Success is possible only for those who have knowledge of the specific Chinese requirements and who work with a proper strategy in this market. At the very beginning, the investor should be aware of the different options for his or her Chinese business. A clear bottom line should be drawn, and crossing that line should lead to an exit. This should include what are acceptable financial losses. Western companies sometimes make the mistake of "forcing" the China business. For the China business, as for all businesses, one should continuously evaluate whether a project can be realized or not.

A business in China should be based on a strategy focusing on a steady, step-by-step building up of business relations. As an example, one could first start with a representative office facilitating indent business, followed by negotiations over a technology transfer leading to a cooperation and a joint venture. It would be unwise to hasten these steps in any Chinese business. Only those who adapt to the Chinese need for a slow building up of sound business relations will succeed. Here, then, are some concrete tips for your Chinese business relations:

- Because of the strict hierarchy of the Chinese bureaucracy, you should contact high-ranking officials and authorities at the very beginning. Lower-level authorities will then be obliged to follow their instructions. The strict adherence to etiquette will lead to close checking by the Chinese side of which hierarchical level would be the correct one for your company. The higher your business is classified, the more privileges you have. It pays therefore to present oneself very well in the initial negotiations. If successful, you will receive a higher classification, and your negotiation partners will have a higher level of competence. The advantage is a much faster chain of decision.

- Essential for business in China is to establish your own *guanxi* network. Building up and nurturing such a network might well take years. Establishing a representative office can therefore be a strong advantage.

- An aid to establishing your *guanxi* network could be a mediator with experience in Chinese business. Often a mutual acquaintance might be a mediator. If a third party has solid contacts on both sides, that fact alone might already serve as a good basis for cooperation. Possible partners might be overseas Chinese with family ties in China or anyone who has worked in China or cooperated with Chinese authorities. International chambers of commerce, business organizations, and international Chinese trade organizations can be of help. One should be careful with international consultants. Their ability might range from excellent to charlatanism. Good contacts may also be found during international trade exhibitions in large cities. In addition to the opportunity of presenting your own company, these exhibitions provide you a good opportunity to meet potential business partners and initiate first contacts.

- In general, you are advised not to initiate the business in China exclusively via Hong Kong. The Chinese give importance to the direct contact, which can be direct to the local office or even to the head office in the West. However, the contact should be held on a continuous basis. Also, consistency of the contact partners is important.

- Be sure that you are not "laying in the same bed but dreaming different dreams"—the basic requirement for a successful negotiation is a definition of common interests. Experience shows that often business relations lack a common base; the interests are completely different. Even with technology or investment contracts, the Chinese side often is interested only in foreign capital, technology, and new jobs, whereas the Western companies are dreaming about the vast Chinese market.

- Be sure to obtain various offers. It is beneficial to negotiate simultaneously with different cooperation partners. The Chinese entrepreneurs do the same and negotiate in parallel with different foreign companies. Important: Keep the negotiations on a general base. Do not offer technical know-how or production details in early negotiations.

The Contract

Chinese and westerners have contrary ideas of the function and definition of a contract. In the West, a contract strictly defines the rights and duties of both partners and regulates consequences of a breach. For the Chinese, a contract is the basic framework for a business relationship and thus can be modified. A contract is not an irrevocable legal document but a sketch of conditions, which can be adapted at any time, in case the basic conditions change. The Western side views a request for a change after signing the contract as a breach; compliance is expected. The Chinese generally reserve the right to renegotiate if negotiation is seen as beneficial. This conduct is regarded as normal and perfectly acceptable by the Chinese, who would have a similar understanding if the Western side also asked for changes.

For a Western partner, a contract is the result and summary of negotiations, describing the rules that all partners must adhere to. The Chinese side sees a contract as the end of the negotiations and the beginning of a mutual and trusting business relationship. The trustworthiness of the partners is continuously emphasized, as is the desire to further strengthen the relationship. In addition, the business partner who conducted the negotiations and signed the contract is more significant than the contract itself. If the Western company changes that partner, that might lead to a different attitude on the part of the Chinese toward the contract—that is, they would see the contract as less strict since they have no relationship with the new partner. As one can see, the cultural divide is tremendous. Conceptions about the functions of a contract and the liability incurred thereby could hardly be more opposite. Constructing a trustworthy relationship is the important thing for the Chinese, whereas business interests are the main emphasis of westerners.

Recommendations for Contract Drafts

Contracts are often drafted in Chinese and English. Check both versions carefully, but be sure that the Chinese version has been exactly translated. If a problem arises later, the Chinese will hold the contract written in Chinese to be valid. Because of lack of basic legal regulations, the Chinese drafts are often longer and more general. Whereas in a Western contract, special paragraphs or phrases from civil and business laws can be cited, only in rare cases can the Chinese refer to such legal expressions or even laws. This means that regulations and basic assumptions have to be clearly formulated.

Tips for Contracts

- Use existing contracts as an example.
- Use simple, clear phrases.
- Define mutual and reciprocal obligations; avoid long lists.

Long catalogs of demands or duties should be avoided. It might well be that you are asked to fulfill your specific duties even though the Chinese partners have not fulfilled theirs. The Chinese partner might for example insist on the second shipment of a partial delivery, even though the first one has not been paid for as agreed upon. One side might be obliged legally to adhere to its list of duties even if the contract does not specifically indicate that fulfillment of a duty by one side does require the prior fulfillment of a duty by the other. In addition, ensure that the contract connects the duties of both partners. View your contract as a kind of zipper system; A contribution from one side leads to a contribution from the other side. Only then is the first side required to act again. This ensures the mutual and reciprocal character of the contract.

Negotiations

Everyone involved in international business must be able to negotiate. Negotiating means more than employing clever tactics to succeed with your own business interests. It is more important to realize that in international negotiations, partners with different systems of logic and strategies of negotiations will come together. It is no secret that negotiating with the Chinese is difficult. Many Western businessmen describe the Chinese as unpredictable, tedious, and not always fair. Westerners observe that the Chinese don't share their logic and rationality at all. With consternation they admit that there are no plausible explanations for the attitudes and proceedings of the Chinese. Quite often a negotiation fails because of the inability of the counterparts to adapt, even after a very promising start.

It is especially true for Chinese-Western business negotiations that successful business undertakings be concluded only by those informed about the culture and habits of their partners. All negotiations must be held while keeping in mind the cultural differences regarding company structure, negotiation style, and discussion strategy. Europeans and Americans will regard the structure of a Chinese delegation, which consists of three groups, as unusual. It might surprise westerners that specialists—for example, very competent engineers—make up the lowest level of the delegation hierarchy. They are very well educated and have a strong interest in Western technological know-how. These experts form the technical basis for the negotiations; they initiate the concrete work on the project. Because of the West's high regard for competence and knowledge, the Western business partners often pay the highest respect to these specialists. In contrast, the functionaries often are shown too little respect, generating a feeling of being passed over. Important: Give face to the decision makers!

Managers rank higher than specialists. They are responsible for the economic and financial side of the project. In contrast to the specialists, managers rarely have detailed know-how about the project. Prior to the negotiations, the managers will collect information about the foreign business partner. This includes an evaluation of the company's worldwide ranking and an investigation into its financial strength, level of research and development, and general image and prestige. It is their duty to evaluate whether negotiations and business relations will become profitable. The managers conceptualize the content and proceedings of the negotiations.

The real decision makers are the political functionaries and the officials from the ministries. They bear the political responsibility and evaluate whether the project is in line with company policy and with the regional as well as the socioeconomic planning policies. The head of the delegation is often an elderly CPC member. He rarely gets involved actively in the negotiations and has basically representative functions. He is superior to the different groups and coordinates the talks. One of his important tasks is to stay back and observe the negotiations, but he still coordinates everything behind the scenes. Here the specialists have his particular interest. The relations among the specialists, managers, and functionaries are intricate and bear a lot of potential for conflict. Because the functionaries have no special knowledge and often don't speak foreign languages, they often envy their younger colleagues. Thus, they show their power by implementing many rules and rejecting requests. A further duty of the head of the delegation is supervising etiquette. At the end of successful discussions, the head of the delegation summarizes the negotiations and presents the results.

Another central role in the negotiations is that of the speaker, who is a mediator between the Western and Chinese groups. He functions as a master of ceremony and is responsible for the cohesiveness of the various groups involved. He specifies statements, summarizes interim results, comments on statements of the Western side, and also forwards questions from the westerners to the Chinese. Quite often, after tensions between the Chinese groups, the speaker is changed. A change of speakers signals that the Chinese delegation is not satisfied with the development of the negotiations but also that they are willing to start anew. The Chinese might be dissatisfied with the negotiations, or about the tensions within their groups. Another reason might be that too many concessions and promises have been made and they are looking for a retreat without losing face. Even in the case that negotiations start right from the last stage, keep your structure of argumentation. Do not point out previous results reached, but keep in mind that some solutions on the table do not satisfy the Chinese.

Protocol

A protocol documents the course of a negotiation. Chinese write mostly a protocol of the course each of their conferences has taken. They like to keep a record of the discussions at every stage of the negotiation. One can assume that each statement, compromise, or promise will be recorded and might well be presented at a later stage. A protocol is especially important for the Chinese to check on the trustworthiness of the business partners. If a partner changes the strategy of argumentation too frequently, he will lose reliability. Keep your chain of argumentation constant; deviations without explanation can be used to your disadvantage. Write a similar protocol, and if possible, ask the other delegation to countersign it at the end of the negotiations. Then you will always be able to verify the statements of the Chinese regarding business conditions, as well as recall your own position.

Translator

Choose an experienced translator. English as an international business language is widespread in China; however, not everyone speaks fluent English. The Chinese side will rarely hold negotiations without a translator and will refuse negotiations in a foreign language for good reason. Thus, the Chinese delegation will always have a translator. Although one of the Chinese delegation might speak excellent English, he will not disclose that fact but try to learn valuable information from the Western delegation. He also might not speak English to avoid taking face from those in his delegation not able to communicate in English. The translator of the Chinese side will always stand for the interests of the Chinese; therefore it is advisable to use one's own translator. However, excellent knowledge of English and Chinese is not enough. A good translator must not only be able to translate but also be able to mediate between both cultures. This requires good knowledge of both the Chinese and the Western culture, whether American, German, Italian or other. Furthermore, as a member of your delegation, your translator represents your company. Thus he or she should learn about the company, business, philosophy, and structures. A good briefing—especially for the technical terminology used—can mean the success or failure of negotiations. A translator rarely will stop and question a statement his or her own delegation makes, but will just translate to show no lack of linguistic knowledge. Try to brief the translator in advance and let him or her recall what he or she has learned about the project.

The Christmas Strategy

The Chinese are well known as clever tacticians, for being able to steer negotiations with a great sense for the achievable. They play masterfully with time, and a special variant of the Chinese negotiation poker is the "Christmas strategy." Here the Chinese combine two points: a penchant for delay and dragging out the negotiations with the full knowledge of the significance that Christmas has for their counterparts. Being aware of the immense meaning Christmas has for the West, of the meaning of the family celebrations, the Chinese like to choose the pre-Christmas season as the time for finalizing negotiations. The Chinese know that the westerner will try everything to finalize the negotiations before Christmas, which he or she would like to spend with family. Here the Chinese tactics start; they delay the negotiations to achieve more favorable conditions and better contract terms. By dragging things out, they build up pressure on a partner who is eager to close the negotiations.

My recommendation: Concessions do not pay. Leave calmly for home. As smart businessmen, the Chinese know very well how far they can go.

Often they are calling for a bluff, and the decision will be made one or two days after your departure. Sometimes the contracts might be signed at the last minute at the airport, or an e-mail or fax will be waiting in your office upon arrival. How widespread this tactic is, is shown in a new phrase of the Chinese: Contracts signed at the last minute are called "car-roof" contracts. A recent Western-Chinese business negotiation went like this:

A German businessman traveled to China for negotiations with a Chinese delegation. The negotiations were lengthy and difficult, developing slowly. Finally the businessman lost all hope, stopped the negotiations and left. On the way to the airport, his car was stopped by a motorcycle on the highway. The driver of the motorcycle came to the car, and the businessman recognized his negotiation partner—to his complete surprise. The Chinese pulled a paper out of his bag and handed it to the astonished westerner: It was the signed contract ready for countersignature.

The example illustrates that the Chinese play poker excellently. Only those who keep a cool head on their shoulders can succeed. As a small tip: Beat the Chinese at their own game and reverse the Christmas strategy. Quite promising is the so-called "Spring Festival strategy." Normally the Chinese will do everything in their power to be with their family in time for the Spring Festival (i.e., the Chinese New Year).

Strategies of Negotiation

Western	*Chinese*
• Result oriented	• Process oriented
• Final goal is important	• The way is the goal
• Time is money	• Good things take time
• Negotiation process is limited	• Negotiation process is continuous
• Fact oriented	• Relationship oriented
• Efficiency	• Mutual consensus

Obviously, westerners, with their habit of planning and calculating in advance, will have difficulties with the Chinese way of business. For the westerner, for example, it is complicated and confusing to understand the different rules of decision making in the Chinese network, which is also influenced by its hierarchical structures. It would be fateful to ignore these hierarchies. The deciding factor in Western-Chinese negotiation might not be the decisions based on the facts but rather the way the negotiations were conducted, which has to respect Chinese peculiarities. It is crucial to show respect for and honor the Chinese managers and functionaries. Very fact-oriented nations, such as Germany or the United States, have problems in this area. Used to arguing according to technical and economic lines to reach conclusions, they favor their technical counterparts. They have difficulty connecting with the managers and functionaries, who often do not understand the details, but make the final decisions. They especially do not take into account that business relationships are more significant to the Chinese than purely purpose-oriented alliances. The high value the Chinese give to the soundness and trustworthiness of their relations is a central point of Chinese culture: For the Chinese, the business and private realms are not two fully independent areas. In the diffuse Asian culture, everything is somehow connected. Therefore, a Chinese partner is interested not only in your scientific competence but also in where you went to school, which friends you have, what life you lead, and what you think about life, politics, culture, music, art, and literature. Westerners, who tend to separate strictly work and private life, regard such questions as being of slight importance to the outcome of their negotiations.

In negotiating in an Asian culture, it is important to put aside any focus on fact-oriented questions and to use the diffuse strategy common in countries such as China or Japan, which is also practiced in southern Europe. At first, one tries to get to know the business partner; only then, after the first contacts are made, can one "get down to business." Those who realize this will see that in composition the delegation is an expression of the diffuse Chinese culture. The presence of high-ranking functionaries shows the importance of the relationship. The role of etiquette can be seen right from the start. Persons of similar or higher rank will receive foreign delegations.

Respect paid to you should be returned to the Chinese participants. You should be sure to pay respect according to a person's rank, rather than according to his or her technical knowledge. Especially in the early phase, give the higher-ranking and elderly managers and functionaries their due honor and respect.

NOTES

1. Forest Lee. "China to Accelerate Its Urbanization Pace." *People's Daily Online*, Dec. 06, 2002. http://english.peopledaily.com.cn/200212/06/eng.20021206_108064. shtml, Apr. 17, 2003; *see also in China Statistical Yearbook 2002*. China Statistics Press, Oct. 2002, table 2–4.

2. U.S. Commercial Service. "Shanghai." 2001–2004. http://www.buyusa.gov/china/en/shanghai.html, Mar. 17, 2004; *see also* Nehru, V., Kraay, A., and Xiaoqing, Yu. *China 2020. Development Challenges in the New Century*. The World Bank, Washington, D.C., Sep. 1997, p. 21.

3. *China Statistical Yearbook 1996*. China Statistics Press, Oct. 1996, pp. 42, 46;

see also "China's economy grows by 9.1%, highest since 1997." *Jakarta Post,* Jan. 21, 2004, p. 16.

4. Nehru, V. et. al, 1997, p. 20, table 2.1.

5. "Statistics about Utilization of Foreign Direct Investment." 2004, Foreign Investment Administration, MOFCOM, 2004, http://www.fdi.gov.cn/state/index.jsp?category = 0201&app = 00000000000000000014&language = en&current Page = 1, Mar. 27, 2004.

6. Liu, M. "Why China Cooks the Books." *Newsweek,* Apr. 1, 2002, pp. 40–43.

7. Maddison, A. *The World Economy: Historical Statistics.* OECD Development Center, Paris, France, 2003. The calculation of the individual growth figures during the respective periods was done by the author.

8. "China's Retail Sales to Jump by 10% This Year." *People's Daily Online,* Jan. 14, 2003, http://english.peopledaily.com.cn/200301/14/eng20030114_110097.shtml, Dec. 12, 2003.

9. "Record U.S. Trade Deficit In 2003." *CBS NEWS.com,* Feb. 13, 2004. http://www.cbsnews.com/stories/2004/02/13/national/printable600034.shtml, Feb. 20, 2004.

10. Hutzler, C. "Future for China May Not Be In Factories, but in Consumers." *Asian Wall Street Journal,* Nov. 23, 2003, pp. M1–M3.

11. Clinton, President William. "Remarks By The President In Address On China And The National Interest." The White House, Office of the Press Secretary, Oct. 24, 1997. *National Archives and Record Administration.* http://clinton6.nara.gov/1997/10/1997-10-24-president-address-on-china-and-the-national-interest.html, Dec. 12, 2003; for statistics see under "Internet World Stats. Usage and Population Statistics." 2003. http://www.internetworldstats.com/stats3.htm, Oct. 13, 2003.

12. Lee, L. "Sohu Posts Sharp Rise in Profit On Solid Advertising Revenue." *Asian Wall Street Journal,* Oct. 27, 2003, A3.

13. ".cn Domain Names May Outnumber Number Of .com.cn Names." DomainsMagazine, Oct 25, 2003. http://www.DomainsMagazine.com/Manage article .asp ?c = 320&a = 4512, Dec. 3, 2003.

14. "China to monitor Internet cafes." *Jakarta Post,* Oct. 31, 2003, p. 11.

15. "VW, GM Sales Surge in China." *Asian Wall Street Journal,* Jan. 6, 2004, p. A3.

16. China's per-capita GDP equaled $4,300 in 2003, expressed in *purchasing power parity* (see Morrison, W. M. "China's Economic Conditions." *Congressional Research Service,* Library of Congress, Washington D.C., May 21, 2003, CRS-4). The average urban household income in China equals thus about $13,760 (China has 3.2 residents per urban household, Census 2000).

17. Ping, L. "China to be fifth largest pharmaceutical market in the world." *Hong Kong Trade Development Council,* Aug. 11, 2003. http://www.tdctrade.com/report/mkt/mkt_030802.htm, Oct. 11, 2003.

18. "Sector report: Road and bridge infrastructure." The British Embassy Beijing, 2002. http://britishembassy.org.cn/english/about_china/business/sr.rab.shtml, Apr. 14, 2003.

19. "State, Private Investment To Rise In China, While Foreign Investment Falls." Chinavista, Mar. 20, 2003. http://www.chinavista.com/business/news/archive/20mar/mar10-03.html, Aug. 29, 2003.

20. "FDI in China up to $53.5 billion in 2003." *Jakarta Post,* Jan. 15, 2004, p. 14.

21. "China strives for accountability in office." *United Press International*, Apr. 16, 2004. http://www.upi.com/view.cfm ?StoryID = 20040416-093051-6129r, Apr. 20, 2004.

22. Supachai P. and Clifford, M. L. *China and the WTO: Changing China, Changing World Trade*. Wiley & Sons (Asia) Pte Ltd., Singapore, 2002, p. 189.

23. Story, J. *China: the race to market*. FT Prentice Hall. Harlow, United Kingdom, 2003, p. 160.

24. Wonacott, P. "Nissan Unveils Bold Sales Drive For China Market." *Asian Wall Street Journal*, Nov. 25, 2003, pp. A1–A8.

25. "GM's Spark Minicar Set for China Debut, Pricing in Dec." *Asian Wall Street Journal*, Nov. 10, 2003, p. A4.

26. Morishta, K. "Industry exodus to China heightens domestic fears." *Nikkei Weekly*, Jan. 14, 2002, pp. 1, 8.

27. ".cn Domain Names May Outnumber Number Of .com.cn Names." *DomainsMagazine*, Oct. 25, 2003. http://www.DomainsMagazine.com/Manage article.asp?c = 320&a = 4512, Sep. 3, 2003.

28. "E-Commerce And Development Report." United Nations Conference on Commerce, Trade, and Development, UNCTAD/SDTE/ECB/2002/1, 2002 http://www.unctad.org/en/docs/ecdr2002_en.pdf, Jan. 17, 2004.

29. Wu Jichuan, Minister of Information Technology. "The Development Of The Information And Network Technology Industry Of China." In: Brahm, L. J. (Ed.) *China's Century*. John Wiley & Sons (Asia) Pte Ltd., Singapore, 2001, p. 332.

30. "McDonald's hungry for China franchises." *Taipei Times*, Sep. 10, 2003, p. 12; *see also* "KFC fast food to wing its way at last to Tibet." *China Daily*, Jan. 15, 2004.

31. "China jumps to third in research, development spending." *Jakarta Post*, Oct. 28, 2003, p. 15.

32. Wu Jichuan, 2001, p. 323.

33. "The State Development & Planning Commission of the People's Republic and Microsoft Corp. Sign A Memorandum of Understanding To Begin the Largest Joint Sino-Foreign Software Industry Cooperation." *Microsoft*, PressPass, June 27, 2002.

34. Karplus, V. "Biotech debate I: Let a thousand GM crops bloom." *International Herald Tribune Online*, Oct. 8, 2003. http://www.iht.com/cgi-bin/generic.cgi? template = articleprint .tmplh&ArticleId = 112731, Nov. 14, 2003.

35. "China's nanotech patent application rank world's third." *People's Daily Online*, Oct. 3, 2003. http://english.peopledaily.com.cn/200310/03/print20031003_125362.html, Nov. 17, 2003.

36. Wonacott, P. "China Will Pump $200 Billion Into Chongqing." *Asian Wall Street Journal*, Apr. 22, 2002.

37. Wozniak, L. "DHL and FedEx Race To Integrate China." *Far Eastern Economic Review*, Feb. 27, 2003, pp. 42–44.

38. Bradsher, K. "China carmakers aim to go global." *International Herald Tribune*, Nov. 3, 2003, pp. 1, 9.

39. Areddy, J. "Citigroup Sets Stake in China Bank." *Asian Wall Street Journal*, Jan. 2, 2003, p. A3.

40. Einhorn, B., and Kripalani, M. "Move Over, India. China is rising fast as a services outsourcing hub." *Business Week*, Aug. 4, 2003, pp. 20–21.

41. "China produces most types of manufactured products in world." Dec. 19,

2002. http://www.xinhuanet.com/english/2002-12/19/content_664775.htm, Dec. 22, 2002.

42. Zinzius, B. *Chinese America: Stereotype and Reality. History, Present, and Future of the Chinese in America.* New York, N.Y.: Peter Lang, 2004, 197 et seq.; see also in Pan, L. (Ed.) *The Encyclopedia of the Chinese Overseas.* 2d ed. Singapore: Archipelogo Press, 2000, p. 172 et seq.; 200 et seq.

43. Yi, J., and Ye, S. *The Haier Way. The Making of a Chinese Business Leader and a Global Brand.* Homa&Sekey Books, Dumont, N.J., 2003, 223.

44. Chang, L. "Anheuser-Busch Raises Tsingtao Stake to 9.9%." *Asian Wall Street Journal.* June 30, 2003, pp. A1–A4.

45. "Legal Brief: Demystifying the PRC Bribery Law." American Chamber of Commerce, 2003 http//www.amcham-china.org.cn/publications/brief/document/LegalBrief03-03.htm, Oct. 18, 2003.

CHAPTER 2

The Chinese Company—
Getting Started

STRATEGIES TO ACCESS THE MARKET

Special Strategies for a Particular Market

The phase prior to a decision is almost always characterized by contrasting optimistic and pessimistic views. It is obvious that China as a marketplace offers enormous business opportunities, and companies might even, for strategic reasons, find it necessary to enter the Chinese market. At the same time, many see direct investment in the Chinese market as connected with significant risk.

Optimists point to the fact that according to calculations by the World Bank, today China is already the world's third-largest national economy; based on spending power parities it is even the second-largest—behind the U.S. and ahead of Japan. Pessimists base their argument against China investment on a variety of macro- and microeconomic risk factors. The obvious absence of a democratic state order and the lack of a secure political basis for a liberal market economy are reasons frequently given against a direct presence. Further reasons cited are the inadequate legal structure, corruption, unemployment, state indebtedness, and bureaucratic arbitrariness.

Those preparing for an engagement in China should take these views into account—both the pessimistic and the optimistic. It is advisable to analyze both views realistically and verify them with facts. Comprehensive information is needed, and the data should come from more than one competent, objective source. It is advisable to proceed with the preparation for the decision already thoroughly done and well coordinated. In obtaining information on China, potential investors should take necessary time and use the necessary resources, and they should listen to more than "bad" or subjective experiences. Those who have been burned by their China businesses often try to generalize their experiences, making them "more objective." But in most cases they have been ill prepared for the unusually complex and difficult market, a fact no one likes to admit. Without thorough preparation for the decision, without a long-term strategy, many investors will pursue unrealistic goals and set the wrong milestones!

It is not enough just to decide "I too will go to China." The why might be obvious: to participate in this megamarket. However, that why is only one of five essential decisive and strategic parameters. What is the investor planning to offer or produce in China? Are these goals realistic? To be certain, one has to ask oneself several questions.

Which products or services, including technologies or expertise, can and will be interesting for the Chinese market? Which of those products and services will Chinese economic policy allow? Both questions require complex answers, as they concern market opportunities in the context of the market economy, that is, offer and demand and political and economic boundaries. These conditions include gaining political admittance to the Chinese market, import and export politics, and the overall state economic control.

It is advisable to get thorough information from China's insiders on both the market and the political environment. The market offers exceptional prospects—however, not for everybody. Foremost, access to it is regulated by many laws and local regulations!

After the potential investor has answered all questions about the market, products, and admission, he or she needs to decide where to set up operations. The question of the best possible site should be answered by site checks, which should not be oriented toward sales possibilities but toward infrastructure and resources. Who should or may be a project partner in the realization of a China project? This question concerns Chinese financial joint-venture partners, as well as production, sales, and logistic partners. The choice of a partner should be closely related to one's choice of investment form—that is, which legal form shall or must be chosen? This concerns legal and tax matters and also depends on current and future development of the industrial sector. Some companies even decide to establish different legal entities to ensure future flexibility. Obtaining and assessing information is therefore the first and foremost basic investment in a China project. Without having complete information in advance, the investor can do no strategic planning and cannot make sound decisions. Risk minimization written in bold? **Yes!**

That being said, investors nevertheless take another, more risky path again and again. Many companies enter the Chinese market as follows:

Figure 2.1
Key Parameters of Doing Business in the New China

Why
- Long-term Strategy
- Vision, Goals
- Risk, Cost and Benefit Analysis

What
- Products, Services
- Technologies, Know-How
- Funds, Assets

Where
- Resources
- Infrastructure
- Investment Climate

Who
- Customers
- Competitors
- Legal Restrictions

How
- Partner(s)
- Investment Form (s)
- Supply/Distribution Network(s)

Arranged by B. Zinzius.

A manager is prepared to enter the Chinese market, and he or she may even be ready to leave as of today. The manager gathers information non-systematically, asking friends and different sources here and there. During an exhibition or a business meeting, or perhaps via an acquaintance, he or she gets an interesting China contact. The manager grabs the opportunity, especially if the contact person offers himself as a partner with good connections. It can be assumed that the partner has sufficient standing in China and is able to collaborate on a mutual project. Access to the Chinese market may certainly begin like that. And with luck and a suitable partner, it might even be successful. However, it will not be according to the plans of the investor and definitely not according to his or her intentions.

The selection of a site especially, but also the offer of know-how and technology transfer, can be one-sided. The investor has to trust almost blindly that the Chinese partner will overcome all hurdles and make the best out of his or her investment. The investor even has to trust that the partner *wants* to make the best out of the investment. The foreign manager can do only one thing: trust and hope that things will go well.

Many investors who were wrecked through their China projects have been responsible for their own failure. The two main reasons for business failures in China are investing too little money in the process of obtaining information prior to market entry and entering the Chinese market without strategic planning, especially contingency plans for upcoming problems. It is a dangerous mistake to try to enter China's business world by chance, so to speak. And clearly even the soundest strategic planning does not replace the tedious task of partner search and selection. However, such planning allows the investor to conduct a much more specific search and to set up rather objective selection criteria. China is a particular market. That fact won't change.

Those who want to invest directly in China's market must realize and accept that Western sales and management strategies do not work there and that practiced models of cooperation cannot be realized in China. A specific planning strategy is necessary for the Chinese market. Essential parameters are shown in upcoming sections.

Costs and Benefits; Risk and Profit

The costs-benefits relationship is the relevant decisive factor for whether a business is viable, and it is the starting point of strategic planning. First, one has to thoroughly consider one's entry into China, with special emphasis on the benefits of such a step. That is the basis for one's economic and strategic plans for entering the market. The costs and benefits must be calculated thoroughly, including the estimated investment, extra costs, and follow-up costs. Finally, the investor should have a clear break-even point and clear profit targets in sight. In Chinese joint ventures, particularly direct investment in enterprises with Chinese participation, the break-even point is generally the final point of the market-entry phase.

Experience shows that for the China investor it takes at least two to three years to break even and four to five years to amortize investments, with only a few exceptions. It is therefore definitely not a quick profit that would motivate somebody to enter the Chinese market. The main motivation for China investors should not be the prospects of fast returns on investment but the prospect of a long-term market presence and share in a market poised to grow continuously and become the largest single market in the world. The growth of the Chinese economy stands, so to speak, on two pillars. The first is the growing investment activity in all industrial sectors and in the service sector. The second is the strongly growing domestic demand for consumer goods, which in itself stimulates the production of and demand for investment goods—a self-stimulating cycle.

Many strong growth factors are present that foreign investors can capitalize on. Besides those already mentioned, there is above average growth in the per capita income of large parts of the population. Studies indicate a doubling of income every six years. In addition, studies indicate improving education levels, rising product quality, increasing productivity, and last but not least, a continued increase of foreign direct investment. Without a doubt, such impressive developments contrast with the existing risks of a China engagement. But it can well be assumed that those risks are decreasing. The yet unbalanced growth, concentrated mainly in the coastal regions, is now spreading into the hinterland. The experiment of a coexisting market economy and planned economy leads more and more to an excellent symbiosis. The state-owned enterprises, or SOEs, are not only being modernized technologically but also gradually reformed to operate economically. Rigid controls and guidance are being partially replaced by decision making on the company level and the possibility of using economic opportunities. The tendency to "discharge" SOEs into the market economy can clearly be seen and seems unstoppable. There are, however, still supply bottlenecks in energy, raw materials, and transportation. There is also the danger of mass unemployment. In most regions development and income differences between the city and the country are still considerable. An estimated 100 to 150 million rural workers have moved to the cities since the 1980s, representing the largest migration in human history. Twelve to fifteen million jobs must be created annually just to keep up with the population growth.[1] The debt levels SOEs carry are a further big risk factor; many nonperforming loans—which are estimated at more than US$500 billion, or 40 percent of China's GDP, are a huge burden for the banking sector. Similar nonperforming loans and bad debts triggered the Asian crisis in 1997 and 1998 and are a major reason for the prolonged Japanese economic downturn in the 1990s. The Chinese government recognizes the aforementioned risk factors, and it is doing everything possible to defuse and improve the situation. Probably, the risk factors will not lead to a crisis and therefore threaten the economy and the further growth of China and the whole region.

However, an important factor in this is the political and social stability of the region. Therefore, the effects of changes in U.S. policy toward China initiated by the George W. Bush government need to be monitored closely—for example, the unambiguous decision to defend Taiwan in case of aggression. In 2003, however, Taiwan's President Chen Shui-bian angered the United States when he used the American support and proposed to rewrite the Taiwanese constitution—a step towards independence that is strongly opposed by Beijing. While firm on his position to defend the democratic Taiwan in case of aggression, President George W. Bush is also firmly determined to recognize the government in Beijing as the government of a single China.[2] A peaceful solution to the Taiwanese question is one of the major political challenges from China in the twenty-first century.

Economic reform, while at the same time maintaining or even strengthening the political status of the country and government, is a strategy that finds its economic expression in the term *socialist market economy*. That reform is described by some Western observers as the main risk factor. This, however, is not correct. The politically planned, initiated, and realized opening of the economy proves to be a factor of reliable safety—especially for foreign investors. Safety for investors in China is rooted in

China's stable political and social conditions, and, vice versa, the Chinese leadership knows that it needs a globally integrated, strong economy integration to assure social stability. And it looks as if those conditions will remain in place in the future, the former Communist leaders will be able to transform themselves into the political and economic leaders of the new China.

Communist China has not experienced the economic breakdown and social mayhem that has afflicted other former Communist states, such as the Soviet empire. China has become an economic powerhouse but has nevertheless remained a communist country. The Chinese socialist market economy was not shaken by the crises of its Asian neighbors; in those times, it maintained the highest economic growth and investment rates worldwide, even as it does today. Therefore, in principle, there is no argument against an investor making a commitment in China. One can confine oneself to an indirect financial engagement—for example, participate in China investment funds or buy shares of Chinese companies, where major American investment companies have already invested. One can also cooperate with Chinese business partners as a representative for their products or services. Or one can invest in the trading firms with a mixture of indirect and direct investment. Depending on the kind of business, its size, and internal resources, these forms might be good steps to start with; however, none of these forms of financial investment offer a direct market presence. Anyone who really wants to be involved in a Chinese business and exert control—that is, establish a solid China presence and produce and sell products or services—must be directly involved. This can be done via direct investment in a joint venture, via cooperation, or via a wholly foreign owned enterprise.

What China Needs

What does China really need? This key topic has already been touched on but will be explained in more detail here.

China needs investors with innovations. Primarily, China needs foreign capital, knowledge, and technology, at best as one package. Obviously, the Chinese prefer that capital and know-how be brought into Chinese-foreign joint ventures. That would, in effect, establish a new, modern enterprise that is basically a Chinese enterprise and more or less closely connected to an existing Chinese company. It is expected that the mutual enterprise would support the Chinese partner and thus modernize and increase productivity and competition.

Are foreign direct investments a tonic, or medicine, for China's economy? They are exactly that! They are therefore lured and pampered, and special conditions are granted. But at the same time they are regulated, and their admittance and "dosage" to the Chinese market are monitored.

Foreign direct investments in mutual enterprises, joint ventures, are not subject to state-controlled or centrally controlled plan figures. However, they are subject to macroeconomic regulations, which are controlled and implemented on all governmental levels, that is, centrally as well as in the provinces and municipalities. It is a canalization of direct investments into state-run sectors and companies according to the needs of the economy. Thus, control is accomplished via the admission and registration policy. Canalization and selection themselves are bound to the targets set by the central government in Beijing. The main emphases are on modernizing and improving industry, supporting export, increasing foreign currency, and leveraging the differences among the regional structures.

From the Chinese viewpoint, all this is best achieved with foreign investment and Sino-foreign cooperation. Companies completely in foreign possession are less desired, but their percentage is increasing rapidly. In general, the admittance of such direct investment is allowed only under strict regulations. As an example, a wholly foreign owned enterprise is contractually obligated to export at least 50 percent of its production and to use exclusively the most modern production technologies. Are foreign investments therefore "offers," for which an almost unlimited demand can be expected in China? Not at all. There are foreign investments that are welcomed (encouraged), generally allowed (permitted), restricted (however, not completely impossible), and forbidden (prohibited).[3]

Investments in mutual enterprises that lead to an influx of modern technology into China and that immediately produce products for export are welcomed and consequently courted. There are only a few areas where joint ventures are forbidden—for example, utilities, telecommunications, transportation, broadcasting and television stations, printed media, domestic commerce, foreign trade, military equipment, and the key areas of heavy industry and mining. All other areas are open to cooperation with willing foreign investors, and the restricted areas are constantly reduced. However, investor preference differs. For example, German investors in China have primarily invested in the automotive industry, mechanical engineering, electronics, the chemical and pharmaceutical industries, and textile production. American and Japanese investors concentrate on housing, electronics, real estate, food and beverages, services, low-technology production, and—especially since the WTO-admission—in the automotive and electronic sector.

Preventing the Investment Site from Becoming a Trap

Deciding on the wrong site can lead to the failure of the China engagement and ultimately to a loss of one's investment. This often happens because of personal or business recommendations and a failure to check out those recommendations thoroughly, and many international investors

have learned their lesson in the last decade. Without a detailed and objective analysis of the conditions of the prospective site and its environment, the project is bound to fail. A thorough investigation must be done
prior to any commitment!

Those who do not thoroughly check the future site, to ensure that it
fulfills all relevant criteria, act with coarse negligence. Whether the site is
a bargain or is expensive, its utility depends very much on region-specific
market structures and sales potential. Regional differences need to be
judged depending on one's product. Companies selling high-priced consumer goods or high-level products need to offer their goods in the
wealthy areas of the coastal provinces, which have a strong spending
power.

Criteria: Site Selection

1. **The region:** Things to consider include the region's markets and
   infrastructure. Who will be the customers and distributors?
2. **The local situation:** Consider the investment benefits, openness
   of the local authorities, and certainly, the site itself, including its
   infrastructure, resources, utilities, and the general environment.
3. **The local living conditions:** Local living conditions include housing, schools, educational institutions, cultural facilities, medical
   supply, consumer goods supply, and so on.

This rule doesn't apply as stringently to enterprises with capital goods.
They may orient themselves in accordance with natural and historical
conditions that were partly influenced by the political planning process
that selected the sites. China's industry, however, is not concentrated only
in the coastal regions. The steel industry has its main locations in the
northeastern coal region. The most dense sites of steel-related industries,
such as engineering, will also be found there.

The main industrialized areas of the inner regions are Shaanxi, Gansu,
Ningxia, Sichuan, Guizhou, Yunnan, and Guangxi, where in the 1960s, a
strategic relocation movement was started to develop these areas. Selected
companies and research institutions were set up, and systematic support
and investment led to further industrialization. Today, in some of these
inner regions, a well-developed industry and increasingly improving infrastructure can be found. A favorable climate for foreign investment has
developed here over the years. Hundreds of special zones have been established, offering direct investors conditions similar to those in the special
economic zones (SEZs) of the coastal regions. These include: tax privileges
and exemptions, customs duty exemptions for the import of raw material
and for production plants, and reasonable charges for leasing land.

It is not only special privileges and growth that make the hinterland regions increasingly attractive for China investors. It is also the flexibility of the local authorities and the more pleasant everyday life today in the medium-sized and smaller inner Chinese cities. Foreign investors and employees of joint ventures are beginning to realize this. It seems absolutely realistic to say with certainty that these regions in the course of the next few years will become popular investment sites. Henan, Hubei, Anhui, and Sichuan in central China and Guizhou, Guangxi, and Yunnan in the south—these provinces already offer a relatively good transportation network. They also offer necessary enterprise resources, including acceptably qualified workers. "Relatively good" traffic infrastructure and "acceptably" qualified workers—these restrictions go along with regional and local differences and should be taken seriously when selecting the site. This is not only the situation in inner China; it is so in all regions: The favorable to excellent macroeconomic prospects do not always correspond to the microeconomic situation. Some of the facts are really claims or promises; they are only in the planning stage or just scheduled to be implemented.

Checklist: Site Selection

☑ Distance to supplier and consumer markets

☑ Local and long-distance transportation; available logistic partners

☑ Flexibility and efficiency of local authorities

☑ Status the possible Chinese partner has with authorities

☑ Property rights of the company, including potential threats

☑ Mutual properties with the Chinese partner, especially detailed rights

☑ Availability and education level of local workers

☑ Banks, including the availability of foreign currency and financial services

☑ Infrastructure, streets, railways, power supply, water supply, wastewater, and waste disposal facilities, including all relevant cost

☑ Local and nationwide tax regulations and exemptions

☑ Telecommunications, infrastructure and cost (e.g., ISDN, DSL, ADSL)

☑ Climatic conditions (e.g., temperatures, rainfall, and flood levels)

☑ Other site criteria

It is best to physically go to the prospective site itself to check, whether it actually has a water, electricity, and traffic connections that guarantee access and efficient transportation of raw materials and finished goods to and from the site. This check should include an assessment of power, water, and wastewater facilities as well as of the capabilities of telecommunication connections. A company's intranet and Internet connections will need sufficient bandwidth. Everything that is or could become relevant to the site, including regional and local features, must be inquired about and analyzed repeatedly at the site. There are many examples of Western companies who have rushed into China business only to discover that the "golden opportunity" was made of sheet metal instead of gold. It is very important to be clear about the presence and capability of local or regional banks. Can they produce foreign currency and financing services? Primarily for joint ventures that do little or no exporting but that import supply materials or semifinished products, the possibility of obtaining foreign currency via a local bank is an important site criterion. It is certain: The success of a China engagement based on direct investment depends fundamentally on the investment site. Success means reaching strategic goals and operating targets. It cannot be repeated often enough: Avoid selecting the wrong site by doing a thorough check and analysis and evaluating multiple criteria. A proven approach is to work out a checklist and use it completely.

In any case, it is recommended that the investor check out more than one site thoroughly, although that might be time consuming. The checklist will provide a good basis for comparison between different sites. Searching for and selecting a site cannot be done from a desk or conference table; it must be done on site. China investors who do not want or are unable to spend sufficient time or effort must later reckon with unpleasant surprises.

Finding a Partner

From the beginning, an investor's objective expectations must be clear. One knows why and when and in what form one would like to commit oneself in China. The markets and sales potential are known; therefore, a business plan including production and sales figures exists. This might well be based on local knowledge.

When the investment's theoretical phase has been concluded, the practical entry into the Chinese market can begin. This may be a long, painstaking process that entails many trips to China. The site checks will cost time and money—both are needed to set up the China business correctly. Those who would like to, or must, economize during the market entry preparation should refrain from going into business in China.

Because it is important, once again we go back to the concrete market entry preparation: site selection and partner selection. Both are closely connected. This applies particularly to direct investments in equity joint ventures: Those who decide in favor of a site also have decided in favor of the Chinese business partner. Whether the decision turns out positively or not is certainly associated with the conditions of the site. But at least as or even more important are the qualities of the partner. Even if all the usual and China-specific site criteria are fulfilled, choosing the wrong partner can nullify their value. How can one know whether the partner is "good" or "bad"? That cannot necessarily be divined from past business successes or from an analysis of balance sheets, which might not even exist.

As a rule, the potential partner is a state-controlled enterprise, and thus is bound to governmental planning. This might be an enormous handicap, which the investor needs to take rationally into account when checking the company's "hard facts." It is often the case that exactly because of this reason, the Chinese partner is willing to set up a joint venture, which offers him a way of loosening governmental control and improving the performance of his company. However, does the Chinese partner have the abilities necessary to meet the expectations of the foreign partner? If not immediately, at least within a short time? To answer those questions, various hard facts must be checked: actual and potential abilities, technical competencies, available resources, indebtedness, profit-and-loss relationship, worker and management abilities, and concrete possibilities for improvement. Only if requested hard data are insufficient, or seem hopeless, should further efforts toward forming the partnership be abandoned. In China, the "soft facts" are more important than the hard facts. The important points here are the Chinese partner's market knowledge and relationships and his creditworthiness at local and regional banks. The banking sector is an area in China where relationships are important. The soft criteria must be fulfilled by the Chinese partner. Fulfillment of these criteria is crucial for him to be able to play his fundamental role: He has to be the "pilot" and the "door opener" at the same time. His good relations must be able to shorten the time of admission at the bureaucracy. Only he is able to open the doors of high-ranking officials and administrators. He knows the heads of administrations and important decision makers. Those decision makers usually never meet with foreign investors, with the exception of a few large-scale investors.

Whether the market entry via a joint venture proceeds without major problems depends—similar to entry into the market—predominantly on the Chinese partner. However, nothing in China proceeds quickly (i.e., quickly according to Western definition). The development of a partnership is no exception. A partnership might happen almost instantaneously, but in reality that rarely happens. "Love at first sight" is possible, for example, at an exhibition booth. But usually such circumstantial contact is almost always followed by further, long and tedious development of the relationship. Chinese companies do not like to get thoroughly checked.

One needs patience to establish a close business relationship—and to learn about one's partner in detail. It is important for the Chinese businesspeople to establish a personal relationship. They practice this by making small talk and at the same time inviting themselves to visit the partner in the United States or Europe. There they will demand hospitality, which requires the host's patience and politeness along with an ample budget. However, in return they invite the potential Western partner to China, where he is treated at least with the same hospitality as expected of him as host.

To develop contacts means to establish relationships. This is a long process that progressively leads to concrete negotiations about the joint venture, based on personal agreement and understanding. Sometimes this might take more than a year, and even then the milestone might still not have been reached. Decisive partnership negotiations are rigidly conducted by the Chinese, and every word will be documented minutely. Again and again, they will add new points and subtopics. The more concrete the negotiations get, the larger the Chinese negotiation team becomes. Furthermore, within the Chinese negotiation team the negotiation partners will frequently change, a point that can irritate the foreign partners, and sometimes is intended to! When negotiating partnerships with the Chinese, it is of primary importance to adapt oneself to the Chinese mentality, to their negotiation tactics and tricks. Without the foreknowledge of what can be expected during negotiations, one might experience a shock. Moreover, it is naive to assume that the Chinese only negotiate with one possible foreign partner. Often they run several negotiations in parallel while they evaluate and compare foreign companies. And they will give all of these companies reason to hope for a future collaboration. Finding a partner and forging a partnership is almost always a marathon of negotiation. Here are some negotiation tips:

- Before the concrete negotiations begin, one has to establish personal relationships. If those don't turn out well, the negotiations do not have a sound basis.

- Creating relationships and holding concrete negotiations will work only if the partners show that they respect each other and take one another seriously.

- Prior to and especially during negotiations, one has to give oneself and the Chinese partner ample time.

- It is advisable to obtain as much information as possible about the negotiating partner before the negotiations. One has to reckon that the Chinese negotiating partner will not shun any means and ways to inform himself about the foreign partner.

- One must always negotiate in a friendly but tough manner.

- If one makes a concession, one should always ask for something in return. Refraining from doing so, even as a kind gesture, will be interpreted as weakness by the Chinese side.

Negotiations can certainly be conducted rigorously around the facts, but they should never become impolite. They should also be used to deepen personal relationships. Chinese negotiating partners might quibble about every word of a contract; in the end, however, the written word does not count as much as the spirit of the contract. This is what brings the Chinese partner alive, the mutual agreement of both partners based on personal relationship. The course and result of the negotiations as well as the contractual agreements finally reached depend strongly on the intensity of personal relationships.

Selecting a Site and a Partner

A recent survey of German investors in China, initiated by a German economic delegation, produced informative results about site selection. One result: Only about one-third viewed Hong Kong as a good site to become active in the Chinese market. Two thirds thought that Hong Kong was not a suitable starting point at all! It seems that Hong Kong has actually lost its importance despite the special status it received after its incorporation into the People's Republic of China. About 25 percent of all businessmen questioned believed that the importance of Hong Kong will decrease; only 13 percent reckoned on an increase.

The most popular sites for enterprise activities for Western investors based on direct investment are Shanghai, Jiangsu, Beijing, Shandong, Tianjin, Liaoning, Guangdong, Zhejiang, Hebei, Sichuan, and Fujian. The industrialization of these sites is well advanced, and the infrastructure can be judged as acceptable to good. Interestingly, the majority of those interviewed did not have their equity joint ventures established in the special economic zones (SEZ). These zones, set up by the central government, have lost their attractiveness primarily because many provinces and autonomous cities have in the meantime established their own development zones. Such zones offer investment conditions comparable to, sometimes even better than the SEZs. Investors are offered tax advantages in the development zones, and, as in the SEZs, they can work in a profit-oriented and market-oriented manner.

It is obvious that foreign direct investment still is concentrated mainly in the economic centers, that is, in the east and the south, along the coast, and in the coastal hinterland. In these areas, industrial and economic centers arise rapidly. Furthermore, the regional and local authorities are more economy oriented, which means more economy friendly. A rough analysis of the Chinese investment climate depicts three large zones that show a rather different climate for investment. The provinces and cities in the "booming corridor" of the east, from Hebei, Beijing, and Tianjin, extending over Shanghai, Jiangsu, Zhejiang, and Shandong in the north to Guangdong and Hong Kong and Shenzhen, show an almost "tropical" investment climate. A more moderate, but not at all unfriendly, investment climate exists in many inland regions. Until today the investment climate has been persistently harsh and cool in northern and southwestern China. One reason for this is the still unsatisfactory infrastructure.

Since 1994–95, it can be seen that the interior parts of the republic are catching up with the coastal regions, especially with regard to industrialization and the logistic infrastructure. This development is strongly supported by the government. Since 1997, investment in the central and western Chinese regions has been strengthened. In 1998, these areas received a 10 percent increase in their overall budget compared with 1997. The budget increase in the west grew to 19.8 percent in 2001, and 20.6 percent in 2002, compared to an increase of 16.2 percent in 2002 in the east.[4] The expansion of existing SEZs and the implementation of new ones are supposed to attract further capital from Chinese and foreign investors. Without doubt, growth is beginning in the interior provinces. Nevertheless, they remain unattractive to foreign investors. For example, investors fear that problems may arise in the transport of raw materials and products to and from inner provinces and that there is a lack of suitable partner enterprises for joint ventures. This opinion is only partly correct nowadays. For all joint ventures, finding the right partner is essential. In addition, joint ventures must fulfill certain prerequisites in order to get the state allowance to found the company. It doesn't suffice that the foreign investor meets the prerequisites; the Chinese partner must also be able and want to fulfill them! An SOE or a state organization is always involved in a joint venture as the Chinese partner, a fact that makes it even more difficult to find the right partner.

It is always important to thoroughly review the contribution of the Chinese partner and to balance that against the capital investment of the foreign partner. Are sufficient company resources available? Are the production plants in good condition? Are educated workers available? Can raw materials be obtained readily? How are the traffic and infrastructure connections? Do buildings need to be refurbished? Can the land be extended? Are all relevant permits available? These are just some of the basic but essential questions, as many western companies tend to overlook essential points, and later realize that the purchased land has no access to roads, or that certain permits cannot be obtained.

Regarding the choice of a partner, the basic questions are these: Does the Chinese partner have sufficient market experience? Does it have contacts with political and economic institutions? Is there strategic planning for production and sales? Is the Chinese partner's management able to think strategically and to turn strategies into operative measures? What is the partner's financial position—overindebtedness, red figures, black figures, bad loans, future write-offs? Are there burdens in the form of social obligations such as pension funds and so on?

Even if almost all questions have been answered satisfactorily, the general attitude of the Chinese partner still has to be checked. The partner's readiness to think and act in response to the market and with an eye toward making a profit is imperative! Another essential criterion is the position of management control, especially if more than 50 percent of the capital is coming from the foreign partner. Is it acceptable that the positions of general manager and chief financial officer are in the hands of the foreign partner?

The investor is more than justified in being very critical and careful when choosing a partner. One should thoroughly investigate the Chinese partner's financial status—for example an SOE may be financially sound or it maybe bankrupt, and the books may not show this at all. Depending on the investment, it is certainly advisable to initiate due diligence twice—one time with foreign auditors and one time with independent Chinese auditors of your choice. It is in the interest of both the investor and the Chinese state to ask for high standards in the Chinese partner in the joint venture—as the government and administration usually does.

Foreign-Chinese joint enterprises have to use modern technical equipment and state-of-the-art management techniques. They must advance the technological and economic development of the Chinese partner. Joint ventures are obliged to educate the technical, managerial, and accounting personnel of the Chinese partner. Their product and sales strategy must be primarily export oriented. Manufactured products must be of high quality and in every aspect competitive on the world market. Joint ventures must have a positive foreign currency balance. This means that their needs for foreign currency, such as imports, interest, royalties, and other payments, must be paid for from the export business. High standards are set for joint ventures in China. Anyone founding such an enterprise must be aware of that fact and should select a partner accordingly.

The Example of Smart Investors

> The man has three different ways to act wise:
> the first is to think, which is the noblest
> the second is to imitate, which is the easiest
> and the third is by experience, which is the most bitter.

This ancient wisdom ascribed to Confucius could well be a basic principle for wise behavior in today's China. Those who want to enter the Chinese market, especially as a direct investor, should start well in advance to think about China. They should also be ready to imitate and adapt to the special conditions of China. However, this will not be easy. They must also be prepared to undergo some bitter experiences.

However, a fourth way exists in addition to those three: One can avoid many a bitter experience if one is willing to learn from others and to orient oneself by following real examples. There are many examples of successful investment in China. The experiences of American and European investors have been analyzed and are well documented; they are easily accessible to anyone interested. However, let's point out some quintessential facts taken from Western experience. It is without doubt that, as a rule, any entrepreneurial engagement in China is connected with problems and difficulties. It is also correct that not all foreign enterprises have been, or are able to handle their problems in China. It is, however, not correct that Chinese joint ventures are in a crisis and it is certainly wrong to talk about a "Chinese trap" for foreign investors.

The most negative experience, that is, without success or even failure, has been made by only those investors who have started out on one of the following four false assumptions:

- Foreigners can fast and easily earn money in China.
- The Chinese are not only hardworking but also inexpensive workers.
- China has opened up to a "pure capitalism" and is beginning to become Westernized or Americanized.
- The Chinese do not think, feel or act differently from us, at least regarding the economy.

These are completely wrong assumptions, which inevitably will lead to cardinal errors. If during the initial access to the market unsuitable scales and values are applied, basic mistakes in the foundation and management of the company will very soon lead to immense problems. Strategic decisions and planning must be exclusively based on Chinese statistics, or on statements of officials and those of the Chinese partners. Often it is not taken sufficiently into account that China is a "socialist market economy." This economy has social and political targets as well as regulations by the state. A foreign investor deals primarily with state owned enterprises and with state organs and institutions.

When founding a joint venture, foreigners often wrongly assume that the interests of the Chinese partner conform to their own. In their dealings and communications with the Chinese partner, they often neglect to spend sufficient time and money. Also, many companies do not take sufficient time for the negotiations to set up the company. Another common mistake is to send managers to China who see themselves as missionaries in a third-world country and act accordingly.

Some foreign investors mistrust the Chinese partner even after making up their minds. This might cause "loss of face" for the Chinese partner as well as for the foreign investor. On the other hand, leniency just to keep face can be wrong too. Some investors trust blindly, which could have disastrous consequences if they have failed to secure the capital majority or management responsibility and thus control of the company.

Successful enterprises avoid preceding mistakes. Let's look at some characteristics of successful enterprises. First, the higher the quota in a joint venture (i.e., the more the foreign partner exerts financial control), the better the chance for success! Second, those who take differences in understanding, and thus the design of contracts, into account will have less problems with their partner, employees, suppliers, and customers.

In China, the understanding of contracts—and even more important, the general attitude toward the law—is not based on a legal system without gaps but on mutual trust and confidence. A "contract" for Chinese people is not absolute or unalterable. Contracts are "helping steps" to create long-term relationships. Therefore, investors should make sure that contracts are negotiated by means of a long process. What is important is not only the details of the contract but the creation and development of relations in the course of the negotiations.

This takes time. Successful enterprises take time. The experience of successful companies shows that all problems that arise clearly decrease in the course of time. The majority of the Chinese joint venture enterprises that are funded by Western investment operate successfully.

At the beginning of 2000, a trade promotion organization in the German embassy in Beijing surveyed 187 German China investors. Ninety-four percent of those questioned were ready to invest in China again. Sixty-one percent would invest at the same site, and sixty-seven percent in the same legal form. It apparently did not disturb these companies that they needed an average of 2.6 years to generate a profit and four years to break even. A similar survey among European companies in 2001–02 confirmed these data. Two-third of all surveyed foreign companies were satisfied with their overall performance; for one-third, the performance of their investment in China was below expectations. Interesting also is the reason the companies most frequently cited for failure: *unrealistic expectations!*

FOUNDING A COMPANY

The Socioeconomic and Legal Background

Deng Xiaoping was a pragmatic politician. He cultivated a language that made use of pictorial, often drastic wordings. Although he was a Communist from the old guard, he commented on the splitting of the gigantic agricultural collectives, the first big step in economic reform, not in the terms of party ideology but with the sentence "It doesn't matter whether a cat is black or white, as long as it catches mice!" He justified the big step toward reform, the allowance and even support of investment by foreign countries, with the metaphor

"Chinese hands milk foreign cows!"

With that he made the point, which holds true today, that foreign investors in China are expected to be milked. Capital and know-how will nurture and invigorate China's economy. But one should note that Deng's words and reforms were unfaithful to Communist ideals and that he wanted to abolish completely the socialist planned economy. Economic reform was initiated and driven forward by *Deng Xiaoping* with the approval of the Communist Party leadership, and it was later consistently continued by Jiang Zemin. It took place, and continues to take place, in a framework and plan that has as its target modernizing the socialist People's Republic of China and making it economically competitive. A major aim is the continued growth of income and consumption, in order to calm tensions and defuse movements that could lead to a real change of the political system. China's economic reform will save China's communism! Therefore, the leadership has deviated from old ideological lines, especially the precept that everything must be determined by central planning and the economy must be controlled through rigorous plan fulfillment. Partial privatization has been allowed. The state and its planning organs have retired from controlling the microeconomy, but they have not given up macroeconomic control and leadership.

There are two essential reasons for partial privatization, a key component of the economic reform: First, China's economy will grow to the strength that, according to Chinese opinion, it deserves to be at. China's self-confidence no longer permits it to accept remaining as a second- or third-ranked country in economic terms. Second, reform is important not only to save but also to consolidate Communist power. Self-consciousness and Communist consciousness have connected the majority of Chinese so closely that one can speak of a Chinese identity. Economic reform is an essential, maybe the most essential, factor of this solidarity. The leadership of the CPC recognized that only a decisive improvement in the economic situation would guarantee the broader acceptance of the system by the population. Economic reform is therefore a legally regulated construction and expansion of the private Chinese economy. The complete process is planned by the government—which basically means the Communist Party—and controlled and monitored via the government's administrative arms. Its primary objective is to develop the People's Republic into a global economic power. This objective is based on long-term planning and is proceeding according to plan. Differently phrased, this development has to be driven forward at least until China can credibly resemble an economic power. The realization of this primary objective is the force behind many activities, including the admittance of foreign investment. The plan could be realized: Cooperation with Western companies brings technology and know-how into the country, improves the quality of Chinese products, makes China internationally competitive, improves the quality of staff and management, and especially revamps the inefficient and unprofitable governmental sector of the Chinese economy.

China investors have to deal with the high expectations of their Chinese partners. Confidence that those expectations will be met determines access for foreign investors and thus progress in China. Confidence is one thing; using guidelines and controls to ensure compliance is better. This is a basic concept of every bureaucracy, and it has been an entrenched tradition of the Chinese bureaucracy for centuries. Authoritative investment guidelines for foreign institutions have been mutually issued by the Chinese State Development Planning Commission (SDPC) and the State Economic and Trade Commission (SETC) of the Ministry of Foreign Trade and Economic Cooperation (MOFTEC). These guidelines distinguish between favored, permitted, restricted, and prohibited investments.

Favored investments are those that will bring a high technological standard to China, improve international competitiveness, and thus also help redevelop the SOEs. However, foreigners are barred from investing in core sectors of the state economy. This clearly shows that China does not want to completely liberalize and open up the Chinese economy. The aim is modernization, increased efficiency, and increased competitiveness, primarily in the state economic sector. For Western enterprises that can contribute to these goals, the way is smoothed by guidelines and laws. They can, moreover, expect to be granted various special advantages. They will pay less taxes, be able to rent land at special discounted prices, be preferred for the allocation of raw materials, and so on.

Foreign investments will receive preferential treatment in joint ventures that have been founded on a contract base of "equality and mutual benefit." The legal form for equality joint ventures was published in law in July 1979, and has been frequently amended since.[5]

It was only in 1986 that the legal framework for wholly foreign owned enterprises (WFOEs) was issued, and it took until 1990 for the execution ordinances to be published. The number and percentage of WFOEs is increasing—at present their quota within foreign countries' investments is around 60 percent—but they are still not very welcome. It is feared that enterprises financed up to 100 percent with foreign capital will contribute little to the transfer of technology and management know-how.

In addition, WFOEs are not as dependent on governmental support as joint ventures. WFOEs cannot be tied, either directly or indirectly, to the central planning system, and they don't contribute to the development of a Chinese partner whose mother is a more or less financially stable state enterprise.

Table 2.1
Company Forms for Foreign Investments in China (foreign investment
enterprises—FIEs)

FIE	Details	Comments
Representative Office (RO) 1 to 3-year term, extendable.	Liaison office for mother company. Limited capital injection needed. Can handle market research, sourcing, project investigation. Can hire local staff via government agents.	Limited activities. No legal person. Invoicing or trading is not allowed. Cost expenses may attract tax liability. First option for start-up companies, or a backup facility for a FIE.
Contractual joint venture (CJV) (Cooperation joint venture) 10 to 30-year term, extendable.	No minimum equity, but maximum of 50 percent. Contribution can be done via assets, profit sharing based on agreements. No duration limits. Manufacturing and sales operations possible.	Capital withdrawal during investment time possible. Trade unions required. Primary form for small business investments. Great flexibility in assets, management, and organization.
Equity joint venture (EJV) 10 to 30-year term, extendable.	25 to 75 percent foreign capital contribution. Debt: equity ratio depends on the investment. (<US$3mio: 70 percent; >US$30mio: 33 percent). Profit and risk according to capital share. Balanced foreign exchange account.	Specific requirements for management structure. Restricted withdrawal of capital during the time of investment. Limited domestic sales. Preferred investment form of Chinese government.
Wholly foreign-owned enterprise (WFOE) 10 to 30-year term, extendable.	Registered as legal person. Limited liability entity, no branch of foreign owner. Employment of Chinese in line with local regulations. Direct negotiations with local authorities. Often converted from representative office.	Intended for high tech or export-oriented industries. No costly negotiations. Control over management and human resources. No import/export license for own products required. Know how remains under investor's control.

Arranged by B. Zinzius.

Nevertheless, the number of WFOEs is growing. More and more regional and municipal administrations are realizing that such companies can bring innovations into the country quickly and efficiently. They can be managed more easily and contribute to the export development of the region. By law, WFOEs must export at least 50 percent of their production. This obstacle was not lowered with the introduction of the execution ordinances in 1990. Joint venture or WFOE? The investor must be clear about that decision. All investments and activities are based on laws, guidelines, and regulations. And the investor should obtain legal advice prior to market entry. It is also important that he or she sees the purpose of the legal framework: It fixes the investor's role in the political plan of the Chinese economy! The admittance of the investment by means of a long, complicated, bureaucratic procedure guarantees that the foreign investor is not only willing but also able to assume the role the Chinese side is offering him or her.

The Way to Approval: A Marathon with Hurdles

As a rule, from preparatory negotiations with the future Chinese partner to the definite foundation permission and enterprise registration, the investment will encounter at least 14 "hurdles." One has to allow six months to two years for getting the final approvals granted. Different competencies of the administrations involved complicate the process even further.

The identity of the responsible authority is in principle determined by the volume of the investment. Local authorities (municipalities, towns) can approve projects of up to a volume of US$10 million. The provincial planning commission handles volumes between US$10 and $30 million. Until September 1996, this regulation applied only in the SEZs and the "open coast cities." Today it applies in all provinces. If more than US$30 million is to be invested in the foundation of an enterprise, in addition to permission of the provincial planning commission, the investor must obtain further approval from MOFTEC. Also, the topmost planning commission, the State Planning Commission, scrutinizes such large investments and presents them to the central government for approval. An approval from a lower administrative level can certainly be canceled "from the top." This may not be due to economic planning reasons; almost always politics comes into the game. Personnel policy practices or politics between bureaucratic authorities may be a factor. A superior authority may want to show a subordinate one its place or its limits. An authority may want to retract delegated responsibilities—from the municipal administration back to the provincial government; from the province back to the central level—a case that is occurring more frequently in recent years. Jostling for position. Power struggles. In the hierarchically structured Chinese bureaucracy, the different authorities are often uncooperative—and maneuvering for position isn't a rarity. If they cooperate, that will happen on a divisional level, and facts are not a decisive factor for cooperation under the circumstances. This situation certainly is changing, but slowly and not everywhere. Decisions based on facts are becoming increasingly important, especially in technical matters. But one should not have too high hopes. What still counts, no matter how supportive and understanding the authorities are regarding the foreign investment, is this: Those investors who want to reach their targets, which means getting the correct seal from the responsible authority on submitted papers, need a lot of patience!

It is quite important that the investor realize this: Everything that is negotiated and formulated has practical value only if the corresponding document gets its official seal. Permission proceedings run literally "from stamp to stamp"! At first, the project submission requires the seal for "general admission" from a competent authority. This submitted proposal, perhaps better termed the *project concept,* is regarded as a *letter of intent.* If the letter of intent is accepted by the administration, the investors must prepare a detailed project description and submit it as a feasibility study to the approving authority. This detailed assessment contains all the technical and business details of the projected joint venture as well as a chance-and-risk analysis. The feasibility study is an important milestone and impacts many later stages. It should therefore be taken seriously and negotiated in detail. Furthermore, it contains the detailed expert opinion of a Chinese authority on the "company design." The State Development Planning Commission or its local authorities will approve the feasibility study.

The commission will cooperate very closely with the prospective founding partners to conduct the feasibility study. A feasibility study consists of three sections: the technical, the economic-legal, and the socioeconomic. As an example, the products the partnership plans to produce and the details of production, including facilities, production procedures, and required raw materials and auxiliaries, are examined and described. The feasibility study describes also many other details, such as the business's legal form, its organization, and profit-loss projections. In addition, the study contains a partner analysis, a market analysis, a risk analysis, and an analysis of the possible influence of the joint venture on the parent companies abroad and in China. The socioeconomic section supplies details on the location, the existing and required infrastructure, and possible environmental problems the joint venture may cause. The acceptance of the feasibility study is the "green light" to both partners to go ahead with the final contract draft. After obligatory approval by the mother companies of the two partners, the contract must be submitted to the responsible approving authority—that is, the State Development Planning Commission or its local authorities.

Even at this stage, new negotiations with the approving authority might be necessary as it has the right to suggest or even require amendments. After all of these battles have been fought, it is time to relax, as normally this means the end of the bureaucratic marathon. A license and certificates are handed out, including the obligatory seals. The joint venture is admitted and almost founded. But the registration procedure is still to come.

Don't Overlook the Differences

In principle, almost everything is regulated in China; however, for every regulation, the Chinese have at least one alternative. The Chinese treat laws and regulations with a certain flexibility. If demanded for practical reasons, the Chinese can react with bamboolike pliability. This is also true for the admission of foreign investments since the admitting bureaucratic authorities are Chinese.

For us it might be simply a paradox: The dreaded bureaucratic stubbornness can be combined with a surprising flexibility—not often, but nevertheless more often than one may assume! The legal boundaries that apply to foreign investments are strictly defined, and the procedures for admission to the Chinese market exactly specified. Nevertheless, it happens that the law is interpreted rather flexibly and regulations are apparently avoided. "Apparently" is the correct expression, since laws are drafted with certain flexibility. Guidelines, laws, or ordinances contain slightly different approaches to or treatments of investments as well as some leeway for the admissions procedures. The authorities have certain flexibility at their disposal and interpret investments case by case. Thus, they can obtain the best possible result for the municipality, city, or province. Finally, permission depends on the actual situation and ongoing or targeted regional developments. The differences between individual regions or even within a province might be enormous, and while some areas are saturated with investments, others are underdeveloped. Those regional differences may already be the decisive factor whether an investment project is allowed or rejected.

The differences between individual regions or even within a province might be enormous, and while some areas are saturated with investments, others are underdeveloped. Those regional differences may already be the decisive factor whether an investment project is allowed or rejected. It is helpful to deal with these factors while planning for admission to the market. Those investing in the "right" region can be assured that the bureaucratic screening process will be much easier. In May 2001, the Fortune Global Forum emphasized China's efforts to develop the Western hinterland. The Chinese president at that time, Jiang Zemin, traveled with several thousand politicians and businesspeople to Hong Kong to meet with

European and American investors. Don't overlook the differences—one has to use them!

Tips for Contacts with Local Authorities

When selecting a partner, one should take care that the Chinese partner is an experienced negotiator and is versatile in his or her contacts with the authorities. It is good advice to use experts on China to analyze whether the desired Chinese partner really knows all the bureaucratic steps to get a joint venture admitted. The partner must be versed in the responsibilities of the different governmental authorities. The Western investor needs a Chinese partner who can initiate the complex admission procedure and correct and carry it over all hurdles.

Personal, direct contact by foreigners with governmental authorities is in general not helpful. Any approach toward the head of an authority is rather detrimental, even if it is possible. It is a huge mistake and could mean the end of the project to make the authorities move quickly or try to push them around. Even worse would be to suggest any incapability. Neither a harsh nor a soft approach is helpful. If and how the admission can be advanced should be left to the Chinese partner alone. In no case should the decisive importance of the required papers and documents be underestimated. Without the official letter of intent of both partners, the admission procedure won't start at all. Moreover, the temporary admission one hopes to receive will be useless if the feasibility study and, later, the contracts are not submitted. It is rather simple, and negotiations of the Chinese partner with the authorities will change nothing. The fact is that the "paper war" is decisive when it comes to admission and thus, finally, registration of a company.

QUALIFIED EMPLOYEES: FOUNDATION FOR SUCCESS

Finding Employees—the Chinese Labor Market

In the early stages of a joint venture, there is often no need to search for employees, as employees of the Chinese partner will be transferred. Sooner or later, however, it becomes obvious that not only does the number of staff have to be reduced but new, better qualified employees have to be found. Thus, sooner or later the company will be forced to search for employees, and it will have to contend with the unusual features of the Chinese labor market. It is essential to mention right from the beginning that the Chinese labor market has hardly been touched by the economic market reforms. As of today, it is basically operating as in a socialist planned economy. For some years it has been possible for joint ventures to recruit and employ staff freely on the labor market, even without a *danwei* (work unit) status. However, it is obligatory to present employment plans to the responsible authorities for approval. This is a tedious and often hard-to-understand exercise; nevertheless, it has to be done.

Since the abolition in 1994 of the migration law that forbade moving to large cities, theoretically a nationwide labor market has been established. But practically it is still rather difficult for Chinese to change their place of work, especially because of the *hukou* system, the Chinese residence permit, which makes migration from rural areas difficult. Maybe one would have to find a new place to reside also, and the question arises of how to get a new or comparable flat. All places that offer attractive jobs have a housing shortage. Furthermore, family, friends, and one's network of relations all would be left behind. A change of workplace can mean falling through the net. For most Chinese, the change from a *danwei* to a private company or Chinese-foreign joint venture means losing the safety net of the danwei; nevertheless, many Chinese have taken this step since the 1990s.

In 2003, the government addressed the enormous burden of the social cost and inefficiency of the danweis. It has therefore announced labor market reforms that may help ailing SOEs to remove welfare burden and lay off staff, or cut health care and retirement allowances. The new regulations were implemented in selected areas, including Liaoning, Zheijiang, Fujian, Guangdong, Beijing, and Shanghai. The reform will help the state-owned enterprises to restructure, while it increases the number of unemployed workers further; the limitations of the *hukou* system, which restricts recruitment opportunities, were also eased in 2003. Plenty of workers are available in the labor market; the difficulty is to find skilled and capable staff.

Recruiting workers from danweis and offering them employment elsewhere is also a function of specialized, governmental part-time agencies. Over 18,000 such agencies exist, and some of those agencies, such as the Foreign Enterprise Service Corporation (FESCO), offer comprehensive, officially accepted or even supported, personnel resource management for WFOEs as well as for joint ventures. For good reason they are called social security danweis—they not only search for and arrange staff, they also offer tailor-made social service packages. Foreign enterprises using FESCO don't have to worry about a complicated social security network that varies from region to region. In addition, they do not have to spend time and money recruiting new, lesser-qualified workers. Higher-qualified employees, where one would expect a certain risk and initiative, do not care too much about social security. So, they must be found somewhere else. In large cities, centers for staff exchange can be helpful. These are private offices controlled by the regional government that offer workers who are willing to change their jobs, mainly middle-management positions. The offices provide employers the possibility of selecting the most suitable staff. But only rarely will one be able to find a qualified Chinese manager in their files. Good Chinese managers have no need to "advertise" themselves via personnel agencies; good managers are rare and can expect hundreds of job offers. To contact them, one needs good *guanxi*, or good connections. Without good connections, the best way to find qualified managers is to place a job advertisement in newspapers with wide circulation. But despite repeated advertisements the number of applicants is usually low, especially for marketing, accounting, and controlling positions. The best way to obtain people for those positions is to hire them from the West.

International personnel agencies are another viable option; however, some Chinese managers use the international agencies to advance from job to job, and they may change to the next available position rather quickly. A critical selection is therefore recommended. Recent Chinese studies show, however, that the salary level of these "job-hoppers" is below that of loyal, long-term employees. A shortage of managers abounds. Because of this, the enterprise should have a long-term human resources plan and recruit young career candidates early. Close contact with universities that offer marketing-related classes is helpful, as these contacts are a good source for the systematic development of Chinese management. University graduates are enthusiastic, energetic, and usually full of initiative; they have a good theoretical background and probably even a reasonable command of English. But they also tend to overestimate their value and skills and demand salaries that are not comparable with their skills. It also has to be kept in mind that within a few years they will demand even more and will be harder to recruit. Currently, there are 82,000 MBA students enrolled in China, and several thousand graduates with master's degrees in business administration leave the 70 plus Chinese MBA-universities annually. This supply of graduates is dwarfed by a strongly growing demand of tens of thousands of managers per year.

Chinese Labor Costs

In general, wages are low in China, but taking only direct wages into account can be misleading. The employment of a Chinese worker is often connected to additional costs. If he or she changes from a danwei to the company, in general compensation has to be paid to the danwei. The change of job is seen as a business transaction! Chinese authorities do not approve such practices, but they can do little to prevent them. Leaving a danwei and moving to a joint-venture company means the employee has to look for new housing by him- or herself. Candidates often solve this "problem" by asking the employer to provide an apartment. This request may even include moving and refurbishing costs. And, as noted earlier, using the services of a personnel agency might not be any less expensive.

The personal agencies, or *social security danweis*, act basically as employers. The current employer, such as a joint venture, pays the salary directly to the agency. After deducting costs, the agency pays the remaining part directly to the employee. Often the employee views his or her part as too small; therefore the employer is asked to pay indirect wages, such as traveling expenses, entertainment fees, gifts, and so on. Chinese accountants are masters of disguising such payments, and such "gray zones" are part of the salary structure in China. But besides these, which official, direct, and indirect salaries should be calculated? In principle, the salary level of a joint venture is about 20 percent above the level of a purely Chinese company. However, that is still far below Western salaries, although the levels are increasing, especially on the east coast.

In 2003, the basic monthly salary for skilled workers was between 1,500 to 2,500 yuan (US$180 to $300). Qualified office staff, foreign language secretaries, or accountants receive between 2,000 and 3,500 yuan (US$250 to $420). The basic salary for personal assistants to executive directors was 4,000 to 10,000 yuan (US$480 to 1,200). Monthly salaries for managers and highly skilled technical staff, especially in joint ventures and foreign companies, can reach up to 25,000 yuan (US$3,000). Salaries in rural areas may be far below these figures, while salaries for foreign-educated managers may well exceed them.

Productivity bonuses and a number of other benefits must be added. But it is difficult to give concrete figures for these payments, as they are partly obligatory and vary from employer to employer.

The westerner's initial joy about low wages might be spoiled by the amount of these additional payments. They can surpass salaries by up to 200 percent! Article 49 of the labor law, which was adopted on July 1994, regulates several cases where the employee has to be insured by the company for retirement, health (including work-related injuries), unemployment, birth, and death. The amount can vary depending on the region. Retirement allowance is the highest (31.5 percent in Shanghai, 25 percent in Sichuan), and the retirement age is 60 years of age for men, and 55 years of age for women. Health insurance can vary from 6 to 11 percent, unemployment from 2 to 3 percent, and maternity payment is about 0.7 percent of the monthly salary. Further expenses that might accrue are commuting costs, one-child-money, kindergarten, housing, and in the winter a cold weather support and in the summer an ice cream fee.

Two further critical points: First, because health insurance pays only for hospital stays, the employer has to take care of all other medical costs. Second, an ordinance passed in 1997 has further cost-increasing consequences. Principally, Chinese and foreign managers in similar positions must receive comparable incomes. Differences that practically exist have to be paid into a social fund for all Chinese employees. It is recommended to monitor the issuance of new labor laws closely, as they may have severe effects on the company's payroll. For all these labor-related topics, it is highly recommended to consult professional legal advisers, at least for the complex and frequent changes.

Chinese Industrial Law and Foreign Companies

The Chinese government, especially the ministries of Finance and Labor and of Social Security, has been working since 1978 on nationwide labor laws and regulatory standards. This is not an easy task, as between 1949 and 1977 alone, about two thousand regulations were issued by Beijing. In addition, economic reform has meant that additional questions have to be addressed, and the existing volume of regulations doesn't make these tasks easy. The new regulations also have to outline directives for Chinese-foreign joint ventures. In the 1980s and 1990s, a special labor law for all companies with foreign capital investment, including WFOEs, was drafted, and the law was made official from January 1, 1995; since then it has been amended regularly. It comprises all regulations applying to companies with foreign investment and Chinese employees.

In principle, all work conditions and contracts of employment must be based on this law. The contracts of employment must regulate the following points: payment, duration of probation period, contract duration, periods of notice, working time, vacation, definition of contract infringements, and results of a contract infringement. The legal working time corresponds to the nationwide regulation, which has been valid since May 1, 1997—40 hours per week. Overtime work should not exceed 9 hours per week and has to be paid between 150 and 300 percent of the normal wage, depending on the circumstances. Vacation for workers in joint ventures must amount to at least 15 working days. Days off must be given for national holidays (New Year, Spring Festival, Labor Day, National Holiday). Maternity leave must be granted as well as special paid leave for visiting parents, marriages, and funerals of relatives. It is stipulated that the salary levels in companies with foreign capital investment cannot be below the levels of purely Chinese companies. Percentages of the salary for indirect labor costs are also fixed, such as contributions for social security, health care, maternity insurance, and last, but not least, taxes.

The role of labor unions is also regulated: They are entitled to voice their opinions but have no voting rights. In joint ventures, a labor union committee must be formed, which can express the opinion of the workers—for example, regarding work safety, overtime settlement, and similar questions. The law also particularly stipulates that contracts of employment can be dissolved by proper or extraordinary notice. Proper reasons for dismissal are as follows: economic circumstances, particularly deterioration of the enterprise's economic situation; restructuring measures; lack of suitability of the employee as a result of his or her physical or psychical impairment; continued lack of professional suitability. As a matter of rule, in the case of extraordinary dismissal the company must pay one month of salary for every year of employment.

Work disputes, especially regarding legal issues, should be resolved by mutual settlement. Disputing parties nevertheless have the right to bring the dispute before a people's court. People's courts are authorities for disputes concerning labor laws.

The Calendar and Holidays

Two calendars exist in China—the official Gregorian calendar and the lunar calendar. In 1912, the Chinese government officially decided to introduce the Gregorian calendar; traditional holidays are nevertheless determined by the lunar calendar.

Chinese Public Holidays

- January 1: New Year
- Late January/Early February: Chinese New Year (3 days)
- May 1: Labor Day
- October 1–2: National Day (2 days)

Optional Public Holidays

- March 8: Int. Women's Day
- May 4: National Youth Day
- June 1: Int. Children's Day
- July 1: Founding of CPC
- August 1: Army Day

A lunar year consists of 354 days and is divided into 12 months of 29.5 days each. The new moon indicates the beginning of the month, a full moon the middle. Because the lunar calendar is 11 days shorter than the rotation of the earth around the sun, a leap month is added after every 30 months. The basis for the lunar calendar is a cycle of 60 years, which is divided into five terms of 12 years each. The 12 years are represented by animal symbols. In China, belief in the influence these symbols have on a person's character is deeply rooted. "Upon birth, the animal symbol burns itself into the heart" is a Chinese saying. Each cycle begins with the year of the rat, followed by the buffalo, tiger, rabbit, dragon, snake, horse, sheep, ape, rooster, dog, and pig. Each animal has its meaning and influences the person as well as the year. The rat signifies diligence and perseverance; the horse stands for activity and a sharp wit. The dragon means wealth and vitality, while the rooster means curiosity and self-confidence.

During the year, traditional holidays are the highlights of social life. As everywhere in the world, China celebrates many national festivals. Traditional holidays stem from mythology and the agricultural cycle. National holidays are based on political ideology. China is mainly an agricultural country; therefore its festivities are a welcome break from the hard day-to-day labor. Furthermore, the holidays are a substitute for a legally ruled vacation. Nowadays, Chinese are entitled anywhere from between 10 to 20 days of paid vacation in addition to a certain number of national holidays. Urban citizens get three days off for the annual Spring Festival; the rural population even longer. Women receive half a day's leave on March 8, International Women's Day. One day's leave is granted on May 1, International Labor Day, and two additional days on October 1, Chinese National Day. Schoolchildren have one day off on June 1, International Children's Day. Traditional festivities are: Spring Festival, also called Chinese New Year Festival; Lantern Festival; Dragon Boat Festival; Middle Harvest (or Moon) Festival; and Ancestors' Remembrance Day.

Management: Everything Chinese?

Who among the venture's senior and middle managers should be Chinese? The answer to this question relies on the joint-venture experiences of Western direct investors. According to their experiences, the least problems arise in the production area if Western staff are able to train and teach the Chinese employees.

According to Western partners, the problem with joint ventures is often not the workers or technicians but the Chinese "management." Generally negative comments arise about Chinese managers' unwillingness to implement mutually agreed strategies. Further problems are nepotism, corruption, and incompetence. Often the Chinese partners make wrong market assessments, lack the ability to motivate staff, reject or even boycott precise financial controlling, or make unnecessary technical investments because of prestige or based on relationships. Too little competence and too little cooperation are judgments often heard from European joint-venture partners, who would like to change their Chinese partners, or at least their Chinese top management. However, these companies contrast with over 50 percent of European companies who judge their partners and the Chinese management as "fair" to "very good." Their concepts are working, their investments are generating a profit, and the problems are acceptable.

Why the more favorable rating? Were these businessmen better able to adapt themselves to the mentality of their Chinese partners? Have they

Table 2.2
Characteristics of Western and Chinese Mentality

Western mentality	Chinese mentality
Individualistic	Collectivistic, Confucian
Prefers individual work or small teams	Prefers team-work
Direct	Indirect
Rejects supervision and strict rules	Prefers supervision and strict rules
Orders are seen as proposals, which can or must be modified and adapted	Follows orders strictly, without questioning their outcome
Competence equals leadership	Seniority equals leadership
Focuses on facts, results, and quality	Focuses on trust and regulations
Favors performance-based pay	Rejects performance-based pay
Delivers bad news, confrontational	Covers up for mistakes, integrative
Ability to self-monitor work progress	No self-monitoring ability
Trust based on contracts	Trust based on relations
Negotiations end with a contract	Negotiations are continuous
Outspoken, especially in meetings	No open expression of opinion
Hard work and honesty are core elements of corporate culture	Loyalty to the superior is very important
The employer is a "co-worker"	The employer is a "father"

Arranged by B. Zinzius.

understood the special Chinese psyche, the intercultural aspects of China business; have they accepted the differences? Knowledge about the intercultural aspects of the business is a major part of their success. A very concrete reason can, however, often be seen in their organizational planning. Right from the start they do the right thing regarding the organization: They have well-balanced management teams consisting of Chinese and Western managers—they do not leave everything for one side or the other to do. Successful China investors start with the assumption that the Chinese side aims for technical know-how transfer but is really in need of Western management know-how.

Managers who for years, or even decades, have held a position in a state-owned enterprise, who have worked in a company that never asked for productivity, efficiency, or profitability and where no marketing was practiced, cannot be expected to be competent managers in the Western sense. They may be able to acquire competence after some years. Until then, the Western joint-venture partners and their management teams will have given them a lot of guidance, training and manifold support. It is ideal if the venture's highest management positions are filled equally by Western and Chinese managers, especially the board of directors. It is also beneficial if a Chinese managing director is the outside representative director, but a Western director with similar authority handles the business's financial and accounting aspects. Experience shows that it is advantageous to put financial control in Western hands. Finally, it is beneficial to have a management team for the operational business—both a Chinese and a foreign manager.

Integration of Expatriates

Even after the enterprise has decided whether a Chinese or a Western general manager will lead the company, the composition of management staff has to be decided. Which management positions are to be filled by Chinese, and which ones by foreigners? The question has to do not only with competencies and qualifications but also with fluctuation and staff turnover. Chinese managers will not always fulfill the requirements of a modern, Western management model, at least not in all areas. It is therefore necessary to get qualified management from abroad, so-called expatriates. Employing expatriates is recommended, but it is also a risk. It is not sufficient that the expatriate has an excellent professional reputation. Success at home, even in the mother company, does not guarantee success in China.

Chinese authorities understand that foreign-invested companies fill certain positions with expatriates. They view such employment as necessary and useful to China. They also see it as proof of the seriousness and the durability of a foreign engagement in China. The enterprise's approval of expatriates is nevertheless connected with expectations, which should be taken into account when selecting the employee. The manager dispatched to China must necessarily have excellent professional knowledge, a mature personality, and good communication skills. Being mature is usually a precondition of what the Chinese expect from a foreign manager: patience and composure when dealing with employees, willingness to teach know-how, understanding of Chinese behavior, and willingness to integrate and empathize. Thus, it is no wonder that finding suitable managers who are willing to take on the "China challenge" is not easy. One's willingness to become an expatriate is connected with one's private or familial situation. Living conditions in China might play a role in the decision, as well as the quality of medical facilities, the availability of international schools or nurseries, and many related questions. The manager's partner, or spouse, must be willing to go along with the overall situation in China. If the manager has children who must attend school, a stay in China is probably only limited anyway from that point of view. Of course, the expatriate can leave a spouse and children at home. But a long separation from family can cause multiple problems. Nevertheless, some expatriates prefer a stay in China without their families, a decision that results often in short, perhaps too short, engagements. A stay of two to three years is usually too short. As a rule, it takes at least two years for the expatriate to acquire a good "cultural" knowledge. There are three different possibilities for employing foreigners in WFOEs or joint ventures:

- A manager gets dispatched for several months up to two years from the parent company. As a rule, his working contract remains with the parent company.
- A manager is sent to China for several years, with the possibility of returning to the parent company. In this case the employment contract is with the Chinese company. Tax and social security matters have to be considered to decide which is the better solution. There are several tax treaties between China and other countries—such as Australia, Germany, Japan, England, and the United States—that regulate details to avoid double taxation.
- A manager enters the Chinese-foreign company as a regular employee with no guarantee of return. Thus, he is per contract an employee of the joint venture.

No matter which of the preceding forms of employment is chosen, numerous papers must be filed and permissions secured before a foreigner is allowed to work in a Chinese-foreign joint venture. A declaration of intent and of the reasons for employing a foreigner along with a résumé and qualification documents must be submitted by the employer to the responsible labor authorities. After a thorough check of the need and the qualifications, the employment permit is granted. This permission is the basis for a labor visa. After receiving the labor permit and visa, the applicant can enter China and complete the admissions procedure. At the responsible labor office, he or she must present the labor permit, passport, and contract of employment in person and apply for a concrete working permit. After receiving the working permit, the employee must go to the immigration office at the local police station and ask for a living permit. The living permit will be granted for the duration of his or her working permit.

This is a brief description of the admission marathon connected with the employment of a foreigner in China. The marathon is routine in joint ventures in China, and depending on the number of foreign employees a company expects to have, it is advisable to have special Chinese staff taking care of these matters. Since July 1998, restrictions have been somewhat lessened, as foreigners are no longer required to live in the extremely expensive foreigner compounds. Since then, foreigners have been able to rent their housing directly from Chinese.

Overseas Chinese: The Best of Both Worlds?

Expatriates—that means, foreign managers, are one way to bridge the divide between international and local mentality, culture, management style, and know how. They are, however, often not well acquainted with the culture and language of the host country. A possible alternative are overseas-Chinese, that means, foreign-educated or born ethnic Chinese. They know Chinese culture and mentality due to their heritage, and Western values due to their stay abroad. Thus, they are able to bridge the cultural divides like expatriates, and—at the same time—are often better accepted by the Chinese than a westerner.

How many Chinese live abroad, and where can one find them? In 2003, over 60 million ethnic Chinese were living abroad, over 90 percent in Asia, including Hong Kong and Taiwan. Chinese emigrated from the southern Chinese provinces in large numbers since the eighteenth century. Poverty, and especially civil wars, triggered their emigration. These overseas Chinese have been highly successful commercially, and many became financial tycoons in their new homelands. The Chearavanont family in Thailand— for example, owns one of the largest conglomerates in Thailand and is the largest individual investor in China (CP-Group); the Riyadi and Liong families from Indonesia own the largest Indonesian banks; Li Ka-shing and Peter Woo from Hong Kong, and Robert Kuok from Malaysia, are US$ billionaires that have prospered abroad and, at the same time, retained close links to their ancestors homeland. Jerry Yang, founder of Yahoo!, and Patrick Soong-Shiong, co-owner of American Pharmaceutical Partners, a drug-manufacturer, are two prominent American examples of ethnic Chinese with multi-billion dollar businesses abroad.[6]

Since 1970, over one million Chinese students studied at foreign universities, 580,000 came from mainland China, a phenomenon often called the *brain drain*.[7] Between 30 percent and 70 percent of these students want to return to China, similar to the Taiwanese students since the 1980s. The Chinese government has started additional campaigns to tap this potential, and President Hu Jintao recently called returning overseas students a "precious wealth" for the country, and is trying to stimulate a reverse brain drain.[8] In 2003, a new green card system was introduced to further attract skilled overseas Chinese; the card is a permanent residence permit and facilitates their return. At the same time, these skilled professionals can maintain their residence status elsewhere, for example in Hong Kong or Taiwan.

Foreign and local companies seek these overseas Chinese, as they are an excellent link to transfer international know how and management concepts to China. These overseas Chinese speak often several languages, and have extensive knowledge about different cultural and management concepts; thus, they are in high demand among multinational corporations and start-up companies in China.

Taiwanese and Korean students started to return after the income level in their home countries reached more than US$3,000. A similar phenomenon can now be seen in mainland China. An increasing number of stu-

Table 2.3
Ethnic Overseas Chinese by Country of Residence, 2003

Country or Region	Ethnic Chinese	Percent of Population
Hong Kong	6.4 million	94.9%
Indonesia	7.3 million	3.5%
Japan	0.2 million	0.1%
Malaysia	5.9 million	26.0%
Philippines	1.2 million	1.5%
Singapore	3.3 million	76.8%
South Korea	0.1 million	0.1%
Taiwan	22.6 million	100.0%
Thailand	8.9 million	14.0%
Asia (incl. HK, Taiwan)	**55.9 million**	**8.4%**
Europe	0.6 million	0.2%
United States	2.5 million	0.9%
America (excl. United States)	2.2 million	0.3%
Total	**61.2 million**	**3.1%**

Source: Internet, country-specific governmental data. Arranged by B. Zinzius.

dents and managers return from the United States to China, often enticed by high salaries and fringe benefits. They see the entrepreneurial opportunities, and compare the current situation in China with the beginning of the twenty-first century with Silicon Valley in the 1980s and 1990s. "China meets Silicon Valley" was the title of a job fair in San Jose in 2002, which attracted over 4,000 Chinese-born engineers. The Chinese Consular General sponsored the event, which is just one example of numerous other activities of the Chinese government and business associations, which facilitate the return of Chinese students abroad.

Ethnic Chinese own about 20 percent of all Information Technology companies that were founded in Silicon Valley since 1980, a number that continues to increase. These overseas Chinese founded numerous networks and professional organizations in parallel during the 1990s as a support network for these enterprises, such as the *Silicon Valley Chinese Wireless Technology Association* (*SVCWireless*), *Silicon Valley Chinese Engineers Association* (*SCEA*), *Chinese Internet Technology Association* (*CITA*), or the *North American Chinese Semiconductor Association* (*NACSA*). These organizations have hundreds, even thousands of members, most of them Chinese. Many services are in Chinese, such as their Web sites, excluding non-Chinese speakers from their circle, while opening the dialog with mainland China. Most of the organizations are non-political, and focus on professional interest, such as information about universities; exchange on job vacancies and internship offers; financial support for entrepreneurs; chat-rooms for engineers; and—an important area—information about trade and cooperation with China. These networks are a strong backbone and an integral part of the Pacific Rim business. In addition, they are a platform for American overseas Chinese that want to return, helping to find entrepreneurial opportunities and jobs in China.

Another source of foreign-educated Chinese is second and third-generation America-born Chinese. In 2003, 2.5 million Chinese lived in the United States, about 40 percent are American-born, 60 percent are immigrants. The American-born Chinese may offer skilled management candidates for China, but it has to be evaluated carefully. Overseas Chinese from other countries provide another valuable source for staff; thousands of Chinese study in Great Britain and Australia, just to mention another potential source. Overseas Chinese are a valuable source for upper and middle management layers in China. An estimated 450,000 overseas Chinese are currently working in China, a fact that confirms their importance and role for the Chinese economy. There are specialized recruitment agencies for overseas Chinese, and the reader should consider using their services, although they may be expensive.

Returnees from abroad are not the only source for new managers. Recent studies confirm that Chinese cultural values are changing, and a new, emerging class of Chinese-born and educated managers and entrepreneurs is showing increasingly Western attitudes and values. These new Chinese managers are quite suited to run operations in China, although they have to be trained thoroughly.

The New Generation

During the twentieth century, the Chinese society has experienced profound cultural changes like few other countries. The Qing dynasty (1644–1911) was dominated by Confucianism and was strongly oriented toward the West. It was followed by several wars and revolutions, which brought the Republican Era (1911–1948), followed by the Communist Era (1949–1965), the Great Cultural Revolution Era (1966–1976), and the Social Reform Era (1977–present).

The most recent transition from Mao's communist reign to the socialist market economy is not only an economic period of drastic change for China. Changes in the educational system, an increased inflow of foreign students and international companies, and the rapid developments in communications—such as Internet, mobile phones, and television—brought an unprecedented information flood and exposure to foreign cultures to China. Economic growth and newly found wealth is also changing Chinese cultural values from collectivist to individualistic ones.

This background explains the recent emergence of a new kind of corporate cultural and management in China. Older generation employees and managers are less educated than their younger counterparts; they avoid taking risks and strictly follow the opinions and orders of superiors and senior colleagues. In contrast, a generation of young Chinese managers is emerging that is more likely to act independently; they are willing to take risks in the pursuit of profits, even if decisions conflict with traditional ways. Nevertheless, these young managers are not simply switching from Chinese to Western values, but they keep their Confucian and collectivist values and combine them with a personal profit orientation and materialism.

This new generation of young managers, that is, those that are born after the 1960s, is becoming known as the *Chinese Me Generation,* or also as *chuppies,* in analogy to the Western *yuppies.* Their values reflect the changes during the period in which they grew up—that is, strong economic growth, and an aspiration for material success, yet they are brought up in the concept of Confucianism. This new generation is, therefore, important for international companies. They are potential managers, as their values and ideals are much closer to the West than that of the older generation. They also form a link between the old and the new China.

The "Old Guard"

Chinese employees enjoy the image of being diligent, eager to learn, and obedient. "Not true at all," groans Peter Jones, the director of a joint venture who came to China hoping for employees who are "Chinese"— that is, obedient, willing to work for little money, and eager to learn from the West. In his mind, it should have been easy to motivate them, if motivation was needed at all.

"I have been extremely mistaken," states a frustrated Mr. Jones after two years in China. "No Chinese is willing to work past 7 or 8 P.M. The Chinese even have a weekly working time of 40 hours, and some use this short time shamelessly for their private businesses or even second jobs!" Most frustrating for Mr. Jones is his feeling that he is talking to a brick wall when he holds his quality circles or gives motivational speeches. He already has the reputation of being a strict, impolite, and basically a bad boss. He feels that an antipathy, even resistance, is being put up against him.

Mr. Jones has a problem similar to that of several of his foreign colleagues: he realizes that he is not well liked. Understandably, he is becoming fed up with the Chinese. More and more he separates his business life from his private, which means his social activities are confined to the American club in the next city and he generally refuses invitations from Chinese business partners. He is becoming isolated from China. Not to put too fine a point on it, Mr. Jones's willingness to communicate with the Chinese, to understand Chinese behavior and their concerns, is basically zero. Of course, a manager such as Mr. Jones cannot motivate his Chinese employees. Can a foreign manager motivate Chinese employees at all?

A manager cannot motivate Chinese employees if he bases his interactions with them on the assumption that the Chinese react and think like people do at home. He also will not be successful if he is of the opinion that the best motivation is to encourage the employees' search for self-realization and to allow personal freedom, as is done in Europe and the United States. Self-realization, a strong motivation for many in the West, motivates only a few Chinese, maybe some younger academics. Most Chinese do not work to realize themselves or out of loyalty to the company. They work because they are obliged to earn money for their families. They work to obtain security and wealth for the family and thus to obtain prestige.

The most important person in the life of a Chinese is and has always been *the father*. Within the family, the most important person is the natural father or the eldest. In the company, this corresponds to a direct superior, provided his age, competence, and dominance are sufficient to play the father role. For the Chinese, a good boss is somebody who can be as strict and as kind as a father. For that person, business must be less important than personal relationships. Certainly, he is supposed to give orders, but he is also obliged to care about his subordinates, not humiliate them or cause them loss of face: on the contrary, he must give them face. A good boss respects his subordinates; he does not criticize them bluntly and in front of others. He teaches employees patiently after they make mistakes and motivates them as a patriarch would. He is supposed to and should earn well and should present himself as a high-paid manager. Nobody will take this negatively. It even increases the quality of relationships. Subordinates want to look up to their boss, to be proud of the boss.

The Chinese employees' personal relationships with their boss, combined with numerous positive experiences, are their main source of motivation. The boss must be a shining example, a leader with whom employees can identify. Those who don't recognize this, who do not use this source, will look in vain for ways to motivate Chinese workers. In other words, the "good boss" is the most important motivational factor. Of course, *boss* basically means the direct superior. In larger companies, therefore, the team leader or department or division manager is the father figure. These personal relationships need close attention and constant, or at least frequent, contact—if they are to motivate. None of this releases the top manager from also being a good boss! By position he is the "godfather," the patriarch of the big family of employees. That reality should not be lost. Such fatherlike managers are rare, and it cannot be expected that among the managers going to China are many with such qualities. The expectations in China do not coincide with Western management needs. But they can be learned. So, there are ways to motivate the Chinese, but the manager must learn them to get results.

The Western company manager ideally is not only a teacher to the Chinese but also an excellent student. Maybe he will even develop a management system that brings together "Chinese thinking" and "Western action." A system that is, to some extent, deliberately unfocused and flexible, where the structures and operating procedures are not completely predefined and thus have some flexibility. A system that does not question but rather strengthens the individual's identification with the group. A system that not only accepts an employee's orientation toward a senior, paternal leader but sees that as the main factor of the employee's success. A paternal leader is the key figure for productivity increase; he provides the essential link between the operating plan and the result. Many problems can be solved knowing this, including the often fruitless approaches to increase productivity. Optimized identification with the group might not increase the productivity of every individual group member, but it will certainly improve the output of the whole group.

THE FACE: AN ESSENTIAL CONCEPT

The Chinese Picture of Humankind

The Confucian picture of humankind teaches that the existence of humans is bound to social relations. A central point in Confucian ethics is the teaching of the unequal relationship between people, upon which the stability of society is based. To be stable, the society can be nothing other than a hierarchical and patriarchal system. The individual is not included in this concept as he or she is outside the five relations of *wulun*. Men and women are defined by their relations, that is, by their positions in the society.

The Chinese language gives special emphasis to the social character of man's existence. The symbol for humankind, *ren,* is a combination of the signs for "human" and "two." From the Chinese perspective, the individual is therefore incomplete. The existence of individual people outside the social community seems immoral and unjustified. Single people, and those acting as individuals, are therefore often stigmatized as low-level subjects; it is regarded as negative to focus on your personal matters, to go your own way, or to live alone. Behind this is the fear that single people could question or threaten the functioning of the family, the basic germ cell of Chinese society. The Chinese deeply pity people who are forced by fate to live alone, as they experience the worst that can happen to a Chinese, loss of the family.

Chinese society is known for its long stability and continuity of almost 2,000 years. From the beginnings of the Han dynasty (206 B.C. to A.D. 220) until the end of the empire, only one doctrine was continuous and important—Confucianism. No other society can demonstrate a similar consistency. A further indicator of the stability of Chinese society is immobility. Very often the Chinese live their whole life in their birthplace. Personal relations to the family, neighbors, and friends remain constant and important, often for the whole life. This is only natural. If one has lived his whole life in one place, he will care for his relations much more than people who are moving (e.g., in case of a conflict or poverty). Social immobility, as well as narrow living conditions, helps to explain the striving for harmony, inherent in the Chinese character.

Keeping, Giving, and Losing Face

"Face" in Chinese society has two meanings. First, it stands for the personal dignity of the individual; second, it is linked to social status. The latter point is very important for the Chinese. Most Chinese pay great heed to their social reputation, the respect they receive from others. Respect, esteem, and dignity are only given if one is accepted and esteemed in society.

The most important rule for social contact with Asians is always to give face, never to take face, and never to lose face. Saving face is not a strange concept in the West; here as well the fear of an embarrassing, disgraceful, or compromising situation exists. However, the concept of face is valued much more highly in Asia than it is in the West. It includes self-definition, self-consciousness, and self-esteem, and it regulates social and moral conduct. The following excursion into Chinese etiquette regarding "giving face," "keeping face," and "losing face" explains something about the Chinese character as well as illustrating the rules one should follow while communicating with the Chinese.

Losing face—Diu Mianzi (Lian)

Open criticism as well as public insult are among the most egregious violations of the Chinese norms. Criticizing someone in front of a third party means embarrassing him or her. The criticized one loses face, and his or her reputation is damaged. It is important to pay one's counterpart respect. In doing this, special emphasis has to be given to delicate hierarchical structures. It would be wrong to treat one's subordinate as one treats one's superior. The hierarchy in a company, as well as in the family, should be strictly respected, even as a foreigner. It is therefore beneficial to check the rankings of delegation members prior to a meeting. With any faux pas, you risk not only taking face from a counterpart but losing your own face. By disgracing someone, you inevitably disgrace yourself. In addition, as a business professional, one speaks as a delegate of a company, even of a country. Negative tensions that arise in a discussion will therefore influence company, or one's country's, relations. One can also lose face by not fulfilling expectations or promises, or by breaking norms or social rules.

Giving face—Gei Mianzi (Lian)

Enlarging someone's reputation—for example, applauding, being in agreement, or giving a compliment in the presence of colleagues or superiors—gives face. Praise obliges and secures loyalty. However, too much praise might generate mistrust. Supporting somebody in a difficult situation is similar to helping him to save face (weihu mianzi). The person is under an obligation to return the favor. The I Ching, an important piece of Confucian literature, deals with anecdotes about correct social conduct, giving multiple examples pertaining to keeping and restoring face. It offers prototypes of compulsory behavior. Most stories end with suicide, which in some cases is the only way to keep one's face after death. Even in case of severe punishment, the face of the defendant is considered. In cases involving governmental officials, for example, it was common to send a silk scarf prior to a punishment, which enabled them to commit suicide. Thus, they could keep their face as well as the face of their family. Any official who did not follow this rule was executed in public and thus lost his face. The concept of face is applicable not only to an individual but also to a group. Great importance is given to the face of the family, which must be kept under all circumstances, as it is even inherited. It can furthermore be applied to the workplace, the hometown, the Communist Party, and even to China.

Especially in contacts with foreigners, the national conscience of the Chinese is very sensitive. Negative opinions about Chinese institutions or customs are not only taken personally but also understood as a national loss of face. The Opium Wars, which were brought by foreigners in the beginning of the twentieth century, were a great loss of face for all Chinese and had a much deeper impact than all economic or political consequences. The consequences thereof can still be felt today, especially in relations with foreigners.

The basic concept of face applies only to persons within the same group—for example, in the family, the danwei, the company, or the party. Within the group, behavior is openhanded, courteous, and respectful; it is based on the principle that one helps the other. Outside the group, the Confucian ethic sees no necessity to give face. In contact with strangers, even if you are from the same nation or area, there are no moral norms that would lead to a certain social conduct.

Personal and Social Face

The concept of face has two dimensions. First, there is personal decency in a moral sense, called *lian*. Second, there is integrity with regard to social hierarchy, called *mianzi*. The latter shows the importance of social relationships in China. Unlike in the West, the society is always thought of as a strictly hierarchical building, not as a community of equal persons. The longstanding Western tradition of individualism, used as the basis for the right to self-determination and individual development, finds little acceptance in China nor any of the Confucian-influenced countries of Asia.

Preserving a hierarchically structured society has an important goal—the single person is of less importance. A person is important in his or her function in the family, society, clan, company, or *danwei* (the special working unit). The way that an individual person behaves within the social relations and dependencies, within the structures of the hierarchical society, is of much higher importance. The most important factor of social face is to integrate oneself as perfectly as possible into the system and to submit personal interests to the request and expectations of the group. The roots of this concept, on which society depends heavily, are based in the Confucian teachings. The concept calls for strict adherence to Confucian norms, such as loyalty, integrity of the hierarchy, reverence, and the desire for harmony. The Chinese view any deviation from these norms as antisocial.

Motivating Employees: Keeping and Giving Face

Giving and taking face, having and keeping face—this is what is important to the Chinese! Every contact with the Chinese is about "face." Face is basically the sum of one's behavior, his or her success in business and fulfillment of duties toward family and friends. The Chinese regard everything taken together as important—the totality of one's reputation in the social environment. Face is a sum that must not be tarnished. Reputation and social position among others give dignity, social value, and a corresponding role. Face is of crucial importance for the individual. From childhood, Chinese are taught that conflicts can lead to a loss of face. Therefore, the Chinese will avoid any and all situations that may lead to conflict. The formal, almost ritual Chinese politeness, the Chinese flexibility, which is not inquisitive as much as it is avoidance of critical questions, and last but not least the unbreakable Chinese composure—all of these are strategies to avoid conflict. Their main goal is to protect the face of individual people and the face of social and business groups. Each group has a face that must be "kept."

Almost all mistakes foreigners make in China are related to face. It might take years of staying in China until one has a good feeling about what can cause loss of face for a person or group. It is to the advantage of foreigners and part of the strategy of avoiding conflict that the Chinese overlook the incorrect behavior of foreigners to a certain degree and for some time. This has nothing to do with being tolerant of foreigners or even being friendly toward them. If foreigners do not realize the importance and meaning of face, they will be ignored and categorized as barbarian strangers. If they learn, however, to behave correctly in China, to integrate with the culture, they will be respected as pleasant strangers, maybe even as friendly strangers.

The general behavior of the Chinese toward strangers applies also—or especially—to foreigners who come as businesspeople or managers to China. They are regarded as civilized strangers if they protect the face of their employees. They are esteemed strangers, if they have a face of their own, which a good boss should have.

This may sound simple in theory, but practically it is very difficult. It will become easier if the most frequent mistakes of motivation are avoided and replaced by the right behavior. Using terms such as right or wrong and correct or incorrect is closely related to face. Wrong forces the employee to be passive, maybe to disobey. He or she won't react that way because of dissent or laziness or passive behavior. The employee is acting to prevent or avoid a possible loss of face. Furthermore, if the boss causes such defensive behavior, he loses face himself! He becomes the unpleasant barbarian stranger.

Motivating Chinese Employees

- It is effective to set or describe examples repeatedly and in a generally intelligible way so that they may be imitated by employees without the risk of disgrace. One cannot motivate employees with aggressive actions or by forcing staff into work, causing loss of face. Also, holding open group discussions on difficult problems or doing role-playing, where employees are forced to open themselves up, are taboo.

- Motivation via questions, where the answers are directly presented, is an efficient tool. It spares the person who is supposed to know the answer a potential loss of face. This face saving might well motivate the indirectly criticized employee to improve. To the contrary, one does not motivate employees by criticizing individuals in front of others or demanding concrete comments. Such tactics might even alienate the complete group, which will sympathize with the criticized employee.

- A group discussion is not a valid means of motivation in China. Such a group gathering should be restricted to rhetorical questions with the answers following directly. Most Chinese prefer to listen and eagerly take notes.

- It is an ineffective, senseless motivational attempt to have employees identify themselves with their company. If there is any identification

among the Chinese, it will be with the working team. Therefore, it may
be a good motivational tool to offer group incentives.

- One does not motivate by referring to abstract principles, but by presenting the concrete advantages of a planned measure or change, possibly
in a pictorial way and in detail.

Western–Chinese Face Problems

A recent example illustrates the problem: The general manager of a
leading German fashion house was visiting an entity in Shanghai. Upon
arrival, she realized that some clothes exhibited in the window were not
ironed. With dismay, she gathered all the employees including the branch
manager to the window, where she delivered a severe lecture and criticized the negligence of the Chinese employees. Without any visible reaction, the Chinese listened to the criticism and went silently back to work.
On the next day, however, many of the staff were late. Some arrived 5
minutes late, others 10, some didn't show up at all. Outraged, the German
manager indicated that the Chinese are altogether unpunctual. She also
renewed her criticism with harsh words about the working attitude of the
Chinese employees. From this point, the working attitude and climate in
the company decreased steadily. Employees arrived late, extended their
lunch break, did not take care in their work, and did not clean up any
more. Normal work was no longer possible; communications between the
German management and the Chinese staff were irreparably damaged.

This example illustrates the difficulties setting up a new company can
create for the Chinese as well as the West. Only those who fully understand the Chinese mentality will be successful. The German manager
made a fundamental mistake. Harsh words in front of all employees will
hurt the Chinese sense of honor, as the Chinese react very sensitively to
public criticism. The behavior also broke one of the most important social
norms of the Chinese—to keep face. The open criticism dishonored the
Chinese, who reacted passively but with complete resistance. Compromise after the confrontation was no longer possible. The example also
shows that public confrontation is inefficient and counterproductive. Experienced managers know one can beat the Chinese only with their own
weapons. Instead of criticism in front of all employees, the manager
should have talked to the store manager in private. In a private setting,
the German manager should have praised the good work of the Chinese
team, and only then should she have asked about possibly improving of
the shop window display.

The value of personal honor in China is more strongly connected to
social standing than it is in the West. The face of the individual gets more
and more dependent on the face of the society; therefore, the social conduct of the individual becomes more important. This counts especially for

all forms of courteous behavior. Social conduct in China is ruled by the etiquette of face, which is full of shades and highly differentiated.

The complex Chinese codes of social conduct might be confusing to, and misunderstood by westerners. Distinct rituals practiced by the Chinese seem superfluous, and against the Western background of open criticism, the aim for harmony is viewed as unnecessary or even a hindrance. Businessmen, who are dedicated to the Western ethic of individualism will regard Chinese behavior—which strives for the homogeneity of the group—as inefficient and outdated. In this misconception, one sees the westerner's lack of understanding of the completely different value system of Asian societies.

Morals, Taboos, and Social Values

China is standing at a cultural crossroad, where two distinct generations with different values, morals, and taboos meet. Older generations were raised strictly adhering to the Confucian concept of submitting one's individualism to the common will; the concept was enhanced by the political and moral rigidity of the Communists. For decades, only one thing was important: the political correctness of the individual. By definition of the Communist cadres, the politically correct were those who submitted their private interest totally to the interests of the people. Therefore, people who intended to marry had to ensure that their partner was a sincere party member as well as a flawless comrade. For some, especially for students, falling in love was not allowed, as that would distract one from learning and concentrating on the important things. Those who dated despite this were regarded as engaged. Divorces carry an even worse stigma as they are seen as an admission of being incapable of having a harmonious marriage.

The relationship between parents and their children was regulated with similarly strict rules. The exchange of tenderness was no longer permitted from the age of three years to school age. This is to teach children to keep a distance and to not grow effeminate; caress was avoided. Children had to learn to get over their individualism and to show no emotions. A Chinese student in Germany once recounted: When I was traveling for the first time after two years from Germany to China, I was extremely anxious and was very much looking forward to see my parents. I wanted to embrace my parents to show them how much I had missed them. In Germany I had learned to show my feelings openly. I even had accepted that some of my German friends greeted me with a kiss. However, when I stood in front of my parents, I didn't have the confidence any more. I briefly gave my mother my hand, although I wanted to embrace her. Suddenly that looked irreverent to me. I couldn't even give my father a hand, although we had a very, very good understanding. He said only, "You are here," and I answered, "I am here."

Younger generations, especially those raised since the 1980s, continue to adhere to Confucian values and concepts. Several factors, however, contribute to a profound value change. The urban flight will strongly change people's behavior, when compared to the rural life of their ancestors. Developments in Information Technology create an unprecedented exchange of information, enabling people to discuss topics that were taboo or unknown just one decade ago, such as political and social activities, entrepreneurial opportunities, and sexual services. The economic growth over the past two decades has raised income levels to a point where about 400 million Chinese belong to a middle-class that can afford to go shopping, dining, travel abroad, or take up kinds of entertainment that were not available few years ago. The government has recognized this fact and eased passport restrictions considerably in 2003. Education has considerably improved over the past two decades, although the level is still below Western standards. Higher education gives the Chinese nevertheless new freedom and experiences, increasing individualism in the younger generation. Economic growth and corresponding social changes are forcing the political leadership to adapt its control over the people. Today, more individual freedom is granted in China, including property ownership, and more personal rights are honored than ever before in history. These changes lead to new social values among the young Chinese, that is, a mixture of traditional Confucian values with a new materialistic and individualistic orientation. The basic concept nevertheless remains Confucian and is not a change toward Western social concepts.

Moral values also change: More and more younger generation managers are willing to voice criticism and raise problems; in public, young couples can be seen on the streets showing their affection; and the extended family is often replaced by a core family. These developments, however, have not only positive aspects. For older generations, and especially political cadres, they are difficult to accept and cope with. Furthermore, a new openness and individualism leads also to new problems, such as corruption, reduced loyalty, or an extravagant lifestyle by the youth. Entertainment industries are thriving, from Internet cafes to nightclubs, from restaurants to travel agencies. Young Chinese are more promiscuous and sexually active than ever before, resulting in high abortion rates among teenagers, and a hidden epidemic of sexually transmitted disease. In 2001, an estimated 1.5 million Chinese were infected with the AIDS virus, a number that could soar to 10 million by 2010.[9]

Confucian traditions versus modern individualism—how will Chinese values, morals, and taboos develop during the twenty-first century? This question cannot be answered today, but the rapid changes of economic, social, and political values suggest that profound social changes will transform the Chinese society. A mixture of Confucian values and money ethics will be a centerpoint of the Chinese society in the global economy of the twenty-first century.

MONEY AND FOREIGN CURRENCY

Restructuring the Banking System

An undisputed principle of the Chinese reform politics is its pragmatism. At the same time, the government must ensure that nothing happens that could destabilize the political order. Privatization is not an end in itself, and it is definitely not a phenomenon of a changed political order. Restructuring is still a precisely monitored means of becoming more competitive and efficient. The efficiency of state-owned enterprises is improved to make them more competitive and to ensure the survival of the state economy. And in contrast to other Communist countries, the dosage of privatization and the way in which it is used work very well in China. The state does not intend to give away control of its core businesses, although direct influence is scaled back. This is especially the case for the core business "monetary economy."

In about 1990, it began to become clear that the main part of China's monetary economy, the banking system, was not able to cope with the country's economic development. Chinese banks, all of them state enterprises, functioned as intermediaries of businesses that were arranged politically. The banks were politically forced to offer loans to unprofitable state enterprises. They remained under political pressure to contribute to a financially unacceptable monetary policy. Furthermore, they did not have the structure to contribute to the economic development of the Chinese economy. The state of the Chinese financial and banking system was a drag on economic reform, and it was doomed to failure. This didn't have any effect on foreign investors. And it also did not affect foreign trade. Internal Chinese problems were matters of concern for the Chinese leadership. They realized that a well-functioning monetary system was a precondition for successfully reforming the economy toward a socialist market economy. Banks had to be able to deliver needed credit to companies. Banks had to be able to do so without governmental support, that is, without state money. It was not the Chinese banks' fault that they could not do so. Political influence forced them more often than not to grant most probably unrecoverable loans to almost bankrupt SOEs. Such "political banking businesses" led to an overindebtedness of the banks. And the worst part of this scenario was that giving credit to unproductive and insolvent state enterprises did not help their recovery, but it did increase the money flow and add to inflation.

The situation forced Beijing in 1993 to begin to reform the banking sector. The aim of the reform was to allow Chinese banks the financial role that financial intermediaries had for a long time assumed in the Western economy. The basic step was to give a new structure to the Chinese banking system. The essential point was to separate politically motivated banking business from purely commercial business. The next step was to newly orient the credit business. Commercial banks should be able to give credit based purely on commercial aspects, such as creditworthiness and credit risk. The awarding of loans, including to Chinese enterprises with foreign participation, had to be put on an economical, profitable, and competitive base.

In 1993, three state development banks were founded, the "policy banks." The China Development Bank (formerly the State Development Bank) is responsible for the financing of large and key projects of national importance. It is the special task of the bank to take on financing tasks in foreign trade, provide loans for import and export businesses, and to ensure the liquidation of foreign government and economic loans. The Agricultural Development Bank concentrates on agricultural development projects. Four special banks account for over 80 percent of all credit: the Bank of China, the Industrial and Commercial Bank of China, the Agricultural Bank of China, and the China Construction Bank. These banks are not supposed to provide any further political-based credit; rather they are to develop into purely business-oriented banks and financial institutions. That process will naturally take several years. These banks face problems, for example, the missing familiarity with financial methods such as credit ratings and due diligence. Other problems include the high number of staff, which causes inefficiency, and the high percentage of unrecoverable loans to overindebted SOEs, which were not made based on sound economic reasons.

Since the end of 1998, China's central bank, The People's Bank of China, has been restructured with the aim of becoming efficient. Among other responsibilities, the People's Bank of China has the following objectives: to control the monetary market, to fix official credit rates, to control state reserves of gold and foreign currency, and to release money. Together with the government, it is the guardian of currency stability, and it oversees all Chinese and foreign financial institutions.

Foreign financial institutions play an increasingly important role and are buying shares in Chinese counterparts, although they are admitted and controlled by the government. In combination with the growing number of foreign financial institutions, which are called "nonbanks," these developments point toward a moderate liberalization of the Chinese financial sector. Investment companies provide and withdraw more and more money to and from the financial markets. Leasing companies spare the private sector the need to invest in fixed assets. Life insurance companies support the private consumer in building up retirement funds.

The mounting bad debt of the state banks has increased the pressure for reform even more. It is estimated that US$300–US$500 billion, up to 50 percent of Chinas annual gross domestic product, are non-performing loans;[10] such loans were responsible for the Asian crisis, and are one of the reasons for Japan's prolonged economic depression. In 2002, the Chinese government therefore allowed foreign banks to establish non-controlling equity joint ventures with local banks. Since then, foreign banks are able to provide financial services in yuan. This solution assures that the control over the banking system remains in Chinese hands, while foreign investors are able to offer local services, such as co-branding credit cards and loans. Several foreign banks have invested strongly since, including Citibank, Commerce Bank, Deutsche Bank, Dresdner Bank, and HSBC. Insurance companies and stock trading are other sectors that have been opened for international investors. This will provide funds and, most important, international control mechanisms and finance management practices to China. In 2004, the China Banking Regulatory Commission injected another US$45 billion in the Bank of China and the China Construction Bank in order to cover non-performing loans. This measure is also designed to attract foreign buyers, as the successful IPO of China Life Insurance in 2003 shows: the IPO achieved US$3.5 billion in New York and Hong Kong. The bailout therefore intends to prepare all four state-owned banks to be listed on overseas exchanges by 2007, an open goal of the China Banking Regulatory Commission.[11]

China's financial economy is polymorphous and, from a Western point of view, well able to function. Will the reform of the banking and financial system be successful? Are the problems of credit institutions declining—or at least on the way to being solved? The answer is that China has made advancements in a short period of time. Partial solutions have been found, whereas other reforms are still in the initial stages. The enormous debt and a string of financial scandals since 2001 have tarnished the image of China's banking system. Nevertheless, with the opening to foreign investors, and thus, to foreign funds and control mechanisms, the overall development of China's financial sector is rather positive, especially given that China has weathered the Asian crisis without any damage.

Financial and Monetary Policies

Besides the Chinese currency renminbi (RMB) with its unit of currency the yuan, until December 31, 1993, China used so-called Foreign Exchange Certificates (FECs). Because this "foreigner currency" was used by more and more Chinese for black and gray market transactions and was also against the monetary policy, it was abolished in 1994. Since then, foreigners as well as Chinese deal only in renminbi. Practically, it is a purely local currency. RMB import and export is restricted to a maximum amount. The import of foreign currencies is subject to no restrictions, although foreign currencies are not allowed in China as means of payment. Imported foreign money must be paid into a current or savings account with a Chinese or an authorized foreign bank. In principle, two types of foreign currency accounts can be distinguished. The opening of an account must be approved by the State Administration for Foreign Exchange (SAFE). A current account is able to handle all daily business transactions. SAFE will determine a maximum amount of foreign currency that can be changed into local currency and vice versa. Thus, the renminbi is in principle freely convertible. This is not possible for the second type of account, the capital account. Capital movements on this account, such as an increase of company capital, credit withdrawals, or liquidation of debt, have to be approved by SAFE.

Small- to medium-sized Western companies that need credit to finance their China investments usually secure it through their Western home banks. Another option is special credit offered by Western governmental institutions such as the German Credit Union for Reconstruction or the European Union's European Community Investment Partners (ECIP) program. The U.S. Export-Import Bank also offers short-, medium-, and long-term programs to support sales of U.S. exports. It goes without saying that foreign currency loans can also be obtained from Chinese or foreign banks in China. As security, the banks more and more often accept mortgages on land holdings. It must be noted that credit obtained in foreign currency has to be registered with SAFE within fifteen days after signing the contract. An advanced debt repayment of such credit also needs the approval of SAFE.

Companies with foreign capital investment can obtain loans in local currency only from Chinese banks. It may be difficult to receive such renminbi loans from time to time. The procedure of the Central Bank assigning credit according to quotas has been officially abolished. Purely Chinese companies receive credit on a preferred basis. The Chinese partner should be able to influence the procedure significantly. Despite official directives, and even if the credit approval has been given, the local bank decides on the release of the credit. It is therefore useful to have good connections with local banks. The Chinese partner should therefore be able to convince all parties concerned of the necessity of the project for which the credit is needed. The funds may be released rather soon, especially if relations are good and the credit is needed for assets produced in China. However, the application for credit may be declined because the credit volume of the bank is exhausted, or because the Chinese partner has lobbied insufficiently. The latter is frequently the case; the Chinese partner anticipates that his foreign counterpart will supply sufficient capital or that he can secure it abroad within a short time. If this is not the case, the Chinese partner will be disappointed and might even think about retreating from the joint venture. Is leasing possible in China? Can cars, equipment, or machines be leased? Yes, and leasing is a frequently used financial tool among foreign investors. Leasing is often much less complicated than receiving credit. But here, also, one has to be careful: Not many leasing companies in China would earn a "good" rating. International companies, such as General Motors, Toyota, and VW have used the new banking regulations to establish finance companies to offer credit services; foreign service providers are, however, still excluded from offering leasing services.

China's fixed exchange rate policy has been under harsh criticism, especially since 2003. Experts see China's currency undervalued by 20 to 30 percent—which gives China's exports a strong competitive advantage. The increasing trade deficit (US$124 billion with the United States in 2003), and the ongoing job losses in the United States prompted the Bush administration to call for import sanctions against a variety of products, including steel, textiles, furniture, and television sets. Other industrial sectors have proposed similar sanctions, a popular call during the Presidential election campaign in 2004.

Trade sanctions, however, are not the solution to the problem, especially as China can be expected to react sharply against such punitive measures. It is estimated that only 25 percent of the three million jobs lost between 1999 and 2002 in the United States are related to imports; most jobs were lost because of improved production efficiencies and restructuring of industries. In addition, many industries are ambivalent about China's emergence as a low-cost producer. While trade sanctions against China may help one company, others will suffer because of their increased business links with Chinese suppliers. Some opinions even suggest that the number of jobs generated in the United States by outsourcing production and services exceeds the number of jobs lost. Pillowtex, a well-known sheet and towel manufacturer, went bankrupt in 2003 and had to lay off 7,500 workers as a result of low-cost competitors; many other American and European companies, small businesses and multinationals as well, benefit from outsourcing their production and development to China. Trade sanctions may therefore have a negative impact on many industries in the United States.

China, at the same time, needs the exports to stimulate the economy and generate jobs for the tens of millions of unemployed farmers. China is therefore approaching any currency revaluation with caution. On the other side, if China does not devalue the currency soon, it's foreign exchange reserves will continue to grow and threaten to increase inflation to record levels at a later time. A moderate devaluation of the yuan would therefore be the most sensible solution to the valuation problem of China's currency.

NOTES

1. Schell, O. "The impressive enigma of China's economic miracle." *Jakarta Post*, Nov. 11, 2003, p. 6.

2. Macartney, J. "Taiwan president's trip draws U.S., China attention." *Jakarta Post*, Nov. 8, 2003, p. 3.

3. "Investment in China FAQ." *China Internet Information Center*. http://www.china.org.cn/english/features/investment /36684.htm, Dec. 12, 2003.

4. Alicic, R. "Asian development outlook 2003: People's Republic of China." *Asian Development Bank*, Nov. 18, 2003. http://www.adb.org/Documents/Books/ADO/2003/prc.asp, Jan. 19, 2004, p. 11 et seq.

5. "Laws on foreign Investment Enterprises." *FDI 24. Invest in China, 2004.* http:// www.fdi.gov.cn / ltlawpackage / index.jsp?category = 0103 & app = 1 & language = en&currentPage = 1. Mar. 12, 2004.

6. Zinzius, B. *Chinese America: Stereotype and Reality. History, Present, and Future of the Chinese in America.* New York: Peter Lang, 2004, 243 et seq.

7. *Open Doors 2003. Statistics on International Student Mobility.* New York: Institute of International Education, Mar. 2, 2004.

8. Zinzius, B., 2004, 197 et seq.

9. "China AIDS a 'titanic peril' " CNN.com, June 28, 2002. http://edition.cnn.com/2002/WORLD/asiapcf/east/06/28/china.aids/?related, Jan. 14, 2003.

10. Kurtenbach, E. "Banks hunting for Chinese partners." *Jakarta Post*, Jan 22, 2003, p. 16; *see also* Arreddy, J. "China Readies Bank Sector For Global Competition." *Asian Wall Street Journal*, Jan. 7, 2004, pp. A1–A4.

11. Richardson, K., and Leggett, K. "Foreign Firms See Chances As China Tackles Bad Debt." *Asian Wall Street Journal*, Jan. 13, 2004, pp. A1–A4.

CHAPTER 3

The Chinese Company— Keeping It Running

MANAGEMENT PROBLEMS—PREPROGRAMMED?

The feasibility study has been tedious, has consumed time and money, and has frayed one's nerves. On the other hand, it has proven that one is ready for the China business. Everything is all set; the company strategy and all macroeconomic factors are well planned. Production, including raw material sourcing; marketing; sales; logistics; cost planning; the five-year business plan, including profit-and-loss statements; environmental issues—everything has been studied; everything is in place.

The foreign joint-venture partner's high spirits at knowing that everything is in place and that things will at least start soon may, however, be replaced by a hangover. Shock follows upon shock; problems come up suddenly. Here are some examples of the most frequent occurrences: Within a short period, the machines that were valued at US$2 million in the feasibility study and included in the joint-venture contract are found to be worth a maximum of US$500,000 and have to be replaced. After six months at the most, it becomes clear that the number of Chinese staff "provided" by the partner is not justified; there are far too many for the planned productivity. Also, their efficiency is by no means comparable with that assumed by the plan: too many staff, too little sales per capita. Both of those key factors jeopardize from the beginning the profit-and-loss projections. Although it had been negotiated that the number of workers can be adjusted according to actual production and sales figures, the unexpected number of employees cannot be sent into early retirement as that would put an unexpected financial burden on the social system. Furthermore, it could trigger problems with the labor union and the administration.

Or, during the start-up phase, it becomes clear that some key positions cannot be entrusted to, or filled by, the installed Chinese managers. Expatriates from the parent company have to be hired, which increases costs and salary levels and leads to additional tensions. Uncalculated costs increase the burden on the balance sheet, finally increase prices, and influence competitiveness. Furthermore, mysterious and unpredictable losses influence results. It is a month before management or financial controllers are able to locate the sources of these losses. As an example, a part of the production is neither sold nor in stock—it is distributed to the employees or partner companies as a benefit. Such additional benefits might not be shown in the books—a Chinese "obligingness." Only a detailed investigation into the differences between raw material supply and finished goods output will detect such cases.

Such practices are common, but they are not seen as criminal acts. Similarly common is the practice of hiding losses or profits in the books, which can be useful and deliberate. However, bookkeeping based on Chinese understanding might be more than a problem in the eyes of a Western company. Western companies should therefore insist that Chinese managers provide a clear profit-and-loss statement as a guiding and controlling instrument for the company. Certainly, one should give the Chinese staff time, but after a year at most, with the first official balance sheet, the accounting and controlling personnel of the joint venture must be able to present the investor with continuous and complete financial information.

One could say that out of duty and as a matter of competence, the foreign partner has to control and manage the joint venture. Concrete influence, however, will be rather limited, especially if the foreign partner owns only a minority share. On the other hand, if the foreign partner owns a majority, theoretical influence will be almost optimal. Experience nevertheless shows that even in that case, overall influence on the Chinese partner is still limited. In general, it is true that the smaller the percentage of shares owned by the foreign partner, the greater the possibility of problems in productivity, profitability, and management. An important part of managing a Chinese joint venture is establishing fully functioning financial controlling—supervision that functions according to Western standards. Such supervision may be unnecessary from the Chinese viewpoint, even unwanted. It may be a strong obstacle for a rotten SOE to be controlled from the macro- and microeconomic perspective by Western accountants. But it is a must for the foreign investor to be in charge of the accounting and controlling if he does not want to get "milked" by Chinese hands, but rather wants to graze in China. It is almost essential in order to establish a profitable business and finally gain market share. The law for Chinese-foreign joint ventures explicitly allows the foreign investor to request and insist on modern accounting. This point must nevertheless be fixed in the feasibility study and included in the contract. Article 11 of the law regulating Chinese-foreign contractual joint ventures (Law of the People's Republic of China on Chinese foreign contractual joint ventures, April 13, 1988) is quoted here as an example:

A contractual joint venture shall conduct its operational and managerial activities in accordance with the approved contract and the articles of association for the contractual joint venture. The right of a contractual joint venture to make its own operational and managerial decisions shall not be interfered with.[1]

Article 14 of the equity joint venture law (September 20, 1988) regulates the same in detail for equity joint ventures.

Efficient Company Operation—Mission Impossible?

The name is fictional; the case, however, is true. Mr. Braun, managing director and co-owner of several furniture factories in Germany, saw his chance to establish a presence in the growing Chinese market in cooperation with Chinese furniture manufacturers. A thorough market analysis convinced him that China was simply the market of the future. For several years, Mr. Braun had established business relations with Chinese importers. Using these relations, he had an attractive opportunity for a production site and a potential partner: cooperation with a furniture factory in Wuhan, a joint-venture contract. The Chinese partner was a state enterprise that did not work profitably but had an established distribution and sales network. Moreover, it offered the proposed joint-venture factory premises, buildings, machinery, and employees. The new enterprise finally started its activities. Mr. Braun knew he had to invest much—the company capital had to be paid, the equipment plant had to be installed, some buildings needed refurbishing. Because major parts of the Chinese furniture factory had been brought into the joint venture, old debts had to be assumed. Mr. Braun quickly realized that it would take years for the investment to be amortized. He nevertheless did not regret having gone to China. He was lucky to have won open-minded, flexible, and reliable Chinese partners. And he found a suitable man from his German managing team to become managing director. It seemed to Mr. Braun the most important thing was that the Chinese side had established sales and distribution channels. The problem was that these channels could not be supplied as planned. Often he had back orders, and there was no customer orientation. For Mr. Braun, it was usual business practice to analyze problems and take countermeasures. So he sent his top financial controller with a consulting team to Wuhan.

Facts and analysis pointed toward a necessary restructuring of the company organization and the joint venture. Productivity and delivery problems were certainly caused by operational weaknesses. The company structure was departmentally organized, not functional. Order entry, production planning, production, warehousing, sales, and logistics—every department was independent and strictly hierarchically organized.

Parallel work was being done, which was slow and labor intensive. The major objective for each department seemed to be to amass work and secure jobs. The result was devastating from a Western viewpoint. The processing of each order involved up to 30 or 40 different people, directly or indirectly. Three workers handled semiautomated equipment, whereas in Europe or the United States, one worker would look after two to three machines. Three workers made adjustments or changes on the equipment, which took two hours per machine and shift! These two hours meant a complete stoppage of the production line. And this was just happening in the first production line; subsequent delays in the second or third lines were even longer.

The restructuring started exactly here: Teams of two to three workers were set up, each team responsible for the handling, adjusting, and maintenance of their machine. The next step was a completely new process workflow. All departments were dissolved, and a process-oriented teamwork was established: order center, order processing, production planning, preproduction, production, materials management and logistics. The order center now controlled the complete process, managing a customer-oriented production. It connected the different customer orders and their processing with the logistics. All of this was possible by introducing new enterprise resource planning (ERP) software that connected the departments—process and production oriented. Today, this joint venture is one of the most modern in the region and a market leader. It is not necessary to focus too much on the reorganization. But it shows that a rational, efficient company organization and management is essential and can certainly lead to increased productivity and competitiveness. It is possible, although not easy. And it is definitely more easily done in a WFOE and more difficult to introduce and fully implement in a joint venture. In this example, one sees that the Chinese workers, technicians, administrative staff, and Western managers have different mentalities and traditions. Although it might seem useful for Chinese to imitate the Western system, that system is nevertheless strange and suspicious for many Chinese.

Pushing Productivity—Without Losing Face

A frequent complaint of Western top-level managers in Chinese-foreign companies is "It is very hard to move the people toward increased productivity, or even to explain the concept of productivity." Productivity to the Chinese means basically that new machines and processes are able to produce more. They don't realize that increased production and productivity do not automatically translate into profit and that it can even mean a loss. Western business management is a strange concept for many Chinese managers and entrepreneurs. To some extent—especially in the younger generation—this is changing. Even those managers who have been educated in the socialist market economy learn that miracle growth—that is, significant increases in productivity—will become profitable only if production efficiency is adequate. Having learned this, they also understand that increased efficiency will only occur based on increased labor productivity. Modern technology, equipment, and procedures—all these are not sufficient to increase productivity and secure efficiency.

Per-capita performance—that is, production result per employee in relation to time, cost, fixed cost, unit cost, and so on—is a possible measure of labor productivity. But the operation has to be benchmarked to be able to compare actual efficiency with target values.

To increase labor productivity, one needs foremost to observe and make critical judgments about general and operational weaknesses and the employees themselves. Furthermore, one needs to introduce measures for improvement that require the acceptance of the affected employees. At least that is how it might be handled in the West! In the West, companies have used countless initiatives, programs, and benchmarking approaches over the past decades to improve operational performance. However, key concepts such as change management, balanced scorecard systems, or Six Sigma management strategy, which all measure operational and strategic performance, have yet to be introduced, implemented, and practiced in many Chinese enterprises. Introducing Chinese managers to performance management concepts and making the concepts work is certainly difficult; but it is also necessary and can be rewarding, as examples of functioning joint ventures show.

The introduction and use of such management systems in China, however, has to be done delicately. For example, criticism can trigger a chain reaction even if it is totally valid and based purely on facts. Criticizing the Chinese means handling nitroglycerin. One must handle criticism with the same caution as one handles an explosive. It must be wrapped and delivered in such a way that it is not judged as a declaration of war. In no way should criticism be used to single out an individual, even if that may be justified. One must also be aware that a Chinese person may feel criticized by words that a westerner would just perceive as a "clarification." Chinese are immensely sensitive people.

A simple questioning of performance or knowledge might tarnish the Chinese workers' personal dignity. For the Chinese, this means losing face, losing personal reputation in their social environment. To take someone's face is an almost irreparable act. What makes the situation even more difficult is that the group, as well as the individual, has face. Blaming a company for having low productivity can mean "taking the face" of the complete management board, causing each board member to lose face. Criticizing team productivity openly or even discussing it openly means causing the complete team and every team member to lose face. On the other hand, it does not help to avoid criticism and just introduce benchmarking tools and measures to increase productivity. The Chinese management will feel ignored and probably indirectly criticized. They may react negatively, maybe even be hostile.

Pushing for productivity is often a rather tough problem. But it can be solved. Experience teaches that criticism does not necessarily trigger a loss-of-face chain reaction if it is delivered carefully and in one-on-one conversations. First, one should speak privately about the matter with the Chinese partner and members of the board. Definite and verifiable facts should be put politely on the table, if possible with proper proposals for a solution already at hand. After an agreement has been reached in individual discussions and the top management is on board, one-on-one discussions with the middle management can begin. Defusing further resistance to the criticism and implementation of countermeasures can be left to the Chinese managers. Take warning, however: The foreign manager should be careful not to get branded as the bad guy. It is a Chinese principle in joint ventures to leave the critical and other negative communication about employees to the Western directors and managers. If the westerner accepts such a position, he or she has a difficult standing with lower and middle management and is often regarded as the hostile stranger.

Implementing Vision and Mission

Solving productivity problems, increasing efficiency, establishing benchmarks, and measuring performances, is a difficult task in any company in China. Even more difficult are the hurdles in communicating and implementing a clear vision and mission that is based on such performance measures, and pursued by all staff. How can one assure that all managers understand and identify themselves with the company's vision? How can vision and mission statements be transferred into the daily operations? How can one ensure that vision and mission are fully internalized in the routine workflow by all levels of staff?

More important than the mutual development of strategic statements is their detailed and repeated communication throughout all levels of the company. The Western management approach would be—for example, to make all employees aware of important corporate and brand values, such as service leadership, quality leadership, or price leadership. It is difficult for Chinese managers and staff, however, to relate to such values or strategies due to lack of concrete actions and orders. Communicating such strategies requires a different approach to work, often a change in attitude, which is hard to achieve in China. Vision and mission statements should, therefore, be translated into concrete building blocks, milestones, and actions, which the staff can relate to. Therefore the involvement of all management levels in the development and implementation of vision and mission statements is crucial. Several steps are recommended to assure the company strategy is understood and implemented throughout the company:

- Develop and communicate the vision with the top management team. Involve the managers directly, and personally ask for their understanding and commitment.
- Mutually develop a mission and strategy with all company managers. Especially middle management must be involved as much as possible in order to assure acceptance, understanding, and follow-through in the daily operations.
- Communicate the mission and strategy throughout the company with persistence, and in detail. Let all sections and departments develop their own and related plans and activities to assure that the daily work is related to the company strategy.
- Define and measure key benchmarks related to the company vision.

Although this may sound trivial, in many cases it is not. Concepts such as vision and mission actually require active participation and contribution by each and every employee, especially the top-management. Chinese social values never encouraged such participation. All corporate and quality related strategies have therefore to be adapted, and their implementation must be done with thorough preparation and involvement of the staff.

Employee Education: Essential for Success

Skilled and qualified employees are essential for a company's success— from individual quality initiatives to corporate goals. This is even more important in China, where the society is undergoing tremendous economic, social, and educational changes. It is therefore advisable for a company in China to establish regular training and education programs for all employees as early as possible.

One of the more successful examples of transforming an unprofitable, run-down Chinese SOE into an international, state-of-the-art company involves Kodak. During the past decade, Kodak has been able to transform Chinese government companies into modern showcase factories that not only have become market leaders in China but export worldwide. Kodak did this using an approach that focused rigorously on highest-quality standards and a world-class organization. At the same time, this happened while the Chinese film market rose from seventeenth to third in the world; it is an ideal environment, one that guarantees further growth. Here are some facts about Kodak in China:

Kodak in China

- In 1993 in China, Kodak employed only 30 people, had 100 Kodak Express shops, and was the third-largest company in the three areas of film, paper, and chemicals. In 2000 in China, Kodak employed more than 5,000 people, had more than 5,000 Kodak Express shops, and was the market leader in all three areas.

- Kodak's in-house software development center in Shanghai develops the latest products, such as the newest digital and one-way cameras for the production lines in Shanghai and Xiamen.

- Kodak's first worldwide internal certification for Six Sigma, the highest achievable quality standard, was awarded in Shanghai. The rigorous safety standards adhered to during the construction of its plant in Xiamen ensured that no accident occurred during 21 million hours of construction. And the general quality standards of Kodak in China are fulfilling the highest international requirements.[2] The products are exported worldwide, even to Japan.

- Initially Kodak planned that the US$1.2 billion investment would become profitable within five years. Kodak was able to achieve profitability within three years, and at that time the company had already paid more taxes than the SOE had paid in 14 years.

- In 1999 the Chinese government officially presented Kodak as a successful model of a foreign investment and the restructuring of an SOE. International business schools, including Harvard, are using Kodak's example as a case study for China.

One of the more important contributing factors in Kodak's success in China is the company's attitude toward employee education. The educational system in China is less developed than in the West, a fact that is explained later in this chapter in more detail. SOEs especially have not offered any further education for their employees, and the level of work and responsibility in those government-owned companies improves neither the professional knowledge nor the attitude of workers.

Kodak selected the dispatched expatriate managers very carefully, including doing a detailed check of their professional, personal, and managerial capabilities. The selection of the Chinese staff was similarly strict, from the top management on down to the fabric workers. Kodak focuses on the continuous, top-level education of all employees. Kodak has established a training and development center in Shanghai to guarantee the good education of all its employees. Hundreds of Chinese and international trainers educate Kodak's employees continuously. Such programs do lead to higher internal costs, and often well-trained staff resign and join the competition. Kodak's example clearly shows that it is quite rewarding to apply quality standards, including the education of employees.

Motorola is another company that has to be mentioned regarding education in China. In 2002, the company's revenue in China was more than US$4 billion; the 12,000 employees generated almost 14 percent of Motorola's worldwide sales. As in the case of Kodak, educating such a large Chinese workforce is an enormous challenge. In 1993, the Motorola University in China was therefore founded with the aim to educate and develop middle and senior managers. The university has agreements with the Chinese government and teaches at 21 universities; more than 200 instructors deliver 130 courses in Chinese. The major topics focus on Six Sigma programs—as a driver for customer satisfaction, and on knowledge management. Motorola is also using Internet-based education tools (e-learning), and over 35 percent of all educational solutions in China are provided via web-based learning; Motorola sees this as a cornerstone for its future education, especially with the strong growth of Internet use in China.[3]

Equipped with knowledge of the Chinese culture and mentality, it becomes a relatively simple matter to implement a successful business plan or to establish corporate human resource guidelines or training programs that fit the needs of all employees. Any such plan is similar to one in the West, but it has to be prepared in much more detail. The implementation and execution has to be followed closely because problems often occur in the minute details and are not recognized or corrected by the staff.

Training should start as soon as the basic team has been employed. It has to be emphasized that there can never be enough training. From professional training about the routine business to corporate culture and language, it is important to build up a competent and motivated team. Hire international and Chinese trainers, establish Chinese training manuals, documents, and other material. Involve outside companies to develop the training content and materials.

IT—Setting Up the Company Backbone

Information technology is obviously becoming more and more important in today's business, and it can enhance and transform company performance in China at least as well as it does in the West. Especially for old-fashioned businesses, IT may well be the magic tool to jump-start their arrival in the twenty-first century. However, the best front-office, back-office, business-to-business, or business-to-consumer commerce solution, the best customer relationship management software, and the perfect enterprise resource planning software, none of these guarantee smooth processes and business success. This is true in China more than in any Western country.

Information technology is never more than a reflection of the company strategy. Therefore, with a company strategy in place, IT has to be implemented in a top-down approach, which must also break with traditional ways of doing business and start a real change in areas such as process flow or internal and external communication. The strategy cannot be a mere handbook; it must be lived by the management to be accepted by all staff. Only if management practices and follows up on its strategies, such as aiming for superior customer service, will the staff be willing to implement them and use the corresponding IT tools in the appropriate manner. Information technology offers an excellent platform from which to implement strategies, but IT can never be the strategy itself.

This may sound obvious, but there are reasons for mentioning this topic especially at this point. Offering critical comments, contributing actively, acting on one's own decision—all these are habits not common to Chinese. One of the more important topics the management of a Chinese company faces is therefore the optimization of process chains, internal and external structures, and especially bureaucratic mechanisms, which are often totally overblown. A comment by Jack Welch, former General Electric chief executive, comes to mind: "Bureaucracy hates change, is terrified by speed, and hates simplicity." One of the main reasons for the existence of large, inefficient bureaucratic structures in Chinese companies is that nobody takes charge to challenge or simplify it. Old processes are just obeyed, never challenged. So the task of management is to break decades-old, inefficient structures and establish customer-oriented, fast, simple processes. Information technology will only be efficient, if organizational changes are effected at the same time that the new IT structures are implemented. Here are two examples:

- An international trading house, whose head office was located in England, decided to improve its customer service in China. One of the reasons was customer complaints about long handling and response times. It was therefore decided to implement new enterprise resource planning (ERP) software with an electronic data interchange (EDI) connection to England in order to enhance data exchange as much as possible. The installation took about a year and several million U.S. dollars; management was certain that this would be the end of most customer complaints. Implementation happened without any major problem, much to the delight of management. But after some months, the statistics were shocking. Many processes had not been shortened, but rather lengthened. What had happened? A detailed inquiry revealed that the new processes were in place and working well but none of the old ones had been abandoned. Instead of only the automatic processes of the new system operating, all documents were still printed in parallel with the office software and signed by several managers in person. If a manager was out of the office, the documents would sit on his table. In fact, the Chinese managers did not want to lose their power and transfer responsibilities. The explanation of the administration was plain and simple: "But that's how we have always done it."

- The marketing department of an American pharmaceutical company decided to target its customer advertisement and install a customer database that would be fully integrated with the ERP system with complete customer relationship management (CRM) capabilities. The module was defined and installed in less than two months, and all marketing departments began using it. During a routine presentation some months later, the American manager asked how the customer database was working. After some excuses the Chinese managers finally said, "Yes, we are entering some names in the database, but you don't expect us to put all our confidential customer data in the central computer—do you?"

These are just two examples of the inefficient and decentralized processes that exist in many Chinese companies. Different causes hinder efficient workflow. One is that Chinese managers are unwilling to exercise power and control. Other reasons are lack of control of subordinates, ignorance, lack of knowledge, understanding, and misinterpretation of company guidelines and visions. The medium, and low-level managers often do not understand the reason or necessity for change. And last but not least, many Chinese fear change, that is, the risk of making mistakes. Where an American is proposing, "Let's change this process to improve it," a Chinese may ask, "Why change it, if it is working?" The American approach demands creativity and self-expression, a rare characteristic among Chinese. Only the younger generation becomes more outspoken. The implementation of a new IT system is an excellent opportunity to optimize or even eradicate bureaucracy, but it needs to be done with the concerted effort of the whole company. And beware, the problems often lie in the details. Excellent local support and flexibility of the local supplier are important, including full language capabilities in Chinese, and the possibility to implement changes in local regulations, such as tax or labor laws.

A major software decision for the company is a back-office solution, the basic support system, which includes the enterprise resource planning system. Its modules include functions such as accounting, finance, production, supply chain management, and warehousing, just to mention the most important ones. ERP software in Chinese companies can be nonexistent, or range from homemade databases to the latest SAP R3 or Oracle software. A functional ERP system is essential for a fully integrated, well-functioning company; therefore one should spare no cost on this decision. Presentations of different local and international companies should give one a good overview of their technical and service capabilities in China. Local advisers should be used to advise on the selection process and coordinate the implementation and training. The final decision about an ERP system may well depend on company size, the cost-benefit ratio, or just be based on a decision of the corporate headquarters. Most of the international systems in China—Oracle, Peoplesoft, SAP, and Scala—all have good references. Most important for the successful implementation and use of the ERP-system is the vigorous and continued training of all employees, accompanied by critical international managers that can identify and streamline the corporate workflow and procedures.

Another major software need is a front-office solution. Today these programs are often combined under the initialism CRM. This includes modules that serve a myriad of functions, such as database marketing, data mining, customer call center, and business-to-business or business-to-consumer commerce, just to mention a few. With falling prices and increasing competition, companies might be tempted to cut internal costs, especially by cutting IT projects that do not seem to contribute to direct sales, such as front-office applications like customer databases and other CRM tools. Several of the aforementioned ERP systems offer also integrated CRM solutions. The decision about the corporate ERP software should, therefore, also take e-commerce and CRM modules of the front office into account.

When companies are getting low prices for their products and services, it is necessary to use marketing as the best tool to create additional value and distinguish oneself from the competition. Customer databases are a great tool to help create additional value. They can be the ear in the market, helping the company to analyze customer trends and fashion developments and to communicate with customers in an intimate, targeted way. Already today several market-leading companies are applying full-fledged CRM. Those who want to stay ahead in China need to apply such tools.

One such company is Volkswagen. Volkswagen in China initiated a customer database and CRM program that went online in 2001. Since then, it has become the most modern CRM solution of the VW group worldwide. Why is this necessary? VW is by far the largest producer of automobiles in China. With about 35 percent market share, VW sold more than 694,000 cars in 2003, a growth of 40 percent. Shanghai Auto Industries is the logistics and marketing partner of VW; it offers more than two hundred sales points all over China. In the past, China's automobile market was a seller's market where demand was stronger than supply. That began to change in 1995, when VW began to continuously lose market share to local and foreign competitors. In 1995 only five manufacturers were allowed to produce cars in China; in 2002 there were more than 20. Import taxes, which have been as high as 100 percent, which will be reduced to 25 percent in 2005. By then, the market will double to at least 1.5 million passenger cars per year. Between 1998 and 2002, VW's market share in the passenger-car market dropped from 60 percent in 1996 to 41.7 percent in 2002, and is estimated at about 33 percent in 2004—an alarming sign for the carmaker. VW had to improve its marketing and services if it was to gain new customers and especially bind existing ones. After long and difficult negotiations with the labor unions, VW was able to restructure the company into a more customer-oriented one. Its six hundred sales people were trained by international trainers, and for the first time in VW all training materials were in Chinese and prepared by Chinese marketing staff, not by European trainers. A spacious design was developed for the showrooms; today more than five hundred new showrooms exist. However, this still did not give VW any knowledge about its 1.9 million customers. For that, a completely new customer database was set up. The database can store demographic data about all customers as well as all repair shop data, which allows the company to evaluate service center performance as well as car performance. The customer database links all VW partners with the head office, such as showrooms, service stations, dealers, production sites, and marketing. This is an ideal tool to use to get many different kinds of market data, such as direct market information or statistics about part or model problems. The database can also be used as a direct-marketing tool—for example, to offer potential customers a free ride in the latest model as a birthday present.[4]

The number of Chinese companies using partial or complete CRM solutions in China is still rather small. According to estimates, about one hundred mostly international companies had a CRM solution in place in 2001, most in the financial, telecommunications, or consumer industries. However, a larger number of international and private Chinese companies are currently installing at least partial CRM software packages. Only the governmental companies see no need, as well as lack the necessary experience, to restructure toward a more customer-oriented organization.

Companies willing to undertake the journey to better customer service—that is, shifting from a product-oriented to a customer-oriented organization, should know that it is a difficult route, but it is by far the most efficient tool with which to turn a company into a customer- and profit-oriented company.

Quality Management and the New Chinese Standard

Most Chinese favor strict rules and clear regulations. A well-planned and strictly executed quality management system, standardization of procedures, and easy-to-understand guidelines can therefore be used to a company's advantage in China.

Benchmarking, change management, best business practices, balanced scorecard, ISO 9000 and 14000 standards, *kaizen*, service performance indicators, Six Sigma—these exemplary management concepts of the past decade stand for business excellence, for optimized business processes and highest-quality standards. Are such processes relevant in China? And which standards should a manager apply? Many managers with the task of restructuring and revitalizing rundown SOEs with decades-old, established bureaucratic systems may ask themselves those or similar questions. New entrepreneurs with the aim of building up a factory or establishing a marketing and distribution organization in China face the same questions. Managers face an enormous number of problems in establishing or restructuring an organization, and many remember the phrase "Made in Taiwan" from the 1980s, when it was a synonym for low price and an equally low quality.

Measured by Western standards, Chinese companies, especially the SOEs, have often produced products of mediocre quality at low efficiency. Furthermore, qualified and reliable staff is hard to find. With few exceptions, the Chinese market does not allow for high prices or large margins, which leaves little room for cost-intensive quality initiatives. Finally, the long, tedious negotiations with local partners and bureaucrats are not only nerve-racking but also time and maybe money intensive. Companies that establish quality initiatives first have to explain them to small local partners and suppliers, who might not have heard about any such concept. And if layoffs or the replacement of unqualified staff is involved, this may even cause problems with the authorities.

So questions remain. How strictly should quality control in China be handled? How high should targets be set for products, processes, or services? In principle, the question about quality targets can be answered rather easily. Without applying the highest demands to quality, staff, infrastructure, products, processes, and services, almost no business will have sustained success in China. Furthermore, to distinguish itself from the competition and also to have a competitive offering for the international export market, the company should aim to achieve the highest quality levels in all operations.

One might wonder how this fits with the low market prices and the mediocre quality that many westerners associate with Chinese goods and services. But this perception of cheap, low-quality products does not accurately reflect the complete Chinese picture. In many areas, improved product quality can be seen. Chinese manufacturers are now on an almost equal playing field in sectors where some years ago Western manufacturers were trumpeting their products' superiority. From automotive parts to pharmaceutical raw materials and international call centers, Chinese product and service quality is improving and the value-for-money equation is quite satisfactory for customers. As an example, the minivehicle market in the automotive industry is currently showing the fastest growth of all car segments, but such vehicles sell for incredibly low prices. Local producers are offering new cars for as low as US$3,000, a price level that can hardly be matched in other countries. This gives first-time customers the opportunity to purchase a really affordable vehicle, building up a connection between the brand and the consumer. Despite the low price, the quality of these cars is good, and foreign companies are investing to secure market share. General Motors recently announced a US$30 million investment in this sector.

So the challenge is to balance cost-efficient production with high-quality products that can compete locally as well as in overseas markets. This is even more difficult when one's enterprise is based on a traditional SOE. Many attitudes and characteristics of the Chinese are the opposite of those of Europeans and Americans. A Chinese factory worker with an annual income of US$600 obviously needs more time to understand the quality aspects of a digital camera with a price tag of US$2,000 or a computer that costs US$1,000, than his or her American counterpart, who is using such items daily in the office as well as at home. Quality criteria that are common in Europe, the United States, or Japan have yet to be understood and established in China. The rationale behind processes such as ISO (International Organization for Standardization) certification or Six Sigma is completely new to many Chinese.

Educational programs are therefore needed to establish quality consciousness among the Chinese managers and workers. It is also important to establish regular in-house processes to examine the knowledge and skills of all staff and to ensure that the company's processes are in line with its plans. Control mechanisms are integral to measure the business performance of all relevant areas. Publish the results and make them accessible for all relevant managers; ideally put them online. This can include data relating to back orders, delivery times, production statistics and defects, and customer satisfaction and loyalty. Only by a broad information flow can it be guaranteed that products, processes, and services are in line with company goals and are meeting market requirements. Only through such analytical tools can internal and strategic problems be seen and corrected and a competitive and profitable organization established. This nevertheless should be done with a modest approach, and one should avoid blaming individual staff or groups for bad key figures. The number of parameters to be benchmarked must be limited so that staff are not flooded with irrelevant numbers and try to improve every little detail right from the beginning.

Although the preceding may sound somewhat like a management manual from the West, it is even more important to apply Western standards and methods in China. Many companies and managers in China have quality initiatives and try to adapt best business practices, but few are doing it very successfully. One reason for that is the lack of implementation by the senior management; another reason is a lack of understanding of such tasks by the Chinese staff. Definitely this is a task for the top management in China. The quality and professionalism of the company, from the international and local managers to the entire staff of the company, are integral parts of entrepreneurial success in China.

Checklist: Quality Management

☑ Apply the highest quality standards right from the beginning to all processes, products, and services. Implement benchmarks to analyze the status of the company regularly, including ISO certifications and compliance with local marks, such as CCC.

☑ Include medium- and long-term quality targets in corporate plans and strategies. Establish a detailed plan for achieving the quality targets. Communicate the plan to all employees; top and medium management especially must be involved to ensure the implementation of quality initiatives.

☑ Apply the highest standards in hiring employees. Be careful about applications as documents may be faked. Several institutions and embassies do careful checks. In case of doubt, contact the applicant's school, university, or previous employer.

☑ Select expatriate managers with great care. Professional knowledge and managerial ability are essential basics; they should be paired with excellent intercultural communication skills.

☑ Make the education and training of staff a core concept of the China business. A strong human resources department with broad responsibilities should assume a leading role. Invite professional trainers from abroad, from within your corporate group, and from the local surroundings, and establish regular exchange programs with organizations in surrounding or Western countries. Valuable training may also be done at the customer site.

At first glance, the quality checklist presented here may resemble one from the West. There are points of difference, however, such as the higher level of attention that needs to be paid to selecting and training employees. But despite the Chinese workforce's lack of quality consciousness, it is necessary to establish benchmarks as high as possible right from the beginning, and certainly to put them higher than most Chinese competitors are doing at present. In a few years, even small local back-alley manufacturers will be able to produce high quality. Therefore any international company must be sure to maintain certain quality advantages. Already today there are numerous examples of Chinese-manufactured products that in quality equal or exceed the international products from which they were copied—reengineering is certainly a strength of the Chinese, where they may even surpass Japanese *kaizen* skills. Electric appliances, food ingredients, medical equipment, pharmaceutical raw material, specialty chemicals, toys, and vitamins are just some products to be mentioned; others are consumer products such as leather bags and clothes. Although there is still a difference between fake luxury goods and the real ones, the original manufacturers admit that the differences are becoming smaller, especially as the fakes might be produced just a few houses away from where the real ones are made. Within a short time, quality differences between China, the West, and Japan will narrow or disappear completely. Therefore, it is even more necessary for international companies to focus on quality and service if they are to maintain a competitive edge over local Chinese companies.

In preparation for accession to the WTO, the Chinese government has also set new Chinese product standards named Compulsory Product Certification System (CPCS), which are comparable to the European Conformity (CE), and the American Federal Communications Commission (FCC) and Underwriter Laboratories (UL) marks. As a part of the CPCS, China has unified its former two compulsory inspection systems, the China Commodity Inspection Bureau (CCIB-Safety Mark), and the Commission for Conformity of Electric Equipment (CCEE-Great Wall Mark), under the symbol China Compulsory Certificate (CCC). Since August 2003, sales outlets or importers are not permitted to purchase, import or sell products that are categorized for inspection, but do not bear the new CCC certificate. In total, 19 product categories and 132 products were affected, mainly electric appliances and tools, telecommunication products, motor vehicle and safety parts, latex products, and medical devices. The State General Administration for Quality Supervision and Inspection and Quarantine (AQSIQ) formulates the regulations and affected items. The Certification and Accreditation Administration (CNCA) is in charge of the nationwide certification and accreditation activities. The mark is more or less equivalent to the European IEC standards for the CE mark, and to the American FCC standards. A vast number CNCA-designated agencies help with the certification process, such as the German "Technischer Überwachungsverein" (TÜVs). As of 2003, 68 laboratories were approved for testing. Final approval for the mark will be granted by CNCA, the fees for the complete approval procedure, inclusive testing, range from about US$4,000 to US$6,000 per item.[5]

Only strict and total quality management, including infrastructure, logistics, production, marketing, sales, and all administrative and service functions, will lead to sustained success in China. Certifications such as the CCC mark, ISO 9000 or 14000 quality benchmarks should therefore be seen as a competitive advantage. To ensure that such quality initiatives are beneficial for the company, they must be a priority of the top management, which has to ensure that the standards are implemented and adhered to, and not just certified on paper. In addition, such internal standards also stimulate suppliers to improve their standards too.

One final warning regarding quality and cost: High quality standards may well lead to excellent products and results. Nevertheless, depending on the product, service, or business area, cost must definitely be taken into account. Various costs, such as general or labor costs, are certainly less in China than they are in the West or Japan. But applying too high or too rigorous quality standards may erode these advantages—for example, in the case of products with low labor costs or high safety requirements. A Chinese manufacturer might not adhere to all Western safety standards regarding production facilities or transportation regulations. There are many examples where the production facilities of a Chinese manufacturer cost only 10 percent of the cost that an international company would have to invest according to international standards. Obviously, international companies have to and should apply international standards. But they should be implemented with local and pragmatic partners to keep overall costs at an acceptable and competitive level for the Chinese market.

LEGAL REGULATIONS

The economic reforms, which lead to major social and economic changes, require China to overhaul its legal system. Many different economic, political, and social groups with diverse interests are trying to influence and stimulate the Chinese legislature, while—at the same time—foreign nations and organizations are also lobbying to implement international legal standards. The political leadership is strongly supporting the economic developments, while it tries to maintain social stability, and assure the survival and transformation of the Chinese political system as its power base. Changes in the legal system, such as private property rights and intellectual property, are therefore only cautiously pursued to prevent any power-decay of the Communist party.

Many new laws in China have brought the country's legal system closer to international standards, and the accession to the WTO in particular triggered the introduction of various trade and property related laws, some of which will be described in the next paragraphs. The existence of these laws does not, however, guarantee their strict implementation or adherence. Chinese social values, political influence, and private interests allow the interpretation and enforcement of these laws according to Chinese rules and cultural attitudes, rather than according to Western standards.

Based on the Confucian principle of the "middle way," there is often no clear "black or white" decision like in the West, but in-between black and white, there is often a gray area, in which courts issue mediating rulings. Furthermore, the perception of laws differs from that in the West, and concepts such as intellectual property rights are not commonly accepted in China. The judicial system itself has also to be developed, as many judges are still closely linked to the political elite or connected to their personal networks; well-educated lawyers and judges are scarce, and many are self-educated. *Guanxi* also plays an important role in the juris-diction, and should therefore not be neglected.

Another set of hurdles comes from the government itself. While the government is willing to adapt to international jurisdiction, it also has to protect the Chinese economy. Within the framework of existing WTO reg-ulations, China is therefore establishing laws and regulations to protect domestic markets, especially in agriculture and manufacturing. The cur-rent trade dispute over soybean imports is just one of many examples. China argues that American soybeans are contaminated with a fungus, and thus cannot be imported. This is a protectionist argument as American soybeans are cheaper than Chinese ones, and the fungus is ubiquitous to all soybeans worldwide, including China. Many similar examples exist, and the development reminds one of the Japanese protectionism of the 1980s and 1990s. Furthermore, there is a divergence between the national and regional interpretation of laws, depending on political and economic interests. While the central government agrees to certain rules, local prov-inces may act differently. Critics predict, therefore, that by 2007, China may be non-compliant to many WTO rules.

Massive economic discrepancies, ethnic tensions, and the vast country itself generate many different interests and political opinions. The gov-ernment, with it's own interests and survival at stake, tries to find the ideal balance between economic growth, control of social tensions and separatist movements, and the assurance of its political power. New laws are an important step toward a free market economy, but the complete implementation may well take years.

Trade Laws: Changing Jurisdiction

Prompted by the need to provide foreign investors with a legal base and security, the Chinese government in the 1970s began to develop a legal system to address that need. Step by step an economic security was established that is today the framework for all foreign and also some Chinese economic activities. In parallel, the government established a la-bor law as a framework for employment conditions in foreign and Chinese-foreign companies.

What is certain? The Chinese economic legislation offers investors in China a legal framework and, at least to some degree, theoretical legal protection. In the late 1970s when this development began, special regu-lations existed for foreign trade and protection of investments. Today, there is a complex set of laws and regulations. The legislation, however, is also constantly adapted to foreign and local economic conditions—a fact that makes the use of such laws difficult and complicated. These com-plex legal conditions lead to a situation in 2002, whereby about 60 percent of all firms in China had more than one legal company form in order to maintain flexibility. The major form is a wholly foreign owned company in combination with a direct representative office, as the example of Hong Kong companies shows.[6] It may also be advisable to separate the Chinese company from legal and tax exposure in China, for example by a flexible holding structure abroad. This makes future spin-offs, realization of profits, and necessary reorganizations easier. Nevertheless, existing laws can be taken as a good basis for reference in case of legal disputes. Laws that regulate the form that direct investment in China may take, or that regulate the foundation of or participation in companies, are of primary concern to foreign investors.

The first "Law of the PR China about joint-venture enterprises with Chinese and Foreign Participation" was issued in 1979, and has since constantly been revised and updated. On April 1, 2002, new foreign investment guidelines of the State Council replaced the provisional guidelines from 1995. The new "Foreign Investment Industrial Guidance Catalogue" specifies four investment categories, which have been modified to suit actual economic developments, support the central and western regions, and thus make certain investment easier. Encouraged projects are generally investments in agriculture, energy, high technology, and transportation. They have been enlarged from 186 to 262 items. Permitted items have not been listed. Restricted projects, specifically backward technologies, have been reduced from 112 to 75 items. The fourth category concerns prohibited projects, related to national security, the environment, and public safety. With the new law, export-oriented industries can expect higher tax-breaks, faster approvals, and can be set up as WFOE. Foreign companies are generally not allowed to enter restricted or prohibited projects.

The new guidelines opened several areas previously restricted or prohibited for foreign investment, such as banking and insurance, telecommunications, international cargo transportation, railway cargo transportation, cinema, medical institutions, printing, and tourism—among others. In addition, specific investment guidelines have been issued for the central and western regions, and will thus help to reduce the disparity between the east coast and the central and western hinterland.

Here, particularly, a typically Chinese conception of the law can be seen. The law must support pragmatic goals! The Chinese want to be assured that joint ventures support the labor market and improve the skills of Chinese workers in local or regional areas. Therefore, almost always, the joint-venture partner has to take over the staff of the Chinese partner. In addition, the venture must support the education of the workers and offer social support that is at least on par with that offered by the Chinese SOE. It must be noticed that on the one hand special regulations exist in many areas, while on the other the integration of the nationwide labor law is progressing quickly. Regulations regarding standard working hours, general working conditions, work safety, as well as regulations about labor disputes, apply equally to all of China.

Intellectual Property Laws (TRIPS)

It is difficult for Chinese to appreciate that immaterial things, including intellectual property, can be the possession of a single person, if he or she is the creator or originator. It is not immoral or even illegal for Chinese to obtain ideas, concepts, methods, or designs and use them. On the contrary, it shows one's eagerness to learn and improve. And it can even be an expression of respect toward the content, or an appreciation of the intellect of someone else. Taking possession of the intellectual property of foreigners is regarded as absolutely justifiable. If that doesn't suit the foreigners, it is their obligation to protect against it. It is doubtful that this attitude, which is not new but ancient and widespread throughout Asia, will change. Illegal copies and branded counterfeits are still widespread. Without any immoral feeling, there are countless activities in China to copy, reengineer, reproduce, and rebuild many types of products and services. During a toy fair in Hong Kong in 2003, for example, copies of toys appeared within hours in the booths of competitors. Chinese companies used "rapid prototypers," three-dimensional digital scanners, to reproduce a model almost instantly.[7]

Based on this background, it becomes clearer what the government has done since the 1980s to protect commercial intellectual property. China became a member of the World Intellectual Property Organization in 1980. In preparation for its accession to the WTO, China has implemented and changed numerous laws and initialized international agreements, such as the Trade Related Aspects of Intellectual Property Rights (TRIPS). The TRIPS-Agreement, which came into effect on January 1, 1995, is the most comprehensive multilateral agreement on intellectual property and covers eight major areas: copyright and related rights, trademarks, geographical indications, industrial designs, patents, layout-designs (topographies) of integrated circuits, protection of undisclosed information, and the control of anti-competitive practices in contractual licenses. Thus, China has committed to amend patent, copyright, and trademark laws to comply with TRIPS.[8] In addition, it provides legal avenues to foreigners in accordance with existing agreements between both countries, and it reports to the WTO council on trade-related aspects.

Foreign and Chinese inventions, products, or trade names today are protected in accordance with international laws, and can be registered with the Chinese patent office (Patent Law from March 12, 1984, effective since April 1985). With registration, the legal protection is countrywide and initially lasts 20 years. The rights of the patent owner are very similar to those under European patent laws. The revision of the Chinese patent law effective January 1, 1993, is basically identical to international legal praxis. This was the precondition under which China could enter the Contract for International Cooperation on Patents in 1993.

According to international standards, a framework was established for the legal protection of copyright. The corresponding regulations and their effective dates are as follows: copyright law (January 1, 1991); regulation for the protection of computer software (October 1, 1991); regulation for the enforcement of international copyright agreements (September 25, 1992); decree of the permanent committee of the National People's Congress on the infringement of copyright protection laws (July 5, 1994); various amendments have been issued since. This legislation follows international conventions and protects a broad variety of works, including computer software.

Most international companies in China, however, believe that patent and copyright infringement is a smaller problem than the abuse of trademarks. Legal protection against trademarks and product designs should therefore be a major objective for all brands before or while entering China. The Chinese trademark law was adopted on August 23, 1982, and the second amendment, which was required due to WTO-membership, was adopted on October 27, 2001. In 2003, about 20,000 Chinese trademarks were registered every month.

China comments as follows regarding trademark protection: "The trademark law and its executive orders offer international trademark protection. In principle foreign and Chinese brands are protected by this law." All in all, today legal protection of commercial intellectual property is basically guaranteed by the legislature and its organs and can thus be enforced in the whole of China. Various different measures are possible: notifying the responsible office at the Ministry for Industry and Trade of a violation, either at the place where the infringement took place, or at the place where the infringing person resides; filing a civil or criminal lawsuit, especially in case of claims; filing a civil or criminal lawsuit to protect intellectual property; notifying customs officials to prevent the export or import of illegal copies.

These measures will start a long, difficult, and costly process, the outcome of which is not guaranteed. Prevention is better, as history shows. Clauses that treat the handling of intellectual property and trademarks should be included in documents right from the beginning of a joint-venture agreement, and they should be declared as strictly legally binding for the Chinese partner. Staff, especially in managerial positions, should also be requested to sign non-disclosure agreements for all corporate secrets, which extend beyond the duration of their employment. It is also recommended that you register patents, product designs, trade names, and logos with the Chinese patent authorities. Nevertheless, infringements happen frequently as part of the risk of doing business in China.

Since accession to the WTO, a better enforcement of trademark registrations can already be seen. In August 2002, Yamaha won a landmark decision against Tianjin Gangtian, who had produced motorcycles for Yamaha and later tried to sell counterfeit Yamaha motorcycles.[9] The court's decision in favor of Yamaha has set a precedent and encouraged similar lawsuits. In 2003, a publishing house connected to China's Academy of Science was fined 350,000 Yuan (US$42,300) for using registered illustrations of Peter Rabbit. A division of Penguin Books copyrighted the illustrations, and the case was a major test and assurance of copyright laws.[10] Lego, the Danish maker of children's building blocks, won a similar suit in 2003.[11] Other companies, such as Cisco, Honda, Lacoste, and Toyota also filed suits to protect their intellectual property rights. The U.S. Chamber of Commerce described the situation in its 2002 report as follows, "To be fair, China has . . . made important improvements in its legal framework by amending its patent, trademark and copyright laws consistent with the provisions of TRIPs. Despite some progress . . . enforcement remains inadequate and infringement continues."[12]

Taxes and Customs

Favorable tax tariffs and numerous tax privileges and exemptions are major factors that attract foreign investors to China. This applies especially to corporate taxes. The basis for the corporate tax is the complete profit of a company coming from operative and nonoperative businesses. The basis for calculation is the company income during the fiscal year less tax-deductible expenses.

Until 1994 the maximum corporate income tax rate amounted up to 55 percent for Chinese enterprises and only 33 percent for companies with foreign capital shares. This inequality, which had immense financial benefits for WFOEs and Chinese-foreign joint ventures, was modified in the tax reform of 1994. Since then, the general rate for corporate income taxes in China is up to 35 percent for Chinese companies, and 15 percent for joint-venture companies. Foreign-invested companies still enjoy various tax privileges. The authority to grant such benefits lies mainly in the hands of local and regional tax authorities. Decisive factors in obtaining reductions or exemptions may include being a strong exporter or the use of innovative technologies. A refund of the corporate tax may be granted if the profit is reinvested in the joint venture or if it is used to set up another joint venture in China. These refunds can be between 15 and 50 percent, but it must be proven that the new joint venture will operate at least five years and be export oriented and technology intensive.

Special tax exemptions are granted to joint ventures that are established in an SEZ, in an economic and technological development zone, in an open-trading zone along the coastal area, or in a new, high-tech zone.

Usually such joint ventures receive a 50 percent tax reduction, the maximum refund of corporate taxes, and the possibility of carrying forward losses on a yearly base. However, all of these measures are not granted automatically—they are decided by local tax authorities. The income of foreign employees of Chinese-foreign joint ventures or WFOEs is fully taxed. It does not matter whether the income of the employee is paid abroad or locally. Not only income from wages but also all additional benefits, such as bonus payments and indirect earnings, are fully taxable as income. The only tax privilege granted to foreign employees is 4,000 renminbi (RMB) as a tax allowance deducted from the taxable income. The tax allowance of the Chinese employees is restricted to a maximum of 800 RMB. The personal income tax rate for foreign taxpayers is from 5 percent (below 500 RMB per month) to 45 percent (more than 100,000 RMB per month). However, there are individual tax treaties between China and several countries that regulate double taxation, and it is advisable to consult a tax lawyer on how to approach this issue. Both foreigners and Chinese are treated as completely equal for value-added taxes or business and consumption taxes. In 2003, value-added tax for food and agricultural products was 13 percent, for all other goods and services 17 percent.

The Chinese customs department decides which products can be freely imported or exported. It also decides on import licenses and import quotas. Import restrictions exist only for a few product groups. These are products whose import does not lie in the public interest or that could endanger the security of the state or the health of the people or the environment. Since the list of products subject to import quotas changes, it is necessary to request actual information from the customs authorities. In principle, customs rates follow two levels, either the minimal or the normal tariff grade. It is correct to assume that the Chinese customs rates are a political measure to regulate the economy. Reduction of or increase in import customs tariffs depends partly on the trade policy toward foreign trading partners, but it also depends on the influence of the imported products on the local economy. In 1996, for example, raw material, supplies, auxiliaries, and components for the production and export of Chinese products were imported by China without customs duties. Today, this tax exemption is canceled. Reduced taxes are still applied to products that are imported into the SEZ. In addition, export-oriented WFOEs and Chinese-foreign joint ventures can expect import tax exemptions all over China. Nevertheless it has to be mentioned that tax exemptions nowadays are less frequently granted compared with the years prior to 1996. In addition, customs inspection and classification today function very well; tax collection is rather fast and the authority of the customs department is enforced—customs can even reach into companies. Without a doubt, the interpretation and enforcement of tax regulations will become even more strict in the future.

Law and *Guanxi*

Today in China the basis of a legal system is in place, especially for business matters. But how does that help if the execution of the law lags far behind its content? According to Chinese legislation, China could well be called a constitutional country. But the basic Chinese understanding of law and general legal practice requires lowering one's expectations. The Western concept of legal "rights" is traditionally not very much esteemed. This starts with the fact that adhering to contracts, a basic concept of our law and a basis of all legal business, has a different connotation for Chinese. Insisting on literal compliance with a contract is quite often regarded as outrageous and hostile, as well as inflexible. In general, most Chinese contracts are the beginning of the consolidation of a relationship. Development of the relationship begins with a contract, and in the course of further interaction, the contract's contents inevitably change. Contracts have no tradition in China. What matters in business relations is what the parties themselves have discussed.

Establishing relations, having and nurturing *guanxi,* is the essence of business in China. Certainly, few Chinese will openly acknowledge this fact. And in principle the Chinese are not "bad" contract partners. They almost love to negotiate and insist on including even the smallest details in the contract. They may negotiate for weeks. This is done mainly to establish a relationship with the potential partner, to test his worthiness of becoming a partner and his ability for *guanxi.* It is advisable to regulate everything in a contract, but one should be clear: This is the beginning, the basic material for a relationship. Western contract partners often do not understand this point of view; in fact, they almost despise it. This difference in understanding is the major source of legal disputes. The Western partner insists on obeying the contract point for point; the Chinese partner does not dream of doing so. Bad feelings arise, maybe even hostility, which the Western partner openly shows and the Chinese partner politely hides.

At such a point, it might be best to go the "Chinese way" of jurisdiction—to involve a third, mediating party. Utilization of relations, *guanxi,* mediation talks, compromises, out-of-court settlements, reinstatement of harmony—this is the legal, traditional Chinese way; it is often used in China and is quite successful. On the contrary, in case of legal problems in the joint venture, many Western partners follow Western legal practice and go to court. And there is a surprise waiting: The court will be seeking a solution based on the "Chinese way." Because westerners often do not know or accept that way, they will make mistakes right from the beginning. They believe it is unnecessary to have a personal discussion with the judge prior to the first official hearing. And it does not seem necessary or correct to propose a compromise to the judge. This fact applies to all civil suits in China: The judge wants to reach a compromise that is acceptable to all parties. Chinese judges do not see themselves as strict guardians of the law. They are mediators. They know and obey the law but do not hide behind it. It is different for criminal lawsuits, especially for acts against the state. There is no mediation, but the state wants to set an example. In such cases as well, judges do not stick firmly to the articles but act based on their political sense and often their faithfulness to the Communist Party. In a criminal suit, guanxi will be of greater help than a lawyer.

Financial Control Mechanisms

A famous dictum of Deng Xiaoping describes the basic philosophy many Chinese follow today: "To get rich is glorious." Human rights, freedom of speech, democracy, personal rights—all these topics are certainly important in China, but not every one of them is important for everybody, and none has the highest priority. Presently, the most important consideration for many Chinese is to become rich, that is, to achieve a better social status.

To understand this completely, one has to look back at China's history. China made the transition from an agricultural society to an industrialized nation basically within three decades, whereas America and Europe needed more than a hundred years. And in those years, China made the transition from an underdeveloped Communist-ruled country to the second-largest economy in the world, based on *purchasing power parity*. The number of impoverished Chinese decreased from 270 million in 1970 to 70 million in 2000. This means that there are still more than 70 million people in China who earn less than US$1 per day. However, 200 million have improved their income above that level; that number equals the number of Americans living in the United States when China's development started in 1970. In 2003, the average annual income in China was about US$1,090; in larger cities it was US$1,500 to US$4,500, whereas in the rural areas is only US$300.

With these developments in mind, imagine the Chinese consumer who had been barred from the free market but now faces its overwhelming choices and countless products. A flood of information is channeled by television, the Internet, newspapers, journals, and even mobile telephone, offering local and international brands, creating new demands and markets. From clothing to perfume, from cognac and wine to the most expensive designer bag—a slew of products is offered by the marketing departments of the consumer industry who are competing for China's consumers and market share. Already the trip from the airport to the city affords one a first glimpse of what is to be expected—oversized billboards line the way.

For decades China did without foreign products and Western advertising, and farmers were the highest class. Thus it is understandable that the Chinese are trying to catch up with the rest of the world and are spending money on luxury consumer goods. BMW, Mercedes-Benz, Rolex, and Luis Vuitton are only a few brands doing very well in China. For several years, China has been among the top 10 Mercedes-Benz importers. This consumer craze is almost understandable in a country that has developed with lightning speed from the Communistic agricultural age to become the second-largest industrial nation in the world.

A prime example of the Chinese dream is Orange County. Orange County, California? No, Orange County, Beijing. This is a settlement of luxury houses about twenty miles outside of Beijing. There are currently about two hundred villas in Orange County, all between 2,000 and 7,000 square feet and decorated with the best the world has to offer, from Italian marble floors to French crystal chandeliers. The villas carry price tags of up to US$2 million. The announcement that China will host the Olympic Games in 2008 has increased the number of and sped up the development of these settlements. Beijing Riviera, Capital Paradise, Dragon Villas, and Purple Jade Villas are just a few examples of the latest luxury enclaves for Beijing's richest. Similar settlements can also be found in other cities, such as Shanghai, Shenzhen, Hangzhou, Chengdu, Chongqing, and Guangzhou. To be rich is glorious, and in China there are many more glorious people than the West might assume.[13] How to become rich as fast as possible is therefore of paramount importance to many Chinese; the phenomenon has wide implications for professional and private matters.

Company loyalty is rather high in the West, as employees see their job as part of their life, and maintaining a good relationship with the company and colleagues is as important as having good relations with one's family. It is different in China. Most important for the Chinese is their family, and after that their friends and acquaintances. Toward these a Chinese establishes a relationship, called *guanxi*. No Chinese wants to establish a relationship with a Western company, unless it belongs to or supports the family. In the employee's view, there are no obligations attached toward the company. This attitude may have consequences for a company. Although infrequent, corruption, fraud, and theft are problems that might occur in China. The earlier advice of an expatriate chief financial officer to thoroughly control the company's financial details is not without reason and should be considered seriously.

"What could happen?" a manager may ask. Many things, probably things one did not imagine at all. Therefore, here are some recent examples of corruption. They also show that nefarious practices are not just the case between Chinese and foreign companies but are common among the Chinese themselves.

In October 2001, three managers of a branch of the Bank of China went on the run after it was discovered they had stolen more than US$700 million. The scandal is probably only the tip of the iceberg and it was an embarrassment for the government, which had to postpone the planned initial public offering (IPO) of the Bank of China; the volume of the IPO has been reduced in the meantime. With the highly successful IPO of China Life Insurance in 2003, and financial support of the bank in 2004, the stage is well set for the Bank of China to issue an international IPO within the next few years.

In early 2002 at a Chinese trading company, managers were found to have embezzled more than US$500 million. Thousands of managers in government companies and party officials on all levels are currently on trial for bribery, fraud, and embezzlement, and many jail terms and even death penalties have been given out. Here are a few more examples. A case of group corruption was discovered in Zhangjiagang, where more than 200 government officials, including 12 leading and 45 medium-level functionaries, took millions of U.S. dollar as bribes. An even larger case of corruption was discovered in Xiamen. This was a case of "fried tofu buildings." State constructions, streets, houses, and even bridges are prone to collapse like tofu because the construction materials have been partially or fully used for other purposes. Corrupt courts subject criminals to very mild sentences because the judges are bribed; even in the Education Ministry, bribery cases have been discovered. Every day new cases are coming up; in the Nanjing province alone, more than three thousand cases of bribery were reported within the first five months of 2003.

Is the current, strict action of the government sufficient to curb the situation, or is it too late? It is probably not too late, but the time to start change is now. Much has to be done before Western values, such as a just legal system or behavioral codes, are firmly established in China. The Chinese government has therefore started a three-step program to deprive corruption of its economic and political base. First and foremost, the legal and financial responsibilities inside the administration are being separated and a controlling body for both is being implemented. Second, the legal system for approvals and permissions is being restructured and simplified to make it more transparent. Furthermore, a new tax system is being established, where all tax income must be reported to the superior tax office. As a third measure, a new system for government projects has been tested, where all official projects have to be published as a tender. This led to average savings of 10 percent in Chongqing, Hebei, Shenzhen, and Shenyang, and in some cases costs were cut by up to 30 percent. The system is expected to be implemented in all of China.

Many Chinese have a very positive attitude toward business favors. This may affect large governmental tenders or small, private orders. Rebates, such as personal rebates, kickbacks, black bonuses, or trade discounts—many ways are used to provide such favors, and many people might be involved to obscure the case. Other employees or relatives may well be used to channel such payments. One might discover that one's company sales level drops sharply, but it is not clear why. Well, the friend of the sales manager may have a similar company, and some of the sales are being routed that way. There are many ways in which a customer and an employee may benefit from such transactions, and as an expatriate one has probably heard of many of them. Nevertheless, one should keep the following in mind: Not all of these payments can be stopped, because the Chinese will categorize many as guanxi—payments in order to maintain a good relationship. But a foreign company has often the necessity, based on its standards of ethics and code of conduct, to prevent any illegal activity or internal or external manipulation.

Checklist: Financial Control Mechanisms

☑ Use internal procedures to ensure the complete separation of the finance, marketing, sales, and order-processing departments. Use internal audits regularly and irregularly to look for problems and inconsistencies.

☑ Hire an experienced expatriate as chief financial officer to control the books thoroughly.

☑ Avoid cash payments from or to the company and reward customers who use electronic money transfer.

☑ In case "special" kickbacks, trade discounts, rebates, or bonus payments are unavoidable, try to use dealers or subdistributors to take care of them. In case of doubt, use third parties to investigate. Use detectives to clarify payments or missing money.

☑ Set people straight regarding the company guidelines and code of conduct, right from the beginning. Lay off staff immediately who are involved in unclear financial transactions. Don't let precedents be set that could later be used against the company.

The Chinese attitude toward networking and the Chinese understanding of relationship—*guanxi*—is one of the main reasons for increased corruption over the past decades. Many Chinese see large amounts of money in foreign and local companies and low income, devotion to the family, and a limited loyalty toward the company may be fertile ground for corruption and embezzlement. It is also understandable that the drastic change from communistic planned economy to socialist free-market economy cannot happen without problems. But when compared with Russia, China has been able to make that transition in a rather proper and professional way.

In 1992, during his famous trip to the South, Deng Xiaoping said, "I believe that it will take another 30 years until a mature, stable system has been developed. Under this system, the politic and leadership will have found its final and firm function." According to Deng's statement, the transitional period will not be over until 2022; but it looks like China is well on its way, with its WTO-membership and the Olympic Games speeding its process.

THE MARKET AND MARKETING

The company has been established, production is under way, the warehouse buildings are running, raw materials are in stock, product quality is good, computer programs are giving the correct data, and even the supply chain is supplying products in reasonable time to distributors and customers—now the main task is to increase sales in China and possibly Asia. Surprisingly and despite the many explosive market segments, that may be more difficult than many Europeans or Americans imagine.

The biggest difficulty in many of China's markets is low market price and strong competition. International and local companies are trying to secure market shares in potentially the largest consumer market in the world by staging a price offensive. China's 1.3 billion people are the market; in that market, about 400 million consumers have a purchasing power similar to that of their Western counterparts.

International companies and brands are as prominent and popular in Beijing and Shanghai as they are in Paris, London, or New York; the Chinese market is certainly becoming globalized. Therefore, some marketing specialists see a globalization of brands and predict that within 20 years, there will be only a generic, global marketing for international brands. To some extent that is correct for truly international brands, such as airlines, luxury goods, or some food and beverage lines. In addition, it may be attributed to changing customer habits worldwide—for example, Western customers assimilating Asian values and Chinese consumers adopting Western tastes and preferences.

But no matter how far globalization progresses, there will still be local values, habits, and customs, creating a need for local marketing approaches for almost all brands. Authors Al Ries and Jack Trout define marketing as "the battle for your mind" in their book, *Positioning: The Battle for Your Mind*. This is true in China as well as in the rest of the world, and the battle in China is full-blown. It is correct that similarities already exist between the Western and the Chinese market, and certain consumers are becoming more global. Nevertheless, there are many differences, which shall be explained in more detail.

Several factors influence marketing in the Chinese consumer and industrial market. The most important element from the customer's viewpoint is price, which is the decisive factor in China triggering a purchase. There are exceptions to this, but they exist mainly in the luxury product segment, which is yet rather limited. One has to keep the average income in mind, and although on the basis of purchasing power parity, about 400 million consumers enjoy purchasing power similar to people in the United States, Japan, and Europe, this is mainly due to the lower market prices. Many companies try to increase not only their market share but also the market by lowering prices. This is especially the case in the telecommunications industry, where the price war is tremendous and many companies are losing money. In many Chinese markets, excessive production capacity is another reason for low prices and strong competition.

Another reason for China's focus on competing via price is lack of marketing experience. Marketing in China is a relatively young discipline, and far less developed than in the West. This is certainly connected to the lack of choice in the past, but it is a function of the lack of education in marketing. The socialist market economy is only a few years old, and practices such as marketing, positioning, and branding were not known in China 20 years ago. Television, radio, billboard advertisement, mailings, print media advertisement—all these marketing communication tools were hardly used in China prior to the 1990s.

Even in greater Asia, marketing is a young domain, but the Asians are learning fast. Despite excellent products, Japanese companies were for decades unable to establish themselves outside Japan because of poor marketing and communication skills. The international automobile market is a good example. American and European manufacturers are well positioned; they are known for brand attributes such as fahrvergnügen (VW), safety (Volvo), sport (BMW), luxury (Mercedes-Benz), and sport-utility (Ford). But for which attributes are Japanese, Korean, or Chinese automobiles and motorbikes known? When Toyota came to the international markets, its only attribute was price. Cost efficiency was the major argument, whereas other attributes such as reliability (Toyota), or innovation (Nissan), came into use later. Toyota was barely able to fight off its original image in the West; it had to establish a totally new brand for its luxury car line, Lexus.

But Asia is catching up, as the examples of Nissan, Sony, Haier, Lenovo, BenQ, and Tsingtao show. Marketing in Asia, especially in China, is becoming more and more professional and creative, targeting exactly the tastes of local customers, rather than a global audience. Local and international Chinese companies are trying more and more to connect with their Asian audience, and in doing so, they are able to outperform their global counterparts. More and more professional marketing support is used; international branding and marketing companies develop local and regional product concepts and marketing strategies for products and services.

Marketing is the battle for the consumer's mind—and so it is obvious that marketing, positioning, and branding have different contents and messages in China than they have in Europe or the United States. Western culture and Chinese culture are obviously different. The tastes, perceptions, and mentality of the Chinese are unlike those of westerners. To successfully sell products in China, one must establish a professional product and marketing strategy based on Western methods, but with a local content and flavor. Chinese companies are already spending US$12 billion annually on advertising, making China the clear number two in Asia, behind Japan. This amount is expected to grow strongly up to US$100 billion in 2020, when China will become the second-largest market in the world, behind the Unites States. Marketing and branding in China—the battle has begun.

Market Research in China

There are many questions to be asked about selling in China: Who are the potential buyers? Where does one find them? What are their interests? How are their purchase decisions motivated? Such questions lead to the need for a thorough market analysis and subsequently a marketing plan. These are tasks for market research, which is another chapter in China. Although numerous governmental and research firms offer extensive reports, they are hardly reliable, comprehensive, and detailed data are available for the Chinese market when compared with what exists for Western countries. There are no reliable sociodemographic data. Approximate figures exist about potential market volumes, but there are no customer target group definitions, customer target group assessments, or even dedicated motivational research. Useful key data for consumer markets are the statistical purchasing power parity data. These data outline a crude differentiation according to low-, middle-, and high-wage earners, and are available for some regions. For example, a manufacturer of high-priced consumer products will find potential customers mainly in the booming regions, such as Guangdong province and the regions of Beijing, Shanghai, and Liaoning. This means that foreign investors who want to manufacture for the Chinese market must do their calculations based on a very restricted market potential, locally limited, comprising a maximum of 40 million customers.

The *China Population Statistical Yearbook,* which is published by the government, is one source of statistics.[14] About 20 percent of the target group identifies as the elderly generation, 30 percent are between 30 and 45 years of age, and 50 percent younger than 30. The latter group constitutes the main market potential for consumer goods. This young generation sets the trends. Children and grandchildren influence the purchasing decisions of their elders. These are practical observations partly confirmed by statistics but mainly based on market experience. Market research in China is possible and service providers exist, but they are just starting to use the market research tools frequently used in the West. Market research uses sources with more or less useful information, that need to be interpreted and finally must be measured on their own or other experiences. But this area is changing rapidly. Chinese market research institutions are emerging that are providing increasingly useful and detailed data. Any data have nevertheless to be treated with caution, as there may be vast discrepancies. Coca-Cola, for example, estimated the soft-drink market at 39 billion liters, while Euromonitor estimates it at 23 billion liters; states sources estimate the TV-advertising market at US$2.8 billion, whereas Nielsen Media Research estimates US$7.5 billion.[15]

The Chinese "market" cannot be described as one market. China has many particular markets, that are separated by vast regional differences. The most important differentiation factor for the marketing of consumer products is purchasing power, which has to be interpreted quite differently from region to region. But this data cannot be a sound base for the estimation of market volumes or efficiencies of marketing campaigns. Therefore, at present, consumer marketing in China is not without risk, but affords a good chance for success.

The marketing of investment products and services, on the other hand, is rather different. Here the market research is less complicated and for joint-venture enterprises, may be not even necessary. The Chinese partner should know the potential buyers, thus market volume is predefined. In case this volume later expands due to new relations, this might well be via *guanxi*.

Despite the limited statistical evidence, objective market research should be done nevertheless. It will ascertain the market and the competitive environment, help develop the different customer sectors, and spot trends in the technology market. However, there are other very essential market parameters. They include the government's plans and budgets, particularly with respect to large-scale, industrial SOEs. Furthermore, development plans for the SEZs and industrial zones and the rapid expansion of the infrastructure are market segments that have big potential but also carry certain risk.

Value-Added Marketing: Think "Chinese," Act "Western"

The price competition in China may be good for consumers, but in the long term such a market is not sustainable. In the past, international companies could separate themselves and their brands by positioning their brands and communicating clear brand values. Thus, they were able to generate additional value and ask for higher prices. Luxury car manufacturers such as Rolls Royce and Mercedes-Benz have done this very successfully; China is one of the best countries in the world for sales of these cars, including the Mercedes-Benz 600. More and more Chinese companies have recognized the benefit and need for strong marketing organizations and have started professional approaches.

Doing business successfully in the Chinese market today includes having a clear positioning strategy combined with a strong product line, quality, and additional values to differentiate oneself from the competition. Only through strategic positioning that targets specific customers will a company gain new customers in competitive market segments, and only through a strong brand with additional features including brand image will the company be assured of customer loyalty. For many companies in China, it is a matter of survival to create such brand values and a strong image. Today, many companies in China resort to diverse methods of creating or enhancing brand value. The questions for foreign companies are these: What are the Chinese product values? What kinds of images and services appeal to Chinese consumers? And what services will enhance brand image in China? Is it necessary for global brands to go local, and which parts of an international campaign can and should be transferred to the Chinese market? Many advertising agencies in China already offer their services to answer these questions. Nevertheless, decisions, such as which image to go for, must be made by the company, and any agency proposal should be looked at very carefully. Quality levels of marketing agencies differ strongly, similar to their market intelligence. Although a large number of market studies exist, their figures often do not reflect the real market situation.

Is specific branding necessary for the Chinese market, and what is its aim? Basically, branding is supposed to create an image. According to *Webster's International Dictionary,* image is the "mental conception held in common by members of a group." The members of this group are obviously Chinese. Thus, their social values and norms must be incorporated in all marketing processes, from product development to marketing to after-sales service.

It is correct that for some international brands, especially luxury brands, local marketing may not be needed. But in most cases, localized advertising and marketing is necessary if not essential, as even the most popular international brands show. Coca-Cola recently hired the Chinese swimming-superstar Fu Minxia, an Olympic champion in 1992 and 2000, for commercials. She is an excellent symbol for the beverage company, targeting a young, sporting audience. This is a case of ideal target marketing in the Chinese market by the world's most valuable brand.

The Coca-Cola example shows that even with increasing globalization, consumer mentality and culture will always have a local flavor. This is important not only for the product itself but even more so for everything surrounding the product, such as added value and image. Image as a mental conception held in common by a group depends not the least on the taste and culture of that group. International brands may be able to shape local culture to some extent, and the spread of McDonald's and

Coke in Asia may be a good indicator of globalization; but the local aspects remain and must be recognized by any marketing organization.

It is therefore important to use Chinese social and cultural values as a basis for developing, positioning, and marketing products and services in China. Table 3.1 compares some of the more important aspects of Chinese culture and Western culture, showing some of the major differences between the two. The lonely Marlboro cowboy is the unrivaled advertising icon of the United States, but he will not be as accepted in China because the image is not in line with Chinese family values. That does not mean it should not be used at all. On the one hand, international companies have to carry their global brand image to the Chinese market. On the other hand, they have to connect with Chinese customers and compete with local Chinese companies, which may be targeting the Chinese audience in more familiar, connective ways. There is no one solution or golden rule, as image is related to taste. But the point should be clear: Brand marketing in China needs to make sure it targets and connects with Chinese customers.

Numerous Chinese and Asian companies are enjoying success in this area, and many international brands are struggling against their local rivals. Here are some examples, which should cover several marketing and sales areas. The British drug chain Boots has for several years tried to transfer its concept from Europe to the Asian and Chinese market—with limited success. The concept—neatly arranged, orderly stacked shelves, clear pricing labels, open spaces, and a good, focused assortment, all

Table 3.1
Chinese and Western Cultural Values

	Western values	**Chinese values**
Family, society Individuality ↔ Harmony	Individualism	Extended family, patriarchy, conformity
Communication Direct ↔ Indirect	Direct and open communication	Subtle and indirect communication
Communication Specific ↔ Unspecific	Focus on concrete topics	Focus on context
Status Success ↔ Position	Status and respect gained through achievement	Status and respect gained by position and the family
Face Low value ↔ High value	"Face" has no special value	Giving, taking, and having "face" (*lian–mianzi*)
Risk avoidance Success ↔ Security	Low risk avoidance, planned risk necessary for success	High risk avoidance, risk perceived as threat
Religion, philosophy Initiative ↔ Harmony	Christianity, democracy	Confucianism, harmony (Five virtues of humanity)

Arranged by B. Zinzius.

mixed with soft music—works well in Europe. But anyone who has been in Shanghai or Hong Kong will see that this is not the Chinese way. The cramped, crowded, narrow Chinese stores seem almost shabby, but the ever-present "sale" and "rebate" signs, the bazaarlike stacks of stuff on the floor, the overcrowded aisles, all this is China, and what is maybe most important, it does not look as expensive as Boots. Although Boots is remodeling its stores in several locations and testing extensively, its initial success seems to be limited.

Particularly in the segment of convenience stores—a market segment that grew 35 percent in 2003 to more than 10,000 stores—China seems to have pulled ahead of the West. Due to various mergers, large local chains were formed. The largest chain is the Shanghai Bailian Group with more than 4,300 outlets. The Dalian Dasheng Group is number two, followed by the Gome Group and the Hualian Group. Various foreign investors try to enter the competitive segment, including the world's largest retailer 7-Eleven from Japan, who opened the first store in Beijing in February 2004; five hundred further 7-Eleven outlets are planned within the next five years. The Japanese retailer Lawson, Thailand-based Charoen Pokphand, and Taiwanese President Chain are other examples of the stiff competition entering the Chinese retail market.[16] Convenience stores have basically perfected their market segment in Asia.

The high population density and use of public transportation in the megacities is an ideal environment for the neighborhood convenience store, as many people will walk by when they are going to or coming from work. To optimize their performance and product range, these shops make use of the possibilities of the modern electronic age. Several chains have fully automated scanning registers, which are connected to the head office. Thus, they not only are able to optimize the logistic supply and ensure stacked shelves, supplying some locations several times per day, but also are analyzing the customers' sales habits—that is, by shop, area, region, time, and product group. Japanese chains even mine their data to analyze for sales patterns and correlations, which opens room to improve shelf arrangement and rebate structures.

Another area of expansion is large supermarket chains, where the French distributor Carrefour is currently the market leader. Whereas convenience stores target the small shopper on his or her way home, the supermarket offers low prices for large-volume shoppers. Carrefour has a strong presence in Asia and is expanding in China. There is tough competition between Wal-Mart, which had 31 stores in 2003, Metro, which had 21 stores as of 2003, and Carrefour, which has the highest market share with 40 hypermarkets in 2003.[17] After some initial struggles, Carrefour redesigned its strategy and cooperated closely with local municipalities. This revitalized its market introduction, and its case is now discussed in marketing universities as a case study. The market, however, is very competitive, and in 2003 the German retailer Metro announced an investment of US$700 million to open 40 new stores across China until 2008.[18]

Starbucks has the vision to become the most recognized brand in the world. However, in the largest consumer market in the world, Starbucks faces the problem that the Chinese simply don't drink coffee. "Too bitter" is one comment. "Coffee keeps me awake until three A.M." says another. China is well known as a land of tea drinkers. Therefore, Starbucks has developed a strategy to target this market and bring its coffee shops to Chinese consumers. The quiet, unobtrusive atmosphere targets a younger generation—students, office employees, and young managers. Despite the high prices, these customers prefer Starbucks to the noisy, smoke-filled tea shops patronized by the older generation. To ensure that its Chinese operation is fulfilling Starbucks' international standards, the company sent several Chinese trainers to California to absorb the American atmosphere and learn about the business in its original environment. Starbucks also hired outside consulting companies, which constantly test and evaluate the Chinese outlets. And to attract new customers to Starbucks' main product, the company has established coffee classes, which explain coffee and coffee drinking to the Chinese. In another move to cater to the Chinese market, Starbucks recently expanded its product line by adding tea. Under the brand name Tazo, Starbucks offers green Chinese and herbal tea. This is value-added and experiential marketing with the highest Western quality standards. There are already more than one hundred Starbucks branches in Beijing, Hong Kong, and Shanghai, and the chain is rapidly expanding into the hinterland. Other coffee shops are following suit, like the Canadian chain Blenz, and the Taiwanese-based chain Dante Coffee, in an attempt to change a nation of tea-aficionados to become coffee drinkers. Similar changes in consumer behavior can be seen in other food-and-beverage market segments. Milk consumption doubled from 1997 to 2002, a reason why Nestle sees China as one of its fastest growing and most important markets worldwide.[19]

General Motors and Roche are two recent successful examples of value-added marketing and customer relationship management in China. In 2002, GM implemented a CRM system which integrated the dealer orders of cars via a Web-portal. The system allows not only order tracking, but also asks for detailed customer information. Thus, GM receives complete information about all its customers. Shanghai Roche, a leading pharmaceutical company in China, faced a different challenge. It has a sales force of almost 500 staff, which details in 35 locations to 15,000 customers. The solution was a CRM-based sales-force automation, which uses mobile devices and simplified Chinese as language. The project carried a high price tag but shows promising results for sales, efficiency, and profit.[20] Both projects were recognized as being among the top 10 companies with the best CRM implementation in China.

Professional local marketing is already practiced by many of the successful Chinese companies to build brand image, market share, and ultimately customer loyalty. These companies spend significant money on their campaigns, which will also affect Western markets, bringing Chinese tastes and brands to Europe and the United States. They are designing their brand identity and bringing it to the minds of their customers. In his book *Designing Identity*, Mark English defines *design* as "the language of verbal and visual communication. Design is the vehicle of memory." To be successful in the Chinese market, it is important to build a good brand image and communicate it professionally to customers. Marketing and advertising should do that by verbal and nonverbal communication that targets and connects with Chinese customers—that is, in a Chinese way.

Company Names in Chinese

Prior to marketing activities in China, a company first has to translate its company name, as well as the names of its products, into Chinese. Only rarely can a Western name be used—for example, an abbreviation such as IBM. The company logo also has to be translated into Chinese characters. Few managers realize how important an adequate and positive translation into Chinese is for the success of their products. A negative or unfitting translation, especially one that has negative associations or that violates taboos, can damage the business.

There are different ways of translating names into Chinese, including direct translation of the meaning, phonetic translation (transliteration), and matching the sound by using Chinese characters that signify good fortune and depict product or company attributes. Brand names that already carry a product description can be directly translated. For example, Volkswagen was translated as *Dazhong Qiche*, meaning "people" and "car," and 100 Pipers Scotch Whiskey became *Qai Diren Weishiji*, meaning "100 pipes men whiskey." A direct translation is suitable only in rare cases; therefore, the name is often transferred phonetically without adding any meaning. For example, Löwenbräu was translated into *Luyunbao*, Opel into *Aopeier*, Adidas into *Adidasi*, and Liebherr into *Libohaier*. These examples show that the language structure allows only a partial phonetic translation. In this regard, Opel realized the importance of the name to successful marketing: The company now operates under the new sign *Oubao*, which means "European treasure."

The most successful translation is to reproduce the name phonetically with an additional positive association to satisfy the importance of the Chinese symbolism. Names that include symbols of luck work very well. The success of the following translations lies in combining the recognizable company name with a product message and a positive association.

The translation for automobiles of Mercedes-Benz is *Benchi*, which means "to run fast, to gallop"; for Porsche it is *Bao Shi Jie*, means "fast and time-saving"; for BMW it is *Boama*, meaning "treasure horse" or "noble horse." A very successful transliteration is the one of Coca-Cola: *Kekou-Kele*, which means "tasteful, delightful"—a lucky meaning, a positive product description, as well as a phonetic translation. Omo is a German detergent brand that has enjoyed virtually sensational market success in China. The Chinese characters *Ao Miao* mean "mysterious and wonderful." Investors hoping to find a similarly good translation for their company or product face a variety of difficulties. Transliteration into Chinese is complicated by the existence of hundreds of dialects that differ from the official language *putonghua* (Mandarin). In addition, the roughly four hundred syllables of the spoken language are accompanied by a hundred times more graphic signs, which have identical pronunciations but different meanings.

Interpretations and associations differ according to the culture. A good example is the translation of the company name Siemens. The German sinologist had good intentions when he translated the name Siemens as *Ximenzi*, or "West Gate Master." This should depict the master coming through the west gate toward China. The interpretation by the Chinese, however, was totally different, but in this case fortunate: They combined the syllables and recognized in *Ximen* an old, honorable family name and in *Ximenzi* a famous figure from a novel. Chinese men like to identify themselves with this figure, a very rich and successful Chinese playboy with many wives. This shows that in arriving at a Chinese name, not only a very good language qualification is needed, but also an excellent knowledge of the Chinese culture.

Because many Western companies entered China via Hong Kong, the names were translated into Cantonese, the dialect of Hong Kong. For example, the phonetic translation of the fast-food chain Pizza Hut into Cantonese sounds like *Bisangha*. In Mandarin, the official Chinese dialect, this sounds like *Bishengke*, and the original name is hard to recognize. An additional point of importance is that company and product names should avoid any negative association. Whereas in the West, for example, associating a brand of perfume with danger, prohibited behavior, or fire is possible, in China this is viewed negatively. A perfume with the name *Poison* could hardly be successfully marketed in China. Toshiba had a commercial song "Toshiba, Toshiba, . . ." which many people made fun of because it sounded like *tou chou ba*, meaning "let's steal it." Today, Toshiba uses the Japanese characters *Dong Ji*, which mean "East" and "nobility." Another interesting example is Oracle, which uses the name *Jia Gu Wen*. This sounds not at all like Oracle, but is the name for one of the oldest languages in China. It was one of the earliest systems to store information and was used for prophecy—an excellent description for Oracle's business.

Advertising in China

China's megacities are flooded with advertising. The impression that every inch has been converted into advertising space is not incorrect. Even telephone booths are completely covered with advertising panels. Public transportation vehicles, buses in particular, are colorful moving billboards. At night, neon lights turn the cities into oceans of light. Countless billboards stretch for miles on both sides of the highways.

Outdoor advertisement can be found everywhere, and the Chinese seem to be particularly smart in finding new spaces. Yes, one is literally surrounded by advertising. Outdoor advertisement in the megacities, particularly in the coastal regions, has a density that surpasses anything in the West. A huge variety of products is advertised—by foreign and increasingly by Chinese companies. The China National Advertising Agency is the highest authority; it is directly under the control of the State Administration for Industry and Commerce. Synovate's Asia Pacific Market Handbook 2003 indicates that total Chinese advertising expenditure in 2001—excluding outdoor, cinema, and Internet advertising—was 98.7 billion renminbi (US$12 billion). Seventy-three percent of this money was spent on television advertisement, 24.5 percent on newspaper advertisement, 1.5 percent on magazines, and 1 percent on radio advertisement. The pharmaceutical industry, with 28 percent, is the largest advertiser, followed by the food and beverage industry (13 percent), toiletry industry (11 percent), retail and services (9 percent), and electric appliance makers (3 percent).[21] A further market boost is expected in 2004, when international cigarette manufacturers will be allowed to enter the market fully. A survey carried out in 2001 for Coca-Cola reflects the current advertising pattern: 47 percent of all buyers of Coca-Cola bought their Coke based on TV advertisements; 44.5 percent on newspaper ads; 42.9 percent on magazine ads; 15.9 percent on radio ads; 11.2 percent on outdoor ads, and 4.4 percent on Internet ads. The expected annual market growth of advertisement in China is more than 20 percent. By 2020, China will become the second-largest advertising market in the world with US$100 billion in revenue, only surpassed by the United States.

An explosion of advertising? The advertising market is the number two growth sector in China, directly behind the total consumer products market. Because growth rates in the consumer market are declining, advertising could well become number one in terms of growth. Advertising is a booming market that supports more than 15,000 advertising agencies. The sheer number of advertising agencies and the growing number of spinoffs in the media themselves make it a rather difficult market. There are also about two-hundred Chinese-foreign joint ventures in the advertising business. In addition, China is the site of many branch offices or WFOEs of large international agencies, such as Saatchi & Saatchi, J. Walter

Thompson, Ogilvy & Mather, McCann Erickson, Dentsu, and Leo Burnett. Currently the largest Chinese advertising agencies are China United Advertising, China International Advertising, Beijing Advertising, Guangdong Advertising, and Grey China.

This is an enormous number of companies from which to choose, to plan, create, and communicate the message about your product to the Chinese market, thus gaining market access and—one hopes, success. But what about quality, and how about advertising laws and regulations? Foreign advertising companies, as well as foreign participation in Chinese advertising companies, are subject to state regulation and require admittance by authorities. The authorities control all advertising, including that of the purely Chinese advertising companies. Advertising must not violate Chinese customs or morals. If it does, it is forbidden, and the producer might be punished. The punishment extends from stiff fines to being closed down. Much can violate customs or morals—a woman's shoulder laid too bare on a poster, for example. Relatively costly fines are used to punish wrong or misleading advertising statements. Superlatives are forbidden in advertisements. Forbidden also is the use of national symbols. It is obvious that nobody can tarnish the "face of the nation" in advertisements. The use of images of poor, handicapped, or ugly persons is frowned upon.

How high are the quality standards in the Chinese advertising business? The design, content, and creativity is always good, but not yet comparable to the best international advertising; the product quality of advertising material is, however, comparable to Western standards. On the other hand, the competence and planning of campaigns or events need to be improved. Admittedly this is a difficult area to judge, and the frequent problems are covered with flexibility. Figures from the advertising media are usually embellished. A print media's circulation or a radio or television station's audience is usually inflated. Claims about areas of coverage and customer structures will rarely reflect the true picture. Even more problematic is the pricing issue. Rarely are unified price lists available. Local advertisers will get different rates for print or TV ads than will foreign companies or even Chinese-foreign joint ventures. As an example, daily newspapers have column prices between US$30 to US$150. In addition, such prices change three to four times per year, almost always increasing.

Negotiating for better rates from advertising firms is only promising with small or medium-sized companies. The big advertisers will hardly move, often just explaining that Chinese prices are far below those of the West. This is correct even when one takes all costs into account—that is, planning, conception, design, printing, and the campaign itself. Compared with the cost in the United States or Europe, advertisement in China is certainly less expensive and the quality is not bad. Any comparison is difficult; still it is clear that advertisement in China is a must. First, the Chinese consumer market still needs to be developed, and it is much easier to invest now and gain market share than to try recover it from the competition later. Second, Chinese consumers seem much more receptive to advertising than their Western counterparts.

Internet advertisement is strongly increasing; there are about one thousand IT service companies offering Internet advertising services. To regulate this area, China's State Administration of Industry and Commerce (SAIC) recently announced it will carry out trial operations in Beijing, Shanghai, and Guangdong province in regulating online advertising. Because this field is rapidly developing and changing, it is advisable to check the very latest regulations. Mass media advertising of investment products is less suitable than advertising those products via catalogs, advertisement in specialized journals, brochures, booklets, or direct mail. Database marketing is therefore a good tool. Participation in exhibitions is widely done, but many experts doubt its usefulness; a careful selection and evaluation of the event is needed.

Chinese Branding and Marketing

Chinese love brands; Chinese love branded products. Chinese suppose that branded products are of better quality and are more reliable, and thus have a higher value. It is a positive from the consumer's viewpoint if a branded product has a high market share. If many people own it, it must be good. If everybody owns it, it must be excellent. And at least it can never be a wrong decision to go with the mainstream. According to a brand recognition survey among Chinese consumers done in early 2000 by a Chinese daily newspaper, well-known brands with large market shares, such as Coca-Cola, Gold Fish cooking oil, Haoliyou pies, Hongtashan cigarettes, and Nanfu batteries, were described by respondents as the best products available.

The survey found that many brands held a market share of greater than 30 percent. Market shares of leading consumer brands in China were as follows: Wrigley's (90.9 percent), Nestle coffee (88.8 percent), Weiwei soybean drink (75.5 percent), Kodak film (53.8 percent), Hoaliyou pies (53.5 percent), White Cat detergent (46.1 percent), Coca-Cola (43.8 percent), Sanxiao toothbrushes (42.8 percent), Nanfu batteries (33.7 percent), and Pepsi (21 percent). Chinese connect mostly positive thoughts and feelings with brand names and logos. This is the same for foreign- and Chinese-branded products. And anyway, the majority of the branded consumer products in China are Chinese brands. It is important that the brand name and the marketing campaign has a Chinese identity. This is almost always decisive for its success, particularly for foreign products.

But even the biggest marketers do not always get it right in the beginning. When Coca-Cola entered the Chinese market, it first tried to keep the pronunciation. However, *Ko-ka Ko-la* for the Chinese means something like "bite the wax tadpole" or "wax-flattened mare," so it was a wise decision to change. And Kentucky Fried Chicken translated its "finger-licking good" initially to "eat your fingers off." As there are many Chinese languages and dialects, it is advisable to choose a product's name and characters carefully.[22]

A positive Chinese identity, induced by Chinese characters and their meaning, is an important success factor in Chinese consumer marketing. A less than positive identity is probably the reason that low-profile brands and products have only a slight chance of success, even if their price is far less than that of their competitors. Brand awareness among the Chinese is not only related to price and quality—overall image is important, and image means customer perception. The following table shows the top 10 companies ranked for overall leadership in 2003.[23]

Other brands named in the survey include TCL, a rising television producer who formed a joint venture with Thompson in 2003, Yuxi Hongta Tobacco Group, First Automobile Works (FAW), Wangxiang Automobile Parts, Broad Air Conditioning, Shanghai Bao Steel, Erdos Textiles, and Lenovo (Legend Group)—China's leading computer manufacturer. After capturing large market shares of the Chinese market, Chinese companies are now positioning themselves for international competition. Legend has recently changed the name to Lenovo, and the Taiwanese computer maker Acer chose BenQ as its new name, both with the aim to increase international brand recognition and identity. The strong competition in many fields, such as mobile phones—where TCL and Ningbo are rapidly in-

Table 3.2
Ranking of Chinese Industrial and Consumer Brands, 2003

Rank	Consumer Brands	Industrial Brands
1	Haier Group	CIMC Freight Containers
2	Tsingtao Brewery	Ancai TV Tubes
3	Tong Ren Tang Traditional Medicine	Shanghai Zhenhua Cranes
4	Yanjing Brewery	NPCP Pharmaceuticals
5	Pearl River Pianos	COSCO Shipping

Source: Forbes, October 20, 2003. Arranged by B. Zinzius.

creasing their market shares against international competitors like Motorola, Nokia, Siemens, and Sony—show that establishing a brand and growing market share are only first steps for an international company in China; defending market share is just as important, and even more difficult than in many other countries.

Is there a different degree of acceptance among the Chinese for a foreign as opposed to a Chinese brand? In principle no, but Chinese brands seem to be getting better recognition recently. According to a brand recognition study carried out by *China Business* in 2000 among general consumers in Beijing, Microsoft was well known by 33 percent of all inhabitants, while Haier was identified by more than 40 percent. Other foreign brands that were well known included Matsushita, Coca-Cola, Motorola, General Motors, IBM, Toyota, McDonald's, Sony, and VW. While they were recognized widely, comparable Chinese brands in the same segment were at least similarly well known.

Whether an international or Chinese brand, an excellent local marketing campaign that hits the tastes and needs of the Chinese consumers is probably more likely to gain market share than a marketing campaign based on a worldwide campaign coming from the corporate headquarters. "Think Chinese—Act Western" is one motto, and we can expect more and more local appeal and influence in the marketing of the twenty-first century.

Therefore, it is certainly worthwhile to invest time, money, and brainpower in the creation of a brand in China—a brand whose effectiveness is based on the name and its meaning, a brand that does not use a logo that would be disapproved by the Chinese. Those who want to build up a brand in China must know the Chinese. Everything has a meaning, a Chinese meaning. Name, character, logo, color, typeface, writing direction—only after the complete package is finished can the next steps be taken, such as advertisement and distribution. As a final reminder—one should not forget to patent or register all design aspects of products and advertisements to protect against counterfeit and theft of intellectual property, including copies of the campaign.

Polite but Merciless—Competition in China

The number of local and foreign competitors in China is growing tremendously year by year. Thus, competition is becoming more fierce. At the same time, the market is growing at a slower rate, especially in the consumer goods sector. One cannot talk about 1.3 billion Chinese customers for consumer products, but about 400 million. By the year 2005, this figure may be as many as 500 million. At the same time, it is expected that up to 22 million businesses, shops, and retailers will be wooing these customers. One thing is clear: The boom of business foundations is met by a consumer spree. At the same time, even the freely spending inhabitants of the megacities have begun to scale down their spending and put more money into savings. A certain level of saturation has been reached. In 2001, urban households had an average of 1.2 color television sets, 92 percent had a washing machine; 81 percent a refrigerator. Other fields promise continued growth, such as furniture (64 percent), mobile phones (33 percent), computers (13 percent), automobiles (0.6 percent), household appliances, health, and perhaps fashion. In addition, 20- to 30-year-olds will spend a lot on leisure and learning.

Almost everybody makes purchasing decisions based on advertising. But this does not change the fact that a rapidly growing supply will be met by a modestly growing demand. That is the situation in the consumer market. It is partially true also for the investment and service sectors. The logical result of this will be increased competition. Similar to many basic strategies in China, this competition will be fought based on ancient Chinese rules of war. They are derived from a book of military theory dating from the time of the Fighting Empires, the third century B.C. *The Art of War* by Sunzi describes the art of fighting as influenced by Confucian behavioral patterns. One approaches the enemy cautiously, circumspect, relaxed, but earnest and brave. At the beginning, one observes politely but meticulously. Based on observations, a strategy is drawn up that includes all possible consequences. One will attack only if it is really clear that the enemy can be defeated. If the attack is launched, it is merciless. Only a defeated enemy is no longer an enemy. Today, Chinese managers are still using this art skillfully and are therefore intellectually fit for competition.

Chinese businessmen are and remain polite people for a long time—including toward their opponents. But they will behave mercilessly if, for example, they feel the time has come to defend or expand their market position. This can be the case if they are confronted with dumping prices, newcomer attempts to establish a monopoly, or they perceive a continued breach of the "Chinese way" of conducting business.

Problem Areas: Distribution and Logistics

Having a good brand policy and using professional advertising are not all that is necessary to market products successfully in China. Products need to be distributed. Supplying one's distributors requires an effective logistical process. What is important to know about logistics in China? Chinese distributors, retailers, and wholesalers are quite successful, but they are also numerous and widespread. It is therefore difficult to establish a regional distribution network. And it is basically impossible to organize sales nationwide via distributors.

A manufacturer of consumer goods in the United States or Europe, for example, would deliver its products to about fifty retail organizations to ensure nationwide distribution. In China that would be equal to about two to three thousand distributors to achieve good regional coverage and a point-of-sales presence. If the manufacturer wants to distribute the products nationwide, it means enormous logistical problems. Furthermore, an inadequate traffic infrastructure does not yet allow for perfect logistics either. In transporting goods by road, one has to reckon with some bad road conditions and great distances. The state railway system has good coverage but completely insufficient capacity, which leads to rather long clearance and waiting times, and thus to back orders. Logistics in China relies on improvisation and needs sufficient safety time—and patience. The fragmented distribution structure, difficult logistics, inefficient local stock management—these are sales barriers which should not be underestimated. Distribution channels are long and narrow and the product flow from manufacturer to customer encounters many obstacles. One solution that is frequently used is a mutual joint venture between foreign joint ventures and local companies. This joint venture will concentrate only on the logistical issues, but this does also not solve the general problems. Another possibility is to restrict sales to regions that have a well-established infrastructure, as such regions are not small and are constantly expanding. Presently, such regions are mainly as follows: along the Bohai Bay on the northeastern Chinese coast, the provinces of Shandong and Liaoning; in the eastern coastal region along the Yangtze river, the provinces of Jiangsu, Zheijiang, Anhui, and Hubei; and along the southern coast, the provinces Guangdong and Fujian.

A BETTER UNDERSTANDING OF THE CHINESE

Increased Individualism—and a Higher Standard of Living

Nothing depicts the end of the Conformism—which was established under Mao—better than the colorful and vibrant life now present in Chinese cities. Where once the *danweis* ruled and ordered everything, the rising complexity and differentiation shows a departure from the almighty party. A striving for individualism and emancipation from ordained lifestyles can be clearly seen. Over decades it was the party that made the decisions and established rules everybody had to follow. For decades, there was only one system for the Chinese—submission, military drills, and state-order thinking. The symbol for the equality of all humankind was the Mao suit, a blue, green, or gray uniform. In this faceless mass, the individual was nothing; individualism and one's own initiative were disregarded; everybody went the ordained way. Nonconformist conduct was punished without indulgence; even the most private decisions, such as the choice of a partner and love, were regulated.

Although the Chinese will toward individualism and freedom of thought and feeling is awake, it nevertheless seems to be broken. As if hypnotized by Western allurements and the promises of a free market, the Chinese desire for individuality and freedom of thought has devolved into a materialistic hunt for wealth and status symbols. The years of renunciation, asceticism, and prudishness have passed, together with the idealism and the enthusiasm for a common goal. What has followed is the desire for materialistic goods, an urge to exhibit oneself and one's newest possessions. Materialism in everyday life cannot be overlooked: The years of Maoist egalitarianism have passed, and more than ever social status has become important, the social status of the individual. Friends, wife, man, lover—all are selected according to their social status as well as their wealth.

Symbols of the new materialism are the *dakuan* (parvenu) and the *baofahu* (newly rich). Their pendant is a class of young ladies who stand out due to their elegant and fashionable style. Both groups have in common an orientation toward the West: He prefers expensive cars, wearing Western suits, striking shoes, sunglasses, and the latest mobile phone or PDA with a camera, whereas she wears dresses from high class fashion houses. The *baofahu* and his companion flaunt their money and their wealth. They spend a fortune to dine with friends in the newest Western hotels, live in upper class areas and drive an S-class Mercedes. China is one of the largest markets for Mercedes luxury cars, and when Rolls Royce opened their showroom in October 2003, six cars were sold in the first week.

Indicative of the new wealth of the Chinese is a new occupation, the *baomu*, the au pair, who sits with the children of working parents. These are mostly young women coming from the country who want to start a new life in the city. The divide between city and countryside can be seen here. Large numbers of *baomu* can neither read nor write, and they use their spare time in the evenings for classes. Another frequently used term for a domestic helper in China is *ayi*, which means "auntie." Whereas years ago ayis were less frequent, today many expatriates and wealthy Chinese employ ayis as maid or nanny; special agencies offer domestic helpers throughout China.

Harmony, the Moral Code of the Chinese

In traditional China, harmony is regarded as ideal ground for any relationship. The Chinese have a strong desire for order and calmness and aim for stable and harmonious relationships. Harmony in East Asian cultures means avoiding open conflicts. In a culture that puts its primary emphasis on the interdependence of all social relations, disagreements must be avoided by all means. In the Confucian worldview, the golden middle way, the harmonization of disagreements, should always be the common goal. Personal profiling, thinking in the extreme, forcing one's standpoint—all these attitudes that are highly regarded in the West, are not valued by Chinese. Not competition but harmonious cooperation is the Chinese way. Therefore, the main goal of the Chinese upbringing is the practice of a conflict-free behavior.

The uncompromising push for one's own interests, at the cost of other members of the group, which is a Western sign of leadership, is unthinkable in China. In a case of conflict of interests, one should proceed with the utmost care. A direct no should be avoided in China, but a yes should not always be taken as a clear confirmation. More often, it is an ambiguous yes, and it is left to the sensitivity of the partner to find out whether or not a no was meant. In this regard, it is obvious why social etiquette plays such an important role in China—to guarantee harmonious relations between people.

These traditional rules regulate social conduct; clear, working regulations create the environment with which to engage in social interaction without conflicts and problems, thus saving one's partner's face, as well as their own. The social rules are closely related to the concept of face. Correct etiquette will retain face; a misstep may lead to loss of face. Spontaneity, individuality in the Western sense, is not possible in this social environment. Harmonious behavior is achieved, for example, through a respectful, disciplined appearance; soft, polite language; and strict self-discipline.

Losing face disturbs the harmony of a relationship and is seen as immoral by the Chinese. Chinese morality is the morality of harmony. Other things that are immoral, even if they are seen as criminal in the West, may be much less severe for the Chinese. Keeping harmony means also keeping face for all parties involved, one of the core principles of Chinese ethics.

Guanxi—the Universal Lubricant

Nothing is possible in China without contacts. The basis of a contact varies. The closest relations will be with one's own family and with relatives. The next area will be within the workplace. One's network of relations is also based on one's hometown and on common educational location. This network of contacts is essential in China, especially in day-to-day business. In matters of licenses, tickets, bank transactions, or living space, only good *guanxi* will help.

Every foreigner has to get used to this well-established nepotism. The foreigner should try from the beginning of his or her stay in China to establish as many contacts as possible. For foreigners, economic interests are most probably the basis of their first contact with Chinese partners. New relations must be nurtured intensively—for example, with invitations for meals and with small presents or favors, as these will keep the relationship going. As an initial test, a foreigner may be asked to provide a job for a member of a group, or arrange an order based on special conditions. This will give him access to the outer circle of the group.

Guanxi

Basically, *guanxi* means "relations," and it stands for connections defined by reciprocity and mutual obligations. A network of family, friends and acquaintances is built up, who can provide material or immaterial support of any means, based on personal favors.

Contrary to practice in the West, where presents are often given without any interest, the Chinese will always try to return any accepted favor or present. In the same regard, the foreigner is obliged to repay favors. Personal engagement is often more highly regarded than material value. The American expression of a "gifting relationship" refers to *guanxi* and emphasizes this dependency of exchanging favors. It would be wrong to assume that the exchange of presents or favors is purely calculating. The value of a present shows one's respect, honor, and trust for a partner. This mutual system of an unofficial accounting for favors and presents works remarkably well. Somebody in need of help with opening a "favor account" with the Chinese will receive an offer of help immediately. This help can be accepted without any bad feeling.

All business is personal: for success or failure it is imperative to have *guanxi* and belong to the social network. In business life and in private life, the Chinese separate people into two groups: *we* and *the others*. *We* is the bigger family, friends, distant relatives, and acquaintances. Hundreds of people can belong to this group. It grows continuously. Also, because of marriages, whole new families and friends join the group. The group, or perhaps it would be better to say the network of interconnected groups, has continuously ongoing business where one person will help the other. Everything is based on mutual trust and support. It is possible that a foreigner may be accepted into a group and thus can use its network of relations, or *guanxi*.

The time it takes to establish such *guanxi* relationships is often underestimated. Westerners should allow for sufficient time in their trips to establish and nurture their relations. Time spent by the Western delegation in establishing relationships is honored by the Chinese side. Take the time to establish business relations! The more time one invests in establishing good relations with business partners, the more important the partners feel and consequently the more face you give them. For the Chinese, these contacts are not a waste of time but an obvious sign of mutual respect. It is important in establishing and maintaining the *guanxi* relations to carefully evaluate the basis of the relations. Much intuition is needed to ascertain whether the Chinese partner feels a moral obligation due to the contact. Unsuitable, expensive presents will put pressure on the partner, especially if he is not able to reciprocate. It is a science in itself to judge the value of a favor. Giving and taking must be in balance. A careful balancing of the relationship is therefore necessary.

One problem with such relationships is certainly their close proximity to bribery and corruption. Often one has difficulty distinguishing between a favor done because of *guanxi* and an act of corruption. Foreigners trying to establish new relationships come relatively close to this border of corruption.

Money Above Everything

"Those who work hard, can achieve everything," says Chen Liang, a young assistant professor at China's elite university, the "Beida" in Beijing. When asked about the meaning of "everything," he answers, "A pretty, modern apartment which belongs to me, later then, if our child comes, perhaps our own house, so spacious that the parents can live with us . . . a German car, BMW perhaps . . . good living conditions, being able to offer the family a good life, which also needs a lot of money. I will not be able to earn this money at the university; therefore a top job in the industry is my goal!"

Working hard, but only where it is worthwhile, where one can earn more, even much more money, is the major aim for most Chinese today. Everything is about money, and it seems to be true that the people do everything to get rich. Money, at least enough money so that one can feel rich, is a motivation for the Chinese to be diligent. Accordingly, they spend their manpower and time very strategically. Those holding a secure but low-income job will spend little time and effort on that work and major time on a second or third job. Officials who are allowed to earn additional income during their working time will certainly do so—without hesitation and with a lot of skills. Bribery? No, according to the Chinese way of thinking, this is just the correct remuneration for the trouble to service a person with an application or petition. Almost everything can be regulated advantageously with money, and with more money, things can be achieved even faster.

Making money through business and through one's career to gain a good reputation for oneself and for the family—this is one of the major thoughts and motivations for the Chinese. They submit everything to this. Acting like a "capitalist," on a small-scale or big-scale, this seems to be the modern Chinese ideology. Everyone wants to live like the new Chinese elite—successful, business oriented, smart, and efficient, without any restraint. How can such behavior exist in a Communist state? Where are the morals, ideology, and ethics? Well, for a long time, the Communist Party has not opposed functionaries' striving for wealth. Rich Communists, rich Chinese—good Communists, good Chinese! It must be the Marxist dialect, that the thesis of community-centered socialism and its antithesis, ego-centric capitalism, find synthesis in China. Business above ideology? It might seem so, but that perception is wrong. Business is part of the ideology and does not tarnish Communist core beliefs. One does not have to be or live like a proletarian in order to be a Communist. That is one reason one sees no indication at all of political change in China. The CPC remains the power in China, not because it is based on military power and reigns over a perfect system of state control, but because the party has been able to find its way with "Chinese capitalism." It even guarantees a safe haven for capitalism, security against global economic storms. Thus, the relationship between ideology and money earners has been forged. This only leaves the question of morality and ethics, which can be answered reasonably from the Chinese point of view, and which still follows a rather traditional moral code.

Managing in China—Learn from Experience

It is true: China is open to the market economy and foreign investors. And many economic and ecological problems the Chinese face are similar to those of Western industrial nations. Chinese attempts to solve such problems are comparable to ours. A part of the Chinese population loves Western consumer products and Western consumer behavior. And it is definitely correct that most Chinese think and act capitalistically in trying to earn money and become rich. All of this should not deceive: The Chinese are and will remain different—that is CHINESE.

The Chinese are not at all underdeveloped or backward. To assume that or to categorize China as a third-world country would be a disastrous misjudgment for anyone doing business in China. Definitely, many things are strange, some even very strange. But nothing is senseless, and many things have been well proven over thousands of years and still work extremely well today. The Chinese are modern people with ancient traditions. They are self-confident, with the conviction that Chinese culture is superior to all other cultures. Going to China means adapting to this attitude. It doesn't suffice to analyze the enormous market opportunities and try to use them. It is very helpful to have a reliable Chinese partner and use him for the start-up phase of one's business. Thus, "Project China" can begin. But a manager is not only a businessman and entrepreneur in China; he also has to live there. And China is definitely an adventure! To make sure that the adventure will be successful, certain inherent attitudes must be brought: openness to other cultures, flexibility, and physical and mental stability.

A China manager needs strong nerves and must be able to sit out the frequent and exhausting negotiations. Negotiations and of course, also internal company meetings drag on. A meeting starts with the warm-up phase, aimed to generate a good atmosphere. General or private information is exchanged; one talks about one's children and hobbies. The real topic slowly comes into focus. Step by step, it is approached; possible conflicting points are shunned or may be touched on some hours later or in the aisle during a break. The discussion can nevertheless be tough, not in form but regarding the facts. But all in all, an easy solution is desired, and often negotiations will lead to a mutual dinner that includes lots of drinking. Having a weak stomach or being afraid of liver problems is not a good precursor for doing business in China. Eating and drinking play a major role in daily Chinese life—business and private. The Chinese love to wine and dine together, with friends and family members, in a good atmosphere with lots of fun and singing. Those who do not participate, because they do not like to or are not able to, are less respected, despite their business qualifications. Something should be said about the cardinal virtue of a Chinese manager: calmness. Calmness makes many things possible: patience, friendliness, disguising anger, and being polite behind an easy smile. Calmness does not mean accepting mistakes of employees, but it is necessary to handle all situations delicately. Addressing problems directly and too harshly will cause only a direct or inner resistance on the part of the recipient. Calmness makes it easier to improvise and to see problems as positive challenges that offer opportunities.

Without the cardinal virtue of calmness, it is not possible to integrate into the Chinese culture. The manager in China must be able to build up efficient structures, but he must also be able to build up solidarity and a company spirit and he must be able to integrate himself. This is absolutely essential if he wants the company to run smoothly. Those who are able to connect partners and employees to a kind of *guanxi* have achieved the masterstroke of any manager in China. These managers have also perfectly understood the art of "keeping" and "giving face." Is it essential for a manager in China to master the Chinese language? It will be difficult to find the time to learn the basic three thousand signs. But he should learn to speak basic Mandarin. First, this shows respect for the Chinese culture and will be rewarded with a better reputation. Second, an ability to have basic communication with those Chinese who don't speak English, which is the vast majority, is a big plus. The best way is to begin learning Chinese prior to arriving in China.

It can be recommended to all, acquire as much as possible knowledge about China prior to arrival. There are many opportunities to do so: Books, intercultural China-seminars for managers, language classes for basic Chinese, or rhetoric and behavioral training.

NOTES

1. "Law of the People's Republic of China on Chinese-Foreign Contractual Joint Ventures." *FDI 24. Invest in China, 2004.* http://www.fdi.gov.cn/ltlaw/lawinfodisp. jsp?id = ABC00000000000004158&appId = 1, Mar. 12, 2004.

2. "Breakthrough milestones in Chinese imaging industry. Kodak grows with China into new millennium." *Kodak Press Center,* Nov. 11, 1999; ibid., p. 3.

3. "Motorola in China: Motorola University." 2004, Motorola Inc. http://www.motorola.com.cn/en/about/inchina/university.asp, Jan. 19, 2004; *see also* Borton, J. "Motorola University scores high grades in China." *AsiaTimes online,* June 4, 2002. http://www.atimes.com/china/DF04Ad02.html, Oct. 25, 2002.

4. Murphy, D. "Old Volkswagen Chases New China." *Far Eastern Economic Review,* Mar. 6, 2003, p. 27–29; *see also* Kahn, G. "Volkswagen Shifts Gears in China." *Asian Wall Street Journal,* Apr. 8, 2002, pp. A8–A9.

5. German Industrial Trade Chamber. [in German language] "TÜV Süddeutschland Informiert: China-Export: Neues Zertifizierungssystem ab 1. Aug. 2003." http://www.ihk-nordwestfalen.de / aussenwirtschaft / bindata / CCC-TUEV-SUEDDEUTSCHLAND.pdf, Nov. 30, 2003.

6. Child, J., Chung, L. Davies, H. Ng Sek Hong. "Managing Business in China." Hong Kong Chamber of Commerce, Aug. 2000. http://www.chamber.org.hk/mbc/organizing71_body.htm, Oct. 9, 2003.

7. Fowler, G. A. "Trouble in Toy Town." *Far Eastern Economic Review,* Feb. 6, 2003, pp. 32–34.

8. "Protecting your Intellectual Property Rights (IPR) in China: an Overview." *The American Embassy in China,* Feb. 2004. http://www.usembassy-china.org.cn/ipr/ovview.html#curt, Mar. 17, 2004.

9. Leggett, K, and Zoun, T. "Yamaha Wins Lawsuit On China Copyrights." *Asian Wall Street Journal,* Aug. 15, 2002, pp. A1–A8.

10. "China Fines Publisher in Peter Rabbit Case." *Asian Wall Street Journal,* Oct. 10–12, 2003, p. A10.

11. "Lego Wins China Copyright Case." *Asian Wall Street Journal,* Jan. 22, 2003, p. M3.

12. Brilliant, M. "US and Japanese commercial Interests Converge Over China's IPR Regime." *U.S. Department of State, International Information Programs, U.S. Chamber of Commerce,* Dec. 2002. http://usinfo.state.gov/regional/ea/iprcn/japanfeature.htm, Mar. 20, 2004.

13. "Rich buyers snapping up China homes. Beijing-area 'villas' draw newly affluent locals." *International Herald Tribune,* Apr. 23, 2002, p. 6.

14. National Bureau of Statistics. *China Population Statistical Yearbook, 2001.* China Statistics Press, Feb. 2002.

15. Kahn, G. "Market Researchers Struggle in China." *Asian Wall Street Journal,* Oct. 13, 2003, p. A5.

16. Chang, L. "Oiling an Old Chain." *Far Eastern Economic Review*, Nov. 6, 2003, pp. 34–36.

17. "China's 44th hypermarket opens in Beijing," Carreefour, Press Release, March 17, 2004. http://www.carrefour.com/english/groupecarrefour/ouvchine 170304.jsp Apr. 4, 2004; Scott, L. "Metro Store Contact." Oct. 20, 2003. http://www.metro.com.cn/Metro_store_contact.htm, Dec. 12, 2003; "Wal-Mart China Co., Ltd." Jan. 7, 2004. http://www.wal-martchina.com/english/news/stat.htm, Jan. 12, 2004.

18. Körber, H. J. "Metro heads for Asia." Press Release, Apr. 15, 2004, http://www.metrogroup.de / servlet / PB / menu / 1004284_I2_ePRJ-METRODE-CMD_ pprint/ May 7, 2004.

19. Chen, K. "Dairy Firms Churn Out Milk Products in China To Culture New Market." *Asian Wall Street Journal*, Feb. 28–Mar. 2, 2003, pp. A1–M8.

20. McDougall, P. "The Place To Be." InformationWeek, Apr. 5, 2004. http://www.informationweek.com/story/showarticle.jhtml?articleD = 18700518 May 11, 2004; "Shanghai Roche's Award-Winning CRM Pays Off." Headstrong, 2004. http://www.headstrong.com/HS/PrinterFriendly/0,6000,1-394,00.html, May 11, 2004.

21. Synovate. *Asia Pacific Market Handbook 2003*. 2d ed. Hong Kong: Synovate, 2003, p. 58.

22. Temporal, P. *Branding in Asia. The Creation, Development and Management of Asian Brands for the Global Market*. John Wiley & Sons (Asia) Pte Ltd., Singapore, 2000, p. 22 et seq.

23. Kim, J. "Special Report: China's Biggest Brands." *Forbes*, Oct. 20, 2003. http://www.forbes.com/2003/10/17/cx_sk_1020chinaintro.html, Jan. 3, 2004.

CHAPTER 4

Cross-cultural Management

CHINA'S HISTORY: CULTURAL KNOWLEDGE AS A MANAGEMENT TOOL

China is like a mysterious castle, and Western businessmen will always struggle to find the entrance. Unfortunately, in today's business with China, this is the bitter reality for many Western managers. The biggest problems stem from the vast cultural differences. Cultural differences exist between the Germans and the French as well as between Americans, Canadians, and Mexicans, despite the fact that their respective nations are close neighbors and they often share a similar cultural background. One can only assume how difficult communications might get between completely different cultures. And even more so, if the people involved come from totally different political, economic and social backgrounds. Few study synonyms for words such as *mianzi, danwei, guanxi*, or *feng shui* prior to their China trip. These words, however, are part of the Chinese behavior, philosophy, and value system, as described earlier. We have to study them, because the individual who does not know his or her customers and business partners will not be successful. Westerners tend to be open and direct, behavior especially attributed to Americans. Chinese, on the other hand, will always be reluctant and cautious, expressing themselves with hints, paraphrases, and symbols. A westerner unfamiliar with Chinese rules and manners will without a doubt put his foot in his mouth. Successful communication without conflict is possible only when reading between the lines and interpreting hints correctly. A social blunder in front of a Chinese is often accompanied by a permanent "loss of face" (*diu lian/*

mianzi). Therefore, an approach of "trial and error" or "learning by doing" is certainly wrong. Anyone thinking about successful communication must deal with the issue of culture beforehand.

One example: Who would not carry the luggage of the only female member of one's company delegation upon arrival at the airport? Unless she is the head of the delegation, involuntarily, the first faux pas occurs. This "polite" Western behavior would disturb the Chinese counterparts, as it is against the hierarchical ranking of the delegation. Also—presents should be chosen wisely. The Chinese often associate an alarm clock or white flowers as symbols for upcoming death. Chinese will ignore such mistakes without any indication, because conflicts are not handled openly in the Chinese society. Therefore, Western businessmen who have lived in China for years often cannot explain why they have not been able to develop relationships with their Chinese counterparts, or why contract negotiations have not been completed or contracts have not been duly fulfilled.

Westerners who believe that the Chinese have to adapt to them, or who expect tolerance of their Western behavior, will receive a fast payback. Regardless of what might be the norm in other countries, no adaptation can be expected from people in China; this is because behavioral patterns are narrow and leave no room for maneuvering. The emphasis of the next chapter is on making people more sensitive to Chinese peculiarities. Realistic examples and practical cases, rather than abstract theories, illuminate the cultural differences. Thus it is necessary to introduce Chinese history, especially with regard to Confucianism and social and cultural interactions. This history influences the current generation of Chinese, illustrates the basic system of Chinese values and views, and serves as a basis for the deeds and thoughts of Chinese individuals and groups. Chinese behavior, as this book demonstrates, is not an intimidating or amusing phenomenon, but a product of their history and origin.

The most effective strategy for the reader will be not only to acquire an understanding of Chinese behavior but to use that knowledge in communication, in negotiations, and in day-to-day contact with Chinese counterparts. Therefore, I recommend undergoing a cultural training. The name China means "Middle Kingdom." This meaning demonstrates the Chinese assumption that their country is the center and origin of civilization. For centuries, China kept its individualism and lived isolated from other states. The Chinese did not have the desire for political or territorial expansion in Europe, nor did they aim for to expand their international trading possibilities. Sending missionaries to convert people of a different faith is also not a Chinese concept.

First Contact with the West (Nineteenth Century)

This world outlook, together with the solid social structure, opened only a few possibilities for external or internal influences or renewals of the social structure. First of all, the court of the Chinese emperor was not interested in diplomatic contacts with the West, as that did not lead to obvious advantages. Furthermore, the Chinese had no need of or desire for Western products, inventions, or sciences. Also, for a land that used silver as currency, foreign currencies were of no interest.

In contrast, the West was very much interested in Chinese products, such as porcelain, silk, tea, and lacquer ware, and viewed China as a gigantic marketplace for Western products. The nineteenth century saw almost a boom for Chinese items. Everyone of a certain social status tried to present "Chinoiseries" to his or her guests—from Chinese tea sets to silk wallpapers to complete Chinese pavilions. For this reason, every Western country tried to establish trade relations with China. But because China did not have a real interest in trade with foreigners, the Europeans encountered vast difficulties in getting trade relations established. After diplomatic channels could not ease entrance to the Chinese markets, the British sent in their military fleet, followed by the French and Americans. First, the colonialists introduced opium to the Chinese, which led to a fast and steep decline of Chinese society. The drug wore down many Chinese physically and psychically, which enabled the colonialists to enter Chinese markets. The Chinese had little resistance against the technique and strength of the westerners, and put up little opposition. The conflicts culminated in the well-known Opium Wars, which saw the Western troops as triumphant winners over a weak and corrupt Qing dynasty (1644–1911).

Consequently, the Chinese trading empire was destroyed. Hong Kong, Shanghai, and other harbors came under Western control. As a reaction, xenophobic and nationalistic tendencies arose among the Chinese, who wanted the foreigners with their imperialistic behavior out of their country. The Chinese were especially angry at discriminatory policies; the sign "No dogs and Chinese allowed" could be read for some years in Shanghai. *Loa wai* (old foreigners) and *gui lao* (devil's fellow) are names the Chinese still use for foreigners.

Opium Wars—Fighting for the Chinese Market

The conflict started with the drug opium, which many Chinese fell victim to. Where drugs are to be found—the mafia is sure to be close behind. The mafia in this case were the British, French, Germans, and Americans. Foreign powers caused widespread addiction among Chinese by smuggling opium into China. Huge profits were earned, especially by the British East Indian Society. Tea for Europe was purchased with profits from the opium trade. The Chinese fought back. The British and French, however, requested free trade and settling allowances. Wars broke out—the Opium Wars. The British and French won various fights, and as a consequence forced China to allow trade in opium and other goods. A battered China bowed to the foreign powers and signed the so-called "unequal" treaties of Nanjing (1842) and Tianjin (1858). In time, huge China was split into zones of influence. The British received Hong Kong, the French received Indochina, Portugal acquired Macao, the Germans Tsingtao, Japan got Formosa and other islands, and Russia received Manchuria. The United States and other Western nations also forced China to sign similar documents, such as the Treaty of Wangxia (1844) on free trade, extraterritoriality, and most-favored-nation status.

Not only the opium trade but also the influence of the Christian Church provoked this conflict. Two powerful forces strongly disturbed relations between China and the West: religion and drugs. Again the Chinese resisted. The great hatred that ensued was mainly instigated by the arrogance of the Christian missionaries, who possessed little consideration for Chinese customs and habits.

Hatred for the foreigners, which the Chinese had suppressed for years, erupted in the Boxer Rebellion (1900–1901). "Boxers," was the name foreigners gave to the Chinese who organized themselves into the group "The Righteous and Harmonious Fists." Their compatriots viewed them as brave fighters, and the foreigners were viewed as barbarian rabble. Uprisings killed christianized Chinese in the provinces and later missionaries and their families. They destroyed railroads, mines, and settlements of foreigners. The West reacted swiftly by mobilizing troops. Under the command of General Graf Waldersee, the Boxer movement in China was suppressed, and the Chinese government forced into capitulation and restoration.

Thus, the fate of many cities was final: They were under foreign rule. In Tsingtao, in the center of China, a city with German timber-framed houses, as well as a police station, post office, and bank, grew. A hotel, butcher shop, and slaughterhouse opened. Even German beer was brewed in Tsingtao. With so much German culture and gemütlichkeit, a strong exchange between Germany and its colony in the Middle Kingdom started: In 1910 one could travel for 536 marks from Berlin to Tsingtao in 13 days. However, this German colonial dream did not endure, as World War I brought it to an end. A few months after the start of the war, the Japanese occupied the territory, and an inglorious chapter of German history came to its end. A reminder of it today is the German art of brewing: Tsingtao beer is still the best-selling beer in the vast Chinese beer market.

The cities of Macao and Hong Kong are similar examples of ports, which were ceded by China to foreign powers in the nineteenth century. Over the years, these colonies developed into major economic centers, transportation hubs, and tourist attractions. In particular, Hong Kong has grown into one of the world's largest free-trade ports, benefiting from mainland-operated manufacturing companies. After decades of negotiation, Hong Kong was finally reverted to China on July 1, 1997 under an arrangement called "One Country, Two Systems." Macao was returned to China two years later on December 20, 1999.

Western and Chinese comments on the return of Hong Kong to China vary drastically. United States politicians, for example, emphasize the historic interest of the U.S. government to develop the democracy in Hong Kong, which actually never existed under the British colonial rule. The Chinese, however, portray the return as the end of 158 years of foreign humiliation which started with the annexation of the territories during the Opium Wars.

Years of Chaos (1911–1949)

During the same period, social revolutionary movements attempted to abolish the emperor dynasty. These movements culminated in 1911 in the fall of the weakened Qing dynasty. The winner of the following power struggle was Sun Yat-sen, who later founded the National Chinese People's Party of Kuomintang (*pinyin:* Guomindang). He was succeeded by Chiang Kai-shek, who was supported by the upper classes and became a president with almost dictatorial power. He tried to unite and renew the country by force. The country nevertheless remained divided by feuds. The arbitrariness of the local rulers terrorized the land, and years of terror and suppression were to come. During these years, the common people became poorer and poorer, and new Communist movements used the mass starvation of peasants to their advantage. Communism developed as the voice that unified the peasants. Thus, Communism gained more and more support by speaking out against Chiang Kai-shek, landowners, and wealthy citizens. The success of the Communist revolution forced Chiang Kai-shek and his followers to flee to Taiwan.

Victory of the Communists (1949–1966)

In 1949 in Beijing, Mao Zedong announced the foundation of the People's Republic of China. He was worshipped by the masses as a salutary; his revolutionary ideas and immense optimism carried them away. The land was captured by mass exodus. After decades of starving and suppression, the people wanted to live in freedom and peace. The socialistic restructuring of the country was accomplished with extreme consequences, even more radical than in the Soviet Union. At the very beginning, all great landowners were expropriated and the land distributed. The peasants were organized in kolkhoz-like communities—similar to the practice in the Soviet Union—and the workers were employed in large government-owned companies. Thus, the collectivization was universal throughout the country. The introduction of the planned economy enabled the government, the party as well as all cadres, to control and guide all economic transactions. The West, with its capitalism and free-market economy, was declared the enemy. Foreigners had to leave the country; the borders were closed. China remained in complete isolation from the West for more than 30 years.

Various crises shattered the republic in its early years. An ideological cleansing followed the economic restructuring of the country. Dissenting people as well as critics were branded as counterrevolutionaries, and many were killed. Often a denunciation by a neighbor was sufficient for a death sentence from the people's tribunal. Official figures speak of four million Chinese killed during these years. Although the political system was stable in terms of power, differences existed within the party about the way to implement social and economic reforms. Mao asked for an open discussion, the so-called Hundred Flowers Movement, about the parties and social politics. The Communist Party could not tolerate such open criticism, and up to four million of these "illegal dissidents" were killed or sentenced to labor camps.

Almost every year new movements were established and new paroles were issued. This unsteady course caused large numbers of Chinese to feel insecure, and it was a terrifying time for many. The power of the CPC was almighty. In the economic arena, this resulted in the suppression of individual initiative and entrepreneurial spirit. The party ultimately secured its power by this policy. The ideology of communism, which had attracted so many Chinese at the beginning, was turned into a weapon against the people.

Great Proletarian Cultural Revolution (1966–1976)

Despite the CPC's established external power, infighting occurred among the cadres. The result was internal cleansing and demotions of many regional party members. Mao intended the Cultural Revolution to mark the high point of this development. In August 1966, the Plenum of the Central Committee of the Communist Party of China declared the Great Proletarian Cultural Revolution as the official party guideline. The simple proletarian life was declared the ideal. In Mao's conception of a permanent revolution, political ideology ranked higher than any economic rationalism. Unification of cultural and political life was the goal. Schools and universities were closed; intellectuals were sent to work on farms. Acquisition of education through the working process was propagated. Strict dress codes were issued—the Mao look with its uniform, blue, green, or gray suits. Art and culture had to follow the narrow objectives of Mao's doctrines. The pillars of the Cultural Revolution were the Red Guards, paramilitary troops, who were recruited from students. The Red Guards functioned as a kind of mind police, ensuring compliance with political guidelines. Soon these troops developed their own dynamic, and many Red Guards went much further than their goal. Thus, Mao's doctrines were enforced by drastic, disproportional means.

At least three million people did not survive the "cleansings," and an unprecedented terror suppressed the people. A strictly organized cadre of functionaries took the lead of the country. Party members replaced knowledgeable staff in factories and government offices. The results of the Cultural Revolution are still felt today; the forced educational gap has yet to be closed. Please be reminded that many of your negotiation and business partners have lived through these times.

First Normalization

Only the death of Mao in 1976 made change possible. The Politburo elected Hua Guofeng as the new chairman. Moderate forces took charge in the country. Hua Guofeng demoted many leftists and arrested the Gang of Four, a group including Mao's widow, Jiang Qing, that was responsible for the terror. During Hua Guofeng's governance, many incarcerated victims were freed and rehabilitated from the accusation of crimes against the state. This included many people who were forced to work in labor camps. One of the rehabilitated was Deng Xiaoping, an extremely important figure in China's new policy.

Reforms and Opening to the West (since 1976)

Moderate forces gained power along with Deng Xiaoping. His way of governing was pragmatic, and a politics of the achievable reigned over the country. In addition, Deng Xiaoping initiated drastic change in China's foreign and economic policies. Economic liberalization in the form of a socialist market and an opening to the West were his key points. This meant private possessions as well as the possibility for free trade for the—until then organized—peasants and workers. Deng Xiaoping also intensified the use of foreign capital to rebuild the economy. The first joint ventures were founded. The people nevertheless mistrusted this new course, as they feared imminent change to old policies. Only the continuity of the reforms managed to convince many. Soon the Chinese realized that the entrepreneurial spirit, trade, and education were no longer stigmatized but encouraged. And with the economic reforms, the desire for political reform grew among the people. The political leadership, however, categorically rejected this. Nevertheless, a democratic reform movement swept the land. Students and workers gathered at the center of the protest, the Tiananmen Square, Beijing.

Massacre in the "Square of Heavenly Peace"

On May 20, 1989, the ruling party invoked martial law in Tiananmen Square as well as over other parts of Beijing. In the struggle for power, the orthodox forces around Deng Xiaoping and Li Peng had emerged. Moderates who had encouraged the economic and social reforms were defeated. With the bloody massacre of June 3 and 4, 1989, the regime tried to curb the uprising for democracy. There were reports that the army shot thousands of demonstrators, but the exact number has never been proven. To suppress further demonstrations, the whole country was subjected to a wave of arrests and executions. Even today, critics of the regime are relentlessly pursued and convicted.

The New China

China's strong economic growth of the past two decades is reflected in its changing society and culture. Improved living conditions, health standards, and an increasing individual wealth are governed by a new political leadership, which shifts from an ideology-driven to an economy-driven leadership style.

One of the important cornerstones of the new Chinese society is the legal system, which is currently being overhauled. A new legal system will provide security to businesses and individuals, and will thus have a profound influence on Chinese society. Whereas for centuries, the personal networks and adherence to classic Confucian principles provided safety and support, in the future individuals and companies can rely also on a newly established legal foundation. This will certainly influence personal attitudes and social values.

Other drastic changes of the new China are even more obvious, such as the rise of new skylines in megacities like Shanghai. The small *hutongs*—back-alley huts—that provided living space for millions in the cities, are being replaced with expensive houses, while hundreds of skyscrapers are growing alongside. Taxi drivers are taking English classes in preparation for the Olympic Games in 2008, something unthinkable few years ago. Uniform Mao-suits have been replaced by colorful dresses and business suits. Chinese and foreign brands advertise new lifestyles, and foreign businessmen and tourists expose the Chinese to foreign cultures. Already today, China is the fifth largest tourist destination in the world with strong growth rates. And Chinese tourists will become the largest tourist group in the world over the next decade, giving the Chinese unprecedented exposure to Western and Asian cultures. This enormous transformation of a nation is in contrast to the changes and challenges in the central and western regions, the shift from an agrarian to a technology-oriented society. Although the government is focusing its efforts on these poor regions, massive problems are certain to arise.

The scale of China's transformation at the beginning of the twenty-first century defies any comparison, therefore the future development is almost impossible to predict. It is clear that the China of today is vastly different from the China ten years ago, and will differ from the China in ten years. To what extent will the Chinese keep their "Chineseness," to what extent will they adopt Western individualism and consumerism? While part of the Chinese mentality and social values may change, other parts will always remain Chinese. Some scholars, therefore, speak about a Neo-Confucianism, that is, Confucian principles combined with Western ethics, while others see the continuation of very distinct cultural values between China and the West.

EDUCATION

The Chinese population stands at 1.3 billion, a vast pool of resources for potential employees. Many of the Chinese workers are highly motivated, flexible, and willing to work. But many are not well educated, and many have profoundly different backgrounds and perceptions than their counterparts in the West. When employing Chinese staff, whether they are graduates fresh from the university or long-term employees of SOEs, one should consider the educational and industrial situation of China, which is not comparable with that of the West at all. To explain the difference, it is necessary to elaborate on the history and current status of the Chinese school and university system.

During thousands of years of imperial reign, the Chinese thought of themselves as superior to the West. Ancient traditions and glorious discoveries, such as the discovery of gunpowder, paper, the letterpress, and the compass, confirmed that opinion. The massive analphabetism was not changed, and real social advance was possible only as a government official. Only China's defeat in the Japanese-Chinese War in 1895 forced the Chinese to rethink their position and to modify the educational system at least partially according to Western models, as the Japanese had done already.

After the fall of the last dynasty in 1911, Mao Zedong and his friends established a system to support the education of the nonprivileged. However, that was stopped in 1930 because of the Japanese invasion, and it was started again only after the Communists freed China in 1949. China adopted the Communistic education model of the Soviet Union between 1949 and 1966, but even in 1956 less than half of all children received a basic school education. A new educational system was established after Mao Zedong's *Great Leap Forward* failed in 1961 and after the start of the Cultural Revolution in 1966. The time of the Cultural Revolution was a disaster for the educational system, as it was for the whole country. Curricula were basically nonexistent and any education was ideologically oriented, if education was carried out at all.

In 1976, after the fall of the Gang of Four and the rehabilitation of Deng Xiaoping, educational reforms were again started. Science, research, and education in areas such as agriculture, national defense, industry, research, and technology were advanced. However, this was supposed to be done based on the *Four Cardinal Principles:* the socialist road, the people's democratic dictatorship, the CPC leadership, and Marxist-Leninist-Maoist thought. The education process comprised the "6-3-3" system—six years of primary school, three years of secondary school, and three years of high school. The general population accepted the system only slowly, and in 1978 less than 5 percent of all students enrolled in high school. This percentage increased to almost 50 percent in 1994.

China introduced a new school system in 1995 that includes nine years of compulsory education. This system shows a clear commitment to a universal education and will produce scholars and scientists as well as skilled laborers. China is irreversibly part of the international community, and developments in China's educational system will have an increasingly profound influence on the other systems of the world, just as so many of them have influenced the present Chinese system of education. It will be especially interesting to see whether Confucian Chinese society, which emphasizes obeying and following, will be able to incorporate new cultural characteristics, such as creativity. Time will tell if China has found a workable formula for its educational system, whether that system's Western contours can be conformed to a patently non-Western environment.

To fulfill the needs of the fast-growing economy, numerous private institutions and international universities have established themselves in China. The Hong Kong University of Management belongs to the best universities in Asia and the China-Europe International Business School (CEIBS) in Shanghai is one of the leading management universities in China and is acclaimed as the gold standard. In 2001, CEIBS ranked 13th among the 50 top Asian universities. CEIBS's full-time MBA program extends over a 17-month period and includes a three-month internship in the industry, either in China or in Europe. The Fudan University School of Management and the Guanghua School of Management are other examples of business schools that offer higher-level business-education programs in combination with international Universities. In recent years, a few hundred MBA-students have graduated from CEIBS, and some twelve thousand students have participated in management courses. However, Bert Bennett, president of CEIBS, has mentioned that the Chinese industry needs about three hundred thousand MBA graduates in order to secure the future growth and successful development of China.[1]

In total there are about sixty MBA universities in China educating some eighty thousand students. In comparison, 90,000 MBA students graduated in the United States in 2003 alone. This shows that the total number of graduates is only able to cater for a fraction of the market's needs, which is a good indicator of the general educational situation in China. And even a graduate with high grades from a top university might not fulfill the market requirements. There have been recent cases where Chinese graduates of Shaanxi University were so fixed on their Western textbook know-how that they forgot the importance of Chinese values, such as *guanxi*. The young managers did not involve the local officials in the correct way and did not build up sufficient connections. Therefore, the officials rejected the investment project, despite the fact that it was very promising. The difficult task is therefore to select the best staff and to guide them correctly in a multicultural environment. The Chinese managers must be able to do the balancing act between Western and Chinese culture, just as foreign expatriates must.

One should keep in mind the history and the present status of the Chinese educational system when employing staff or setting up an organization. Few older Chinese have had the opportunity of a school or university education, and fewer still have a business background in the Western sense. The education of the younger generation has improved in the past two decades; since then, the rate of illiteracy has dropped significantly. The younger generation is more able to adapt to a new system, including at work. A larger number of students can be found who have studied abroad and are willing to return to China. These students are sought after in the market, as they can be excellent cultural bridges between westerners and Chinese. Human resources is definitely an important topic in China, and it is worthwhile to make it a top priority. Employees should be selected according to strict criteria, paying particular attention to those who have worked in SOEs. If you are forced to take over Chinese employees from your SOE partner, try to use an employment, perhaps a part-time employment agency, as a go-between.

As mentioned earlier, continued education should be one of the main components of the human resources system in China. This can start with internal training and end with full-time university programs and bilateral exchanges with partner organizations in other countries. Currently many Taiwanese companies are sending their staff for limited periods of time to China to educate and support the Chinese staff, although at times this is difficult because of visa problems. One trade-off of a good in-house education and training program might be a higher turnover rate of staff. Other companies are always looking for well-trained employees, and many Chinese might seize the opportunity to increase their salary by changing their job frequently. Certainly money is a motivation for many younger Chinese. However, knowing already that high turnover is a possibility, it is easy to educate sufficient staff to have replacements at hand.

And there are other means to curb staff fluctuation, such as social and fringe benefits or incentive payments.

LEISURE TIME

The traditional Chinese society has little in common with Western society regarding leisure time, as the Chinese spend most of their time securing their living. Nevertheless, the Chinese have hobbies, the main one of which is their family. With much enthusiasm, they keep in contact with relatives and attend various social gatherings. Scarce leisure time is often used for family activities at home. Widespread, for example, is an enthusiasm for collecting, such as of coins or stamps—from China or even from Europe and the United States. Even less wealthy people use it as an investment, which can be passed on to their heirs. Favored also are board games such as chess or mahjong.

Many people breed goldfish and singing birds. Men carrying a cage with their bird can often be seen in parks and other public areas. One can also attend singing contests of these birds. The Chinese also love dogs and with the economic changes a new hobby is on the increase: dogs. Forgotten is the Mao decree that marked dogs as unnecessary and bourgeois, as a waste of time. More and more Chinese want to keep dogs. Often it is only a small one, such as a Pekinese. Still it is only a few who can afford this hobby, as the food and especially the registration tax are quite costly. One has to pay 1,000 yuan (US$120) registration fee for a dog, and 500 yuan (US$60) in the year thereafter, whereas the dog by itself is only 170 Yuan (US$20). The fees were as high as 5,000 yuan and 2,000 yuan since 1995, but were lowered in 2003 to encourage people to register.[2] That there are now over 1.4 million dogs in Beijing alone clearly shows the increasing level of wealth. Of great importance in China is mealtime. The Chinese enjoy eating well and often, and three warm meals a day are usual. Thus, not only the dining but also the purchasing and preparation of fresh ingredients takes a lot of time.

Since the 1990s, however, Chinese consumer habits are changing. Increasing disposable income levels and fast-growing choices in consumer products and services change the traditional leisure habits of the Chinese. Especially in the eastern coastal regions and among the younger generation, people are spending more time and money for themselves and their family. Shopping is increasingly becoming a pastime of the Chinese, especially for the younger generations. They are brand-conscious, fashion-oriented, and the number of shopping malls and retailers that are mushrooming in Chinese cities is indicative of the newly discovered consumerism of the Chinese.

The Chinese practice sports, but modestly. In the past, athletics as they are known in the West are rejected, as it is against the Confucian ideal of being modest. Soccer and table tennis, but also basketball, volleyball, and shadowboxing (or tai chi—*taijiquan*), are widespread. One might be astonished by the popularity and enthusiasm for soccer. Many Chinese follow closely the regular matches of the European soccer leagues via satellite TV; in 2003—after acquiring their new superstar David Beckham, Real Madrid made its first trip abroad to China. The international tennis leagues also are watched closely, and the U.S.-born Michael Chang is still a great idol. A victory by Chang is considered by millions of fellow countrymen as a Chinese victory. Basketball is becoming increasingly popular since the end of the 1990s. The transfer of the Chinese superstar Yao Ming to the Houston Rockets in 2003 created a basketball craze in China. The Chinese national sport, however, is morning gymnastics in the public places of towns and cities. In addition, couples often can be seen playing tape recorders and dancing; standard and disco dances are among the most popular.

Golf is one of the latest sports that are becoming increasingly popular in China, especially among businesspeople. Presently, there are almost 200 golf courses in China, and up to 1,000 are under construction. The number of golf courses in Beijing alone grew from 3 to 30 between 2001 and 2004, and the world's largest golf complex opened in 2004 in Shenzhen in Guangdong Province—the Mission Hills Golf Club with 180 holes. It was designed by world leading players such as Greg Norman, Jack Nicklaus, Ernie Els, Vijay Singh, and Annika Soerenstam, and includes a David Leadbetter golf academy.[3]

Holiday or educational trips—very popular in the West—are less common in China, even though the landscapes and cultural points in China are often gorgeous. The average Chinese is quite stationary and travels only for business reasons. Since the end of the 1990s, this attitude is changing very fast—triggered by the increasing living standards and easier access to passports. 24 of China's 31 provinces have made tourism one of their pillar industries. Another growing area is amusement. Major cities in the eastern seaboard are setting up entertainment destinations, including aquariums and marine parks, theme and amusement parks, zoos and wildlife parks. Overseas travel of Chinese increased from 1.5 million travelers in 1993 to more than 12 million in 2002. The World Tourism Organization estimates that in 2002, Chinese spent more than US$16 billion abroad—mainly in Asia. Europe expects a big boost over the coming years: The German airline Lufthansa predicts more than 1 million annual Chinese visitors by 2009, up from 20,000 in 2002.[4] First shops serving specifically Chinese tourists are emerging in Europe, a déjà vu with the Japanese tourists of the 1980s and 1990s.

Hiking is also less common; however, those practicing this sport will inevitably climb the five sacred mountains of China. This has little to do with the Western kind of hiking as steps; rather, the paths lead to a sacred place. Almost unknown are seaside trips. Dark skin, a sign of sportive youth and dynamism in the West, is unseemly in China. Even more—dark skin is a sign of the hardworking peasant, a reason for state-weary Chinese to avoid the sun. Sunbathing Chinese will hardly be seen; often they will walk with umbrellas at the beach—fully dressed. Sun clothes, such as bikinis or shorts, are almost unknown. Chinese women will wear broad-brimmed hats and long gloves as protection against the sun, and skin-whiteners are a growing market in China.

Western forms of socializing and entertainment, such as pubs, restaurants, discotheques, or nightclubs, were deemed improper for a long time. This changed only after the economic opening. For the last several years, karaoke bars and discotheques have flooded the cities. More and more Chinese enjoy Japanese forms of entertainment. The rich and superrich enjoy themselves here. An average evening in a karaoke-bar costs at least 200 yuan (US$25), whereas the monthly income for a worker is about 600 yuan (US$75).

Much cheaper are the get-together parties of the *danweis,* marriage markets, which are known throughout China. Here the government influences the private life of its people. Amusement halls with less serious intentions are the many workers' clubs and cultural palaces, where many concerts, musicals, and Peking operas are conducted. The Chinese passion for gambling is proverbial; gambling is officially forbidden in China, but many still play. Board games are widespread, and legendary is mahjong, where often large amounts are bet. The pragmatic Chinese resort to a ruse: Sunflower seeds are used during the game, and the accounting is done later.

CHINESE FOOD

Chinese cuisine is known worldwide. Exotic menus, an endless parade of spices and sauces, and the imaginative preparation fascinate the West. Diversity is a trademark of Chinese cuisine, even in a single menu.

Chinese cuisine as such doesn't exist: In the East sour dishes are eaten, in the West spicy, sweet in the South, and salty in the North. Each province has its own style. The cuisine of the North, in the Beijing area, is rather rural and simple. Its attractions are Beijing duck and the Mongolian firepot. Northern cooks favor wheat dishes in endless and curious variations. Pastries, dumplings, and filled noodles are the specialty. Garlic is also widely used. During one banquet, large raviolis were served, and the German guest commented that they were nearly as good as in Germany. The piqued Chinese host indicated that Marco Polo exported these noodles from China to Europe. The Sichuan cuisine in the West is spicy—sometimes very spicy! Red, hot chilies are often used; the spicy soybean product *mapo-dofu* is a delicacy.

Best known is the Cantonese cuisine of the South, which has many varieties. Occasionally cats, dogs, and apes are on the menu. The dishes are less spicy than in the North; more importance is paid to the taste of the ingredients themselves. A true and renowned delicacy is the Cantonese *dim sum*. These small dainties, delightfully arranged, often accompany tea: filled dumplings, piquant or with a sweet mousse, spring rolls, rice balls in lotus leaves, or shrimp dumplings. The Chinese cuisine is piquant and exotic, sometimes too exotic for the Western palate. The Ming dynasty (1368–1644) differentiated between eight precious food categories. 'Precious objects from the mountain' were bear claws and swallows' nests, whereas eagles and swans belonged to the "precious poultry." The ape-headed mushroom, wooden ear mushroom, as well as the straw mushroom belonged to "precious spices."

These delicacies are not included in the meals of an average Chinese family; the daily cuisine is much less spectacular. Breakfast, for example, is often a variety of cold and warm dishes, accompanied by *xifan,* a warm, watery rice milk. Piquant side dishes are served: roasted peanuts, fresh vegetables, smoked fish, water glass eggs, fresh tomatoes with sugar, and cucumber slices with garlic paste. Also, fried noodles or steamed dumplings are served. The basic food in China is rice, especially in the North, and it is often served with a variety of delicate dishes, not only for breakfast but also lunch and dinner. "A meal without rice is like a pretty woman with one eye" as Chinese saying goes.

Meals are often finished with soup or vegetables. The Chinese consider the Western habit of serving soup as a starter rather amusing. "A soup served first is only good for a diet" is the Chinese judgment, as this only fills the stomach. The combination of dishes and a well-balanced menu are essential. For example, one dish of seafood, one of vegetables, and one of meat harmonize, especially when the methods of preparation and taste vary. The harmony of the body is based on the harmony of the food. A menu's combinations therefore are in accordance with aspects of health, because the Chinese view food and medicines in a similar way to the body and the soul. It is an old Chinese saying that medicine and nutrition have the same roots.

BANQUETS—SEATING ARRANGEMENTS— TOASTS—DELEGATIONS

The day-to-day things in life quite often can be problematic in intercultural relations. Seemingly trivial things such as a dinner with Chinese guests, a private invitation, or seating arrangements at a banquet have no international, generally practiced rules. One problem is the assumption that normal practices are used everywhere. But the habits and customs of a country—such as those surrounding eating and drinking—can well document its culture.

Eating and Drinking

One of the most favorite Chinese occupations is mutual dining. Dining together means more than eating and being together. The Chinese prefer exquisite and exotic food on a round table as a form of communication and to establish and harmonize relations. Every new relationship is initiated with a dinner invitation and must be nurtured with continuous banquet invitations. Delicious and abundant food is one of the greatest pleasures for the Chinese. Generally nourishment is a central factor of Chinese life.

A relationship must taste good.

Mutual meals—whether they be with the family or as a result of a formal invitation—are an important part of social life in China. Other forms of social gatherings, such as cocktail parties or going to a pub, are much less common than in the West. Instead, and especially in southern China, there are the teahouses. Teahouses are informal establishments and can well be compared to an American music bar or the British pub. The reason an invitation to a banquet is so earnest is shown by its importance in social relationships. Considering all the stress involved in arranging such a banquet, it is even more astonishing how exuberantly the Chinese enjoy these festivities.

Another sign of the communicative character of the banquets is that the Chinese order for the complete group and eat all dishes together. It is very rare to order individual menus and eat them individually, as in the West. During a visit by a Chinese delegation, it might very well be that the Chinese order several dishes as they are used to doing in China. When the first Western restaurants opened in China, one could see, for example, chuppies in Minims ordering several dishes, such as cordon bleu, goulash or sausages, and placing them in the middle of the table—in order to split and eat them in the Chinese manner.

In most cases, all dishes are served at once and placed in the middle of the table. A small revolving round tray (lazy Susan) allows everyone access to all dishes. If you are hosting a banquet, the menu should be selected well in advance. Different countries, different customs—nowhere else is this more true than for Chinese table manners. Those not knowing Chinese manners might well be embarrassed: Slurping, burping, spitting, and smacking, as well as picking one's nose and teeth, are not improper. Burping is quite popular as it shows that the food tasted good. Europeans and Americans think that the Chinese have no manners, eating soup with loud slurps. Chicken meat is not separated from the bones but cut into small pieces. The bones are spat out or thrown onto the table or floor. Even though you might be irritated by these manners, do not look down on them. React with tolerance and keep in mind that even Luther asked, "Why don't you burp and fart, was it not delicious?"

A Chinese Banquet

The Chinese go to bed quite early, and therefore a dinner in the wintertime should start at around 6 P.M. and end at 8 P.M.; in the summer a 7 P.M. start is fine, but the dinner should end at 9 P.M., nevertheless. Westerners consider the way the Chinese say farewell unusual. Without prior indication, a guest states that he or she has to go now. Normally the guest will rise and walk toward the door. This procedure also applies for banquets. When the dessert is finished, everybody departs. For Europeans and Americans, this happens rather suddenly. A proposal from the Western side to go for a final drink at the hotel bar is often rejected by the Chinese. In westernized cities, the Chinese might go to a karaoke bar. Don't be shy—try it! You will gain their respect.

At a banquet, shortly after the guests' arrival, hot tea will be served, except during warm weather, when cold drinks are served. Often snacks such as peanuts or sweets are offered. The host will inform the guests when to sit down at the round table. You should never sit by yourself without invitation. Dishes are often beef, chicken, vegetables, and seafood. The number of dishes is always even, and normally there are at least as many dishes served as guests present. During large banquets, rice is often served last, or as the second-last dish, to avoid the impression that the host was too miserly to serve something other than basic food. One should nevertheless take care when rice comes in small bowls toward the end. It should be left on the table, because the host might lose face if you eat it with appetite: He would assume that you didn't like the specialties, or that the portions were not sufficient. Soup is often served before dessert to ensure that even the smallest space in the stomach is filled. Sometimes, fruit or ice cream follows. Finally tea is served; coffee or digestives are uncommon.

During formal banquets, speeches and toasts are popular. Normally the host will welcome everybody after the dinner has started, and the second-in-rank host will follow later. The etiquette requires that the highest-ranking guest thereafter proposes a toast to the host. Other guests can agree by nodding or smiling politely. If you are the host, you should rise 5 to 10 minutes after the meal has started to present a short speech, honoring the highest-ranking guest. Should there be several tables, you should visit every table and give a short toast there, too. These speeches should please the partners and praise the Chinese culture. Give a toast to the Western-Chinese friendship and talk about how enthusiastic you are to have the opportunity to learn more about China. Express your respect for the Chinese culture and praise the good food.

As host, you have the duty to occasionally toast the guests with a *ganbei*—which literally means "drink out (dry) glass." Every remaining drop means a new glass, resulting in a favored and efficient drinking game. Drinking with the Chinese is a real challenge, and be warned— *moatai* is a 60 percent millet liquor, which works quickly! If you don't drink hard liquor, mention your "alcohol allergy," or you might well hire a "drinking clerk" from upcountry. Shortly before the banquet ends, the oldest or highest-ranking guest should give a short speech, giving thanks for the excellent dinner and the invitation. Some further toasts to the Western-Chinese friendship as well as hints at the counterinvitation should be included. The banquet is finished as soon as the host thanks everybody for coming and presents the last toast. Similar to the start, at this time often hot towels are offered.

The host's farewell to the guest follows strict but polite rituals. Etiquette requires accompanying the guest to the door and even further to the taxi stand, parking place, train station, or bicycle stand. The host gives the guest more face by accompanying him or her in this manner. Similarly after an office meeting, the guests are accompanied to the elevator, or even to the entrance of the building to show respect. For business partners, one should always make sure that the guests reach their home without losing face. If necessary, organize a car to ensure their safe and easy return.

Table Manners

With a polite *qing!* (Please) the host gives the sign to start the meal. He will not say "Bon appétite," as is common in the West; rather he will announce, *manman chi duo chi dian*—"Eat slowly but much." The guest of honor is requested to start first, and the host personally serves food to his guest. The guest of honor normally will be modest; therefore it is the duty of the host to serve him the best pieces. It is impolite to put large helpings on the plate. The most important rule is to make sure there are always sufficient food and beverages on the table. As the host, you serve yourself last.

It is very typical for the polite Chinese to serve others. Thus, it is the duty of the host to ensure that the plates of the guests are always filled. The host will serve those sitting directly next to him. If no special chopsticks are available, he may turn his chopsticks and serve with their unused ends. Guests who are not seated directly next to the host will be served by their neighbors to the right or left. It is quite usual that your neighbor will not ask about your taste but serve you whatever he or she thinks is the best. In case you dislike a course, just leave it on the plate. The same is fine if your plate gets filled repeatedly. You could say you're not hungry anymore, but the Chinese will interpret this as politeness and serve even more. A small portion of food signals much better that your stomach is full and that you are no longer hungry. In general, you should always leave a small portion on your plate. A Chinese host will feel ashamed if no food is left over. Empty bowls and plates are a sign of a stingy host. It is essential to be able to use chopsticks in China. This is one of the few ways to gain the respect of the Chinese. When eating rice, you should lift the bowl and shovel the rice into the mouth.

You should be careful not to leave your chopsticks in an upright position sticking in your rice. This position—celebrated as a death symbol— is regarded as a bad omen. The Chinese want to make sure their deceased are well in the beyond, and thus they offer rice bowls with chopsticks and incense in a vertical position. Usually, Chinese dishes are prepared so that all foods are already cut in bite-sized pieces. Thus knives won't be found on the table. Most dishes will be eaten with the chopsticks; only some soups—such as consommé—as well as dishes such as ice cream will be eaten with a spoon.

There are nevertheless exceptions. The meat of the famous Beijing duck— duck together with sauce—is rolled in very thin pancakes and then eaten with the fingers. Prior to the meal, the fingers are washed in lime water, and during the course wet towels are served. This also applies to fruit and seafood.

It is important to say several times during the evening how excellent the meal is; mentioning this just once at the end of the dinner is insufficient. In China it is common to smoke during the meal. Even the non-smokers will usually not protest this. Among smokers, it is common to take single cigarettes from the package and offer them to one's neighbors. In case the neighbor declines, the package is just thrown or laid in front of that person. In China it is considered impolite not to share a package with all other guests at the table. Therefore, the host should have some packages prearranged on the table, whether he or she is a smoker or not.

It is typical in the face conscious Chinese society to quarrel over who is allowed to pay the bill. This question will not be raised during a banquet but becomes an issue in a restaurant. In general, the bill is paid by one person. Sharing the bill, as is often done in the United States, is not practiced in China. One simply knows when it is his or her turn to pay. One settles the bill in a quiet corner with the waiter, or you may hand the credit card to the waiter when entering the restaurant—to ensure that the other side cannot pick up the bill. Often a discussion will start about who is allowed to pay the bill; one should see such discussion as a game to test which side is more hospitable.

Seating Arrangements

Chinese dining culture is a very typical expression of the Chinese social character, with a strong emphasis on solidarity. The hierarchical thinking

Figure 4.1
Seating Arrangements at Chinese Dinner Tables

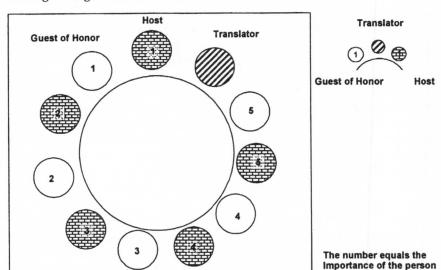

The number equals the
Importance of the person

of the Chinese is, however, apparent in strict regulated seating arrangements. The important role of etiquette in a Western-Chinese business relationship can again be seen in the following German-Chinese example.

Following long, difficult days of negotiations, Mr. Z., as the head of the German delegation, is organizing a dinner for the Chinese partners. He chooses the menu and arranges the seating. At his right, he seats a Chinese engineer with excellent professional qualifications as well as good English knowledge, as he wants to discuss things more with him. Shortly before the banquet, the Chinese translator arrives and changes the seating arrangements.

Mr. Z. has made a basic mistake. He overlooked that according to Chinese rules, the seating arrangement cannot be chosen freely but is very strictly organized. Anyone who does not stick to this principle violates a basic rule of Chinese social conduct: keeping face. The seating arrangements Mr. Z. proposed would result in a loss of face for him, as he has not respected the hierarchical ranking of his guests. Guests seated below their rank would also lose face, thinking they were being treated with disrespect. Likewise, guests seated above their rank, would lose face by taking inappropriate seats, higher than they were allowed to do. By recognizing these mistakes as well as the precarious situation, the translator prevented Mr. Z. and his guests from losing face. Mr. Z. saw in the dinner primarily a good chance to converse with the highly regarded engineer.

According to Chinese rules, he made the big mistake of not heeding Chinese etiquette, but pushing his own preferences and interests. He also would have violated the social structure, which is of utmost importance in traditional, hierarchical China.

The immense importance of banquets can also be seen in their time-consuming preparations. The Chinese often discuss endlessly the hierarchical seating arrangements. In authority-conscious China, the most important guest sits on the right side of the host, facing the door. The view of the door ensures that his back is covered, that is, that he is in the most secure place. In a large group, an alternating pattern is used (e.g., guests and hosts, men and women). Only after the guest of honor has taken his seat are all other guests supposed to sit. In general, an even number of guests is invited.

FENG SHUI

Nothing personifies the spirituality of the Chinese better than the teachings of *feng shui,* that is, godlike powers that control life. Feng shui means "wind" and "water" and is the teaching of creative and destructive powers, the teaching of cosmic energies, which determine if a person gets healthy, happy, and—most important—wealthy. The Chinese have an extreme belief regarding the omnipresent and almighty cosmic powers, called Qi; harmony with all of nature's powers is of utmost importance. Feng shui means that nature's power, hidden between the glass facades and skyscrapers in the form of good and bad demons as well as ghosts, influence our lives. Belief in these powers is so strong that everybody tries to comply with them. One of endless examples is the hotel and apartment building at Repulse Bay in Hong Kong. The building has a huge hole in the middle, which was made just after the shell construction was finished. Thirty apartments were removed because the feng shui master said the house obstructs the way of the mountain dragon to the sea, as he was living behind the building on the mountainside. This could have had serious consequences for the inhabitants of the house.

Feng shui is the art of seeking a location for men, buildings, or events that is enhanced by the surrounding forces. Feng shui was not allowed for a long time in the PRC. The large number of "geomancers," the feng shui experts, is indicative of the immense belief of the Chinese in feng shui, despite a 1979 law prohibiting superstitious practices. Even in the former British crown colony of Hong Kong, in Singapore, Taiwan, and many other Asian countries, feng shui experts play an important role. Everybody planning to build a house in Hong Kong first has to contact a feng shui master, known in the vernacular as "those who ride the dragon." These feng shui masters will evaluate the cosmic location of a house with a geomantic compass, called *luo pan.* The luo pan is a requisite tool in the practice of authentic feng shui, and is made up of 7 to 36 rings encircling a center compass needle. The number of rings and symbols depend on the school and system the luo pan is designed for. The luo pan helps the feng shui practitioner to locate, measure, and predict natural earth energies.

Nobody wants a building with bad feng shui. Those who dare will arouse the anger of the neighbors: Bad feng shui in the neighborhood leads to mishaps and bad sales. And if the feng shui of a location changes, countermeasures must be taken. Recently a new road was constructed leading directly toward a large building of a Chinese company. Because this means bad luck, the company built an enormous dragon on the outside of the building to fight the bad spirits of the road. There are many Chinese examples of buildings that are designed according to feng shui principles, such as the Forbidden Palace in Beijing, the headquarters of the Hong Kong Bank or the Shanghai Bank, and even new communities are planned according to feng shui.

A businessman starting a company is Asia should never neglect the importance of feng shui. Prior to opening an office or contructing a new building, one should consult a feng shui master. Chinese partners and employees who pay attention to feng shui will proceed more actively with the project. On the contrary, bad feng shui is seen as a negative omen. Some even refuse to enter a building with bad feng shui. Businessmen and government officials, for example, may choose an auspicious date and time selected by a feng shui master when opening a new building, or entering a new office. Often it is this spirituality that gives the Middle Kingdom its exoticism. And although the Western world sees feng shui as a mixture of belief and superstition, it has its roots in the Chinese philosophy, especially in the two books Tao Te King and I Ching. The Tao Te King was written by Lao Tzu and describes a way of living that leads to harmony with nature; it is one of the oldest written works of Taoism. The I Ching, the Book of Changes, was written by Kung Fu-tse (Confucius), and it is one of the most important works on Chinese philosophy, culture, and spiritualism. Feng shui is deeply rooted within the I-Ching.

The classification into yin and yang is one of the central ideas of the Chinese Philosophy, and it actually stands for the polarity and dynamic of natural phenomena, such as winter and summer, day and night, cold and heat, humidity and dryness. The cosmos, human society, and the human organism incorporated into the concept of these antipodes, which complement and support each other.

NOTES

1. Thompson, M. "China adopts East-West MBA." *International Herald Tribune*, May 14, 2002; *see also* Steinborn, D. "A Business Degree from China Is The Hottest New Commodity." *Asian Wall Street Journal*, Dec. 1, 2003, p. A8.

2. "Beijing loosens leash on pet dogs." *China Daily*, Sep. 06, 2003.

3. "Mission Hills Golf and Country Club." Website, 2003. http://www.mission-hills.co.hk/, Mar. 17, 2004.

4. Buckmann, R., and Neuman, S. "Cashing In on Chinese Tourists." *Asian Wall Street Journal*, Sep. 30, 2003, p. A1–A4; *see also* Neuman, S. "China Adds EU to Destinations Approved for Tour-Group Visits." *Asian Wall Street Journal*, Oct. 31–Nov. 2, 2003, A3.

The Expatriate Package

This section provides some general information about what you can expect in a contract as an expatriate. The information herein is based on an equal net salary between the home country and the host country—a concept that is increasingly used internationally. No matter whether you are going abroad for the first time or are already an Asia or even a China specialist, the contractual details of your dispatch to a host country will always be one of the more important topics of your stay abroad. And as you have read this much of this book, the topic is certainly of interest to you.

The topic is quite complex, as it touches on many professional and private matters, and almost every company handles them differently. Here are some of the more important issues (the Internet is a source of further information):

Checklist: Foreign Assignment Contract

☑ All details of the net salary should be defined, such as basic salary, variable bonuses, annual leave bonus, savings contributions, stock options, retirement allowance, company pension fund, social contributions, hardship allowance, foreign country allowance, position allowance, and other allowances. After deduction of personal income tax, this should result in a total net salary. Fringe benefits in the home country should be detailed, such as support for housing and mortgages, insurance, and other payments, such as membership dues.

☑ The details of how the net salary is to be calculated should be explained in full. This should include the local cost-of-living offset in the host country (i.e., the international shopping basket), the currency fluctuation off-set, the split between local and foreign currency, and the basis for income tax, inhabitant tax, and other taxes.

☑ In case the company is not taking care of the taxes, either locally or in the home country, the employee has to decide what the best way is for the company and the employee. In principle, inhabitant taxes can be paid in the home country, paid in the host country, or split. In several Euro-pean countries, there are no double taxation laws, which regulate inhab-itant tax payments as well as corporate social benefits. Because of the complexity, it is advisable to consult a tax specialist.

☑ Local fringe benefits in the host country should be detailed as much as possible, which can also be done in side letters. This should include housing; additional housing costs such as water, electricity, telephone, gas, and so on; memberships; travel allowance and regulations; company car and driver; moving costs and details, including special moving sup-port; insurance support; and holiday regulations. Other topics such as language and cultural training in the home or host country, home leave for the expatriate and his or her family, transportation in case of serious illness of the employee or of his or her family, and transportation in case of serious illness of relatives in the home country should also be covered.

These are some of the more important aspects of expatriate contracts, although there are many more. Details depend on the individual company. Therefore, it is advisable to start negotiations with the human resource department as early as possible to address all questions and personal is-sues as fast as possible. In addition, you should allow time to start cultural and language preparation prior to departure, which can then be continued upon arrival.

More and more international companies have changed their expatriate salary system to the home-based net salary approach—for example, many European industries use this approach now. It has several advantages; first and foremost, salaries between the countries become more transpar-ent and comparable. In addition, the expatriate does not have to take care of taxes, currency fluctuations, or changes in the local cost of living; all will be calculated and balanced against the theoretical home-based salary. Therefore, the expatriate is able to have the same net salary available, plus location and hardship bonuses, which depend on the company's willing-ness to honor the stay abroad.

A certain disadvantage of this model is the calculation for all the dif-ferent factors, such as local cost of living. Already for this so-called inter-national shopping basket several different models exist. The same is true for the cost-of-living, housing, and exchange rate fluctuations. Housing, for example, is particularly expensive. A 100- to 150-square-meter apart-ment can cost as much as US$3,000 to $10,000 per month, and a small three-bedroom townhouse in Beijing or Shanghai costs over US$10,000

Figure 5.1
Home-Based Net Salary Approach for Expatriate Salaries

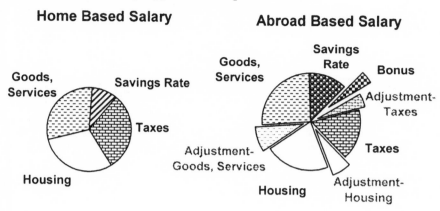

per month. At the other end of the scale, you will probably pay around US$1,800 for a one-bedroom apartment, or US$4,000 for three bedrooms.

One model was developed in the 1980s by Organization Resources Counselors, Inc. (ORC), which also provides standard tables and information for most countries worldwide; other companies, such as Mercer, provide similar data on a regular basis. These models can be used to calculate the total remuneration package, for example to assure that the expatriate has adequate living standards and an income at least comparable to the one in his home country.

Conclusion

Doing business in the new China is a great opportunity and challenge at the same time. Many challenges and upcoming changes, that are unknown today, will play a role in China's business over the next years. Major changes will come from the restructuring of the economic, political, social, and judicial systems in China—a gigantic task in a country with 1.3 billion people.

China's leadership has learned from past mistakes, internally and abroad. Thus, it was able to build a strongly growing economy that attracts the world's largest foreign direct investment and the latest technologies. Thousands of international companies are doing business in China and want to benefit from China's growth. They cover a broad spectrum of industries and company forms. Returning overseas Chinese and expatriates also play an important part in China's growth; about 450,000 westerners and overseas Chinese work in mainland China, an enormous resource that enables China's transition from a planned communist economy to a socialist market economy.

Based on the strong economic data and foreign investment, it is very likely that China's economic success will be a prolonged one. The continued economic growth will help to develop China into the largest economy worldwide, balancing off the negative impact of the hundreds of millions of unemployed farmers and laid-off employees, which are expected over the next decades. Economic setbacks may happen, possibly a banking crisis due to nonperforming loans. China's economic strength, however, seems sound enough to control possible setbacks and prevent an economic meltdown, like Japan is able to prevent since the 1990s. Furthermore, the globalization and growing link of China with other economies will assure that Western nations, including Australia, Canada, Europe, Japan, and the United States, will support and assure the continued and sound development of China. Thus, China is well positioned to become the world's largest economy in the twenty-first century.

For Western companies, it is important to position oneself as a part of this development. To be present in China is not sufficient. It is important to be successful in China, to grow market shares and adapt products, marketing strategies, and services to Chinese consumer needs and tastes, while—at the same time—defending the position against emerging local challengers, such as reverse engineering.

This success in China must also be transformed into a global strategy to compete with the growing number of Chinese exporters on a worldwide base, and especially in Asia. This will be an immense challenge for every Western company in the twenty-first century, as the real impact of China's enormous growth will only be seen within years to come.

Doing business in the new China requires more than technical, financial, marketing, and management know how. It requires the ability to understand the Chinese, their mentality, business style, and ethics, including their Confucian values. It requires understanding of the magnitude of the transition that China is undergoing: The largest economic, social, and political change in the world's history. Only those that are able to understand the concepts, values, and motivations of the Chinese will be able to do successful business in China, and to cooperate or compete with the Chinese.

Good luck for your China business, which means hard work ahead . . .

APPENDIX 1

Recommended Web Sites

Because the Internet changes so rapidly, it is difficult to assure accurate information. Here, nevertheless, are some facts:

- There are about 68 million Internet connections in China, amounting to 12 percent of all worldwide users. The number of Chinese users is probably the fastest growing worldwide, for the end of 2004, 120 million are predicted.[1]
- In 2003, about 300,000 Chinese Web sites were registered with ".cn" and even more with ".com.cn."
- It is predicted that in 2007 Chinese will become the number one Web language.
- Check the latest Web information at: *http://www.cnnic.net.cn*

The fast-growing Internet sector offers immense business opportunities in China, but also obstacles. First and foremost is the language issue. There are many sites about China available in English, but within a few years, there will not be just "the World wide Web," but different cultural and language environments. Just to read Chinese characters special operating systems are needed, such as Chinese Windows. Regarding domain names, not only does China tightly control the .cn sites, but also domain names have already been issued with Chinese characters, which are inaccessible for the West. The Chinese Web authority CNNIC has more than one million applications already and will most probably control the Chinese domain names.

Beside the language issue, there is also the issue of governmental control. The Chinese authorities monitor all activities and recently started the first trial against a human rights activist based on his Web publications.

The Internet is another facet of the Chinese economy that has yet to develop fully. But already many good sites offer plenty of information—from basic facts about China to detailed business data to information on personal matters for the Western expatriate. See the following section for some selected English sites.

BUSINESS AND GENERAL INFORMATION ABOUT CHINA ON THE WEB

One of the most comprehensive portals on China, including business, art, Internet, politics—a good site to start a China search:

http://www.gateway2china.com/

Another portal to more than 700 sites:

http://gochina.about.com/travel/gochina/

Asian resources and business directory:

http://www.accessasia.com/

Administrative search portal for China:

http://www.china-adminet.com/

A good business portal:

http://www.surfchina.com/

Another good business portal and information source:

http://www.ultrachina.com/

General data on the Chinese economy:

http://www.chinavista.com/business/consulting/oldeconomy.html

http://www.uschina.org/china-statistics.html#us-china-trade

Good overall information on economics and China business:

http://www.usembassy-china.org.cn

Information and data on foreign direct investment, including laws:

http://www.chinafdi.org.cn/

Statistical data about the Chinese economy on a monthly basis:

http://www.china.org.cn/e-company/web1.htm

An excellent site with information on news and business in China:

http://www.chinaonline.com/

Comprehensive trade and promotional data of the China Council for the Promotion of Trade and the Chinese chamber of International Commerce:

http://www.ccpit.org/

Ministry of Commerce:

http://english.mofcom.gov.cn/

Ministry of Foreign Trade and Economic Cooperation:

http://www1.moftec.gov.cn/moftec_en/

Chinese chambers of commerce links:

http://www.cee-mail.com/camere/cina.php3

English Web services (China product information for businesspeople):
   http://www.chinapt.com/
Friedl–China-based business and economic information:
   http://www.friedlnet.com/about_us.html
The official state news Web site—comprehensive and good:
   http://www.xinhua.com/
News sites (mixed):
   http://www.cnd.org/
   http://www.china.org.cn/english/
Good overall information on Hong Kong:
   http://www.info.gov.hk/
   http://www.hongkong.org/
Good overall information on Taiwan:
   http://www.gio.gov.tw/
   http://www.roc-taiwan.org/
China National Accreditation Organization (CNAO):
   http://www.cnca.gov.cn/
Legal information and advice:
   http://www.aqsiq.gov.cn/
   http://www.lehmanlaw.com/indexx.htm
   http://www.novexcn.com/index.html
   http://www.qis.net/chinalaw/prclaw10.htm
State General Administration for Quality Supervision and Inspection and
   Quarantine (AQSIQ):
   http://www.aqsiq.gov.cn/

These sites contain the English translations of most of the Chinese investment-related laws. They include, among others, information about numerous joint-venture areas (i.e., advertisement, banking, franchising, retailing, transportation), intellectual property rights laws (TRIPS), labor laws, and wholly foreign-owned enterprises. They are therefore a useful source for actual and future managers doing business in China.

Useful information for expatriates
   http://www.expatriate.com/
   http://www.newcomersclub.com/cn.html
   http://www.expatsinchina.com/
   http://www.expatexchange.com/
   http://www.expatsh.com/ (Shanghai)
   http://www.chinainstitute.org/ (information on art, culture, and history)
   http://www.echinaart.com/ (good site on Chinese art)

NOTE

1. Hutzler, C. "Wide Swath of China Is Surfing the Web. Social, Economic Impact Is Expected as Internet Use Spreads Beyond Big Cities." *Asian Wall Street Journal,* Nov. 18, 2003.

APPENDIX 2

Abbreviations

CCC	China Compulsory Certificate
CCOIC	Chinese Chamber of International Commerce
CCPIT	China Council for the Promotion of International Trade
CJV	contractual joint venture
CNNIC	China Internet Network Information Center
CNCA	Certification and Accreditation Administration
CPC	Communist Party of China
DPP	Democratic Progressive Party
ECIP	European Community Investment Partners
EJV	equity joint venture
FEC	Foreign Exchange Certificate
FESCO	Foreign Enterprise Service Corporation
FIE	Foreign Investment Enterprise
GDP	gross domestic product
GITIC	Guangdong International Trust and Investment Corporation
MII	Ministry of Information Industry
MOFCOM	Ministry of Commerce

MOFTEC	Ministry of Foreign Trade and Economic Cooperation
PPP	Purchasing Power Parity
PRC	People's Republic of China
RMB	Renminbi
SAFE	State Administration for Foreign Exchange
SAIC	State Administration of Industry and Commerce
SETC	State Economic and Trade Commission
SEZ	special economic zone
SOE	state-owned enterprise
TRIPS	Trade-related aspects of intellectual property rights
URL	uniform resource locator
WFOE	wholly foreign owned enterprises
WTO	World Trade Organization

Recommended Readings

Backman, Michael, and Charlotte Butler. *Big in Asia. 25 Strategies for Business Success*. New York: Palgrave Macmillan, 2003.

Batey, Ian. *Asian Branding*. Singapore: Wiley (Asia), 2002.

Blackman, C. *China Business. The Rules of the Game*. Chicago, IL: Independent Publishers Group, 2000.

Brahm, L. J. *China's Century: The Awakening of the Next Economic Powerhouse*. Singapore: Wiley (Asia), 2001.

Fairbank, John King, and Merle Goldman. *China. A New History*. Cambridge, MA: Harvard University Press, 1998.

Hofstede, Geert. *Culture's Consequences: Comparing Values, Behaviors, Institutions and Organizations Across Nations*. 2nd ed. New York: Sage Publications, 2003.

Kottler, P., H. A. Swee, M. L. Siew, and T. T. Chin. *Marketing Management: An Asian Perspective*. 3rd ed. Singapore: Prentice Hall, 2003.

Nolan, Peter. *China and the Global Economy*. Basinstoke, England: Palgrave, 2001.

———. *China and the Global Business Revolution*. Basinstoke, England: Palgrave, 2001.

Ogden, S. *China's Unresolved Issues: Politics, Development, Culture*. 2nd ed. Englewood Cliffs, NJ: Prentice Hall, 1992.

Pan, Lynn, ed. *The Encyclopedia of the Chinese Overseas*. 2nd ed. Singapore: Archipelogo Press, 2000.

Panitchpakdi, Supachai, and Mark L. Clifford. *China and the WTO: Changing China, Changing World Trade*. New York: Wiley, 2002.

Richter, F.-J., ed. *The Dragon Millennium: Chinese Business in the Coming World Economy*. Westport, CT: Quorum, 2000.

Schütte, Hellmut, and Deanna Ciarlante. *Consumer Behavior in Asia*. New York: New York University Press, 1998.

Seagrave, S. *Lords of the Rim: The Invisible Empire of the Oversea Chinese*. New York: Putnam, 1995.

Sheef, David. *China Dawn: The Story of a Technology and Business Revolution*. New York: HarperBusiness, 2002.

Story, Jonathan. *China: the race to market*. London, England: Prentice Hall, 2003.

Synovate. *Asia Pacific Market Handbook 2003*. 2nd ed. Hong Kong: Synovate, 2003.

Tang, Jie, and Anthony Ward. *The Changing Face of Chinese Management*. London: Routledge, 2003.

Terrill, Ross. *The New Chinese Empire and what it means for the United States*. New York: Basic Books, 2003.

Vanhonacker, Wilfried R. "A Better Way to Crack China." *Harvard Business Review*, July–August 2000.

Wong, Y. H., and Thomas K. P. Leung. *Guanxi: Relationship Marketing in a Chinese Context*. New York: International Business Press, 2001.

Zinzius, Birgit. *China Entdecken*. Munich, Germany: Beck Verlag, 1999.

———. *China Business*. Berlin, Germany: Springer Verlag, 2000.

———. *Sino-America: Stereotype and Reality. History, Present, and Future of the Chinese in America*. New York: Peter Lang, 2004.

Index

A. T. Kearney, 36
Accenture, 36
accounting, 114, 136; CFO, 97, 114;
    controlling, 63, 136, 160–63;
    expenses, 109; favor account, 183;
    financial control mechanisms, 163;
    staff, 108, 114, 136
Acer (BenQ), 177
addressing, 50–54
Advanced Semiconductor
    Manufacturing, 31
advertising, 174–76; agencies, 168;
    Internet, 174, 176; market size, 166;
    television, 14, 167; urban, 174
agriculture, 2, 20, 153–54, 198
Airbus Industries, 35
alcohol, 206
Allianz, 36
American International Group, 36
America Online, 28
Ancai TV Tubes, 177
Anheuser-Busch, share in Tsingtao, 38
Anhui, 91, 180
anti-piracy laws, 155
Art of War, The (Sunzi), 179
Asia: body language, 61–64;
    education, 198; GMO food, 33;
    harmony, 181; marketing, 164–66,
    169; negotiations, 78; overseas
    Chinese, 38, 116–17; population, 4,
    38; telecommunication, 9
Asian crisis, 2–5, 87–88, 131
auditing, 97, 163
Australia, 40, 115, 118, 218; Chinese
    investments in, 40
automobile industry, 12–13, 35, 89,
    146, 148; overcapacity, 39
ayi, 181

B2B, B2C-commerce, 23
Bain & Company, 36
bamboolike character, 105
banking system, 36; crisis, 87, 96, 129,
    130, 217; reform, 36, 131
Bank of China, 36, 130–31, 161
banks, 36–37, 129–32; Bank of China,
    36, 130–31, 161; Bank of Shanghai,
    36; Central Bank, 3, 130, 132; China
    Banking Regulatory Commission,
    36, 131; China Construction Bank,
    36, 130–31; China Development
    Bank, 130; Deutsche Bank, 36, 131;
    Dresdner Bank, 36, 131; foreign
    access, 36, 131–32; HSBC, 36, 131;

restructuring of, 129–32; state
banks, 131
banquet, 57, 202–8; alcohol, 206;
delegation, 205; eating and
drinking, 204–7; seating
arrangements, 207; table manners,
206
baofahu, 181
baomu, 181
beer industry, 12, 38–40, 177, 192
Beida University, 184
Beijing: as government of a single
China, 87; Beida university, 184;
high-speed train connection, 35;
real estate market, 161, 214; rent,
214
Beijing Centergate Technologies, 29
BenQ, 177
Best Buy, 38
biotechnology, 27, 32–33
Blenz, 171
BMW, 161, 165, 173, 184
body language, 61–62
Boots, 169, 170
Boston Consulting Group, 36
Boxer Rebellion, 192
brain drain, 31, 116
branding, 165, 167–68, 173; co-
branding, 131; Mercedes-Benz, 173;
Oracle, 173; Siemens, 173
brands, 12–14, 38, 160, 164, 168–69,
176–77; brand war, 12; Chinese,
12–13, 176–77; cultural values, 168;
globalization, 164; international, 38,
160, 164–65, 168–69; legal
protection, 156; loyalty, 168; luxury,
13, 168; market shares, 176;
positioning, 167; ranking, 177
BrandsMart, 38
break-even point, 86, 99
bribe, 24, 27, 63, 83, 112, 128, 161–63,
184
British crown colony, 40, 49, 209. *See
also* Hong Kong
BSW Household Appliances, 12
bureaucracy, 19, 66, 71, 101, 104, 144
Bush, George, 62; and Deng Xiaoping,
62

Bush, George W., 87; Taiwan policy,
87
business cards, 48, 59
business culture, 113, 143
business relations, 66, 71–72, 94, 159,
183

Caihong Electronic Group, 12
calendar, 111
call centers, 37, 39, 148
Canada, 218
Canon, 28
Carrefour, 170
case studies, 142–46, 170–71;
Carrefour, 170; Kodak, 142;
Starbucks, 171; Volkswagen, 146
cash-on-delivery systems, 10
Cathay Pacific, 35
Central Bank, 3, 130, 132
chain stores, 170
change process, 17; political, 19, 185
Changhong (Sichuan Changhong
Electronic), 12, 176
Charoen Pokphand (CP) Group, 116,
170
checklist: acquisitions, 90; financial
control mechanism, 163; foreign
assignments, 213; quality
management, 150; site selection,
90
chemical industry, 1, 15, 27, 38, 89
Chengdu, 31, 161
Chen Shui-bian, 87
Chiang Kai-shek, 61, 193
China Banking Regulatory
Commission, 36, 131
China Compulsory Certificate (CCC),
13, 151
China Construction Bank, 36, 130,
131
China Development Bank, 130
China Europe International Business
School (CEIBS), 198
China Life Insurance, 131, 162
China Mobile Communications, 30
China Netcom, 30
China Telecom, 30
China Unicom, 30

Chinese Americans, 31, 37–38, 115–18;
    organizations, 117
Chinese capitalism, 185
Chinese cuisine, 202–3
Chinese culture and mentality, 7, 39,
    42–48, 50, 113–14, 119–26;
    Chineseness, 197; Confucianism,
    42–44; face value, 43–44, 121–26;
    family values, 7, 119; guanxi, 39,
    63–64, 159, 161, 182–84, 199;
    history, 189–96; integration in, 186;
    knowledge and respect, 205;
    language, 58, 173, 186; loyalty, 113,
    161–63; networking, 7, 39, 57, 163,
    182–84; presents, 63–64, 183;
    superiority, 13, 185; tourism, 201;
    trustworthiness, 78, 113; wulun,
    42–44, 121–22
Chinese emigration, 37–38, 115–16
Chinese foreign investments, 40–41
Chinese Me generation, 119
Chinese tourism, 201
Chongqing, 34, 161–62
Christmas strategy, 76–77
chuppies, 119, 204
CIMC Freight Containers, 177
Cisco, 157
Citigroup, 36
Clinton, Bill, 9, 63
Coca-Cola, 168, 173–76; advertising,
    168, 174; brand awareness, 176;
    naming, 173, 176
code of conduct, 163
Commerce Bank, 131
communication, 44–48, 55–74;
    intercultural communication, 45,
    50, 150, 199
Communism, 16–17, 194; and
    economic reform, 88, 100; Cultural
    Revolution, 118, 194–95, 198;
    Hundred Flowers Movement, 194
Communist Era (1949–1965), 118
Communist Party of China (CPC), 16,
    194; restructuring, 19, 88, 152
company names, 172
competition, 12, 28, 178; local, 146,
    165
conformity, 46, 68, 169, 180

confrontation, avoidance of, 47, 126
Confucianism, 42–44, 169; and
    patriarchy, 11; economic growth
    and, 43; five relations of (wulun),
    42–44, 121–22; harmony, 50, 169;
    Neo-Confucianism, 197; social
    interactions, 190; unequal
    relationships, 42; values, 50, 128
Confucius (Kongfuzi), 42
construction industry, 15
consumer behavior, 160, 200–202
consumer market, 7–9, 12–14, 20, 28,
    128, 164–65, 178
contacts, 38, 94, 106, 182, 184
contracts, 72, 77, 102–3, 106, 110, 113,
    159, 190, 214; car-roof, 77
contractual joint venture (CJV), 26–27,
    102–3, 137
conversation, 44–46, 57;
    characteristics of, 68; keqi hua, 68
corruption, 24, 27, 63, 83, 112, 128,
    161–63, 184
COSCO Shipping Company, 177
counterfeiting, 29, 155–57, 178;
    Chinese attitude to, 155;
    Legislation (TRIPS), 155–57; rapid
    prototypers, 155; software, 29. See
    also intellectual property
credit cards, 10
crisis. See Asian crisis
criticism, 120–28, 133, 139–40, 144
cross-cultural. See intercultural
Cultural Revolution, 118, 194–95, 198
currency valuation, 131, 133
customer relationship management
    (CRM), 143, 145–46, 171
customer satisfaction, 143, 149

dakuan, 181
Dalian, 32, 37, 170; Dasheng Group,
    170
Dante Coffee, 171
danwei, 17–18, 107–9, 120, 124, 180,
    social functions of, 17, 107, 109
database marketing, 145–47, 171
decentralization, 18
Deloitte, 36
Deng Xiaoping, 19, 195–98; and

George Bush, 62; "Chinese hands milk foreign cows!," 100; educational reforms, 198; foreign investment, 100; political reforms, 163, 195; "To get rich is glorious," 1, 160; trip to the south (Shenzhen, 1992), 2, 163

Deutsche Bank, 36, 131

Deutsche Post, 34–35

devaluation, 133

DHL, 34–35

direct marketing, 147

discussion styles, 68–71

distribution, 179. *See also* logistics

Dongfeng Automobile Group, 12, 22

double taxation, 115, 158, 214

Dresdner Bank, 36, 131

drinking, 186, 204–6

due diligence, 97, 104, 130, 163

eating, 204

e-commerce, 9, 23, 146

economic growth, 1–7, 14, 16, 20, 22, 27, 37, 42, 88, 119, 128, 153, 196, 217

economic reform, 19, 24, 99, 100, 110, 129, 152, 194–95

education, 142, 197–99; Beida, 184; CEIBS, 198; compulsory, 198; e-learning, 143; knowledge management, 143; MBA studies, 198–99; reforms, 198

e-learning, 143

electronic industry, 1, 6, 12, 27, 37, 39, 89

employee, 106–10; education, 142; loyalty, 113, 120, 163; motivation, 120, 124–25; selection, 106; types, 112

enterprise resource planning (ERP) software, 145–46

equity joint venture (EJV), 26–27, 102–3, 137

Erdos Textiles, 12, 177

ethical standards, 128–29, 182, 185, 197, 218

Europe: automotive industry, 12, 22, 33–35, 165, 172; banking industry, 36–37; economic growth, 4; foreign direct investments, 21–24, 36–38, 89, 98, 176; overseas Chinese, 117; telecommunication industry, 9; quality control (QC) systems, 151

European Community Investment Partners, 132

expatriates, 115, 213; consulting, 215; employment forms, 115; housing cost, 214; integration, 114; permits, 115; requirements, 114; salary concepts, 213

expectations, 92–93, 97–99, 101, 114, 121–23, 159

export, 24, 37–39, 132–33; surplus, 6, 133

face (lian, mianzi), 43, 47, 121–26; concept of, 124; loss of (diu mianzi), 122

Falun Gong, 10, 49

family, 37, 42–45, 57, 63, 76–77, 107, 114, 120–24, 128, 161, 183; values, 7, 37, 169

feasibility study, 97, 104, 130

Federal Express, 35

feng shui, 39, 189, 209–10

financing models, 133

First Automobile Works (FAW), 177

Forbidden Palace, 210

Ford, 165

foreign currency, 24, 89, 92, 97, 129–33, 213–14

foreign direct investment (FDI), 1–7, 20, 24–29, 38, 89, 132, 142, 154, 171; Chinese selection of, 89; company forms, 102–3; encouraged, 89; favored, 101; forbidden, 89; Hong Kong, 24, 38, 116; laws, 16, 103, 154; letter of intent, 106; Taiwanese, 31, 38; Western, 24–27, 29, 142, 171

Foreign Enterprise Service Corporation (FESCO), 107

Foreign Investment Enterprise (FIE);

guidelines, 154; legal forms, 102;
number of, 1
foreign reserves, 130
foreign trade, 14, 37–39, 132–33;
growth, 14; with the United States,
21; volume, 6; world share, 4
Four Cardinal Principles, 198
franchising, 27
free-market economy, 16, 194
fried tofu buildings, 162
Fudan University, 198
furniture industry, 133, 137, 179

Gang of Four, 195, 198
Gansu, 90
GAP, 21
General Electric, 40, 144
General Motors, 22, 133, 149, 171, 178
genetically modified organism
(GMO), 33; patents, 33
geomantic, 209
Germany: automobile industry, 35;
foreign investments, 89
gestures, 61–62
gift giving (shou huilu), 63
gifts, 63–65, 183–84
Giordano, 40
globalization, 48, 66, 164, 168, 218
Golf, 201
Gome Group, 170
Grace Semiconductor Manufacturing,
31
Great Cultural Revolution Era
(1966–1976), 118
greetings, 56–57
gross domestic product (GDP), 2, 5, 15,
87, 131; per-capita income, 14, 86
Guangdong, 12, 13, 95, 107, 166, 175,
176, 180, 201
Guangdong MD Holdings, 12
Guanghua School of Management,
198
Guangxi, 90, 91
Guangzhou, per capita income, 2
guanxi, 39, 159, 161, 182–84, 199;
network, 182–83
Guizhou, 90, 91

Haier, 12, 30, 38, 40, 165, 177–78; in
Camden, South Carolina, 38; in
New York, 40; investment in the
United States, 38–40; Zhang
Ruimin, 40
Han dynasty (206 B.C. to A.D. 220), 42,
122
Hangzhou, 161
harmony, 43, 50, 169, 181–82, 203,
209–10
Harvard Business School, 142
Henan, 91
Henkel, 12
hierarchy, 66, 122
high-speed train, 35
hinterland: development programs, 6;
income disparity, 2, 154; invest-
ment in, 31; logistic problems, 34
history, 189–96
hobbies, 186, 200
holidays, 111–12
Home Depot, 38
Honda, 21–22, 36, 157
Hong Kong, 192–93; as business hub,
95, 173, 192; British crown colony,
40, 49, 209; foreign direct investment, 24, 38, 116; free-trade port,
192; history, 191–93; overseas
Chinese, 24; return to the
mainland, 192–93
Hong Kong University of
Management, 198
Hongtashan (Yuxi Cigarette Factory),
13, 177
HSBC, 36, 131
Hua Guofeng, 195
Hubei, 91, 180
Hu Jintao, 19, 116
hukou system, 107
human resources, 102, 108, 150, 199
Hundred Flowers Movement, 194

IBM, 29, 172, 178
I Ching (Book of Changes), 210
import duties, 20, 31, 158
income: annual, 160; per capita, 7, 14,
86

individualism, 46, 68, 124, 127–28,
    169, 180–81, 190, 197
Indonesia, 37, 39, 41, 116, 117;
    overseas Chinese, 116
information technology (IT), 23, 27,
    143–44; CRM, 143, 145–46, 171; as
    economic motor, 23; ERP, 138, 144;
    percent of GDP, 28
infrastructure, 35
Intel, 30
intellectual property, 152–55, 178;
    TRIPS, 155
intercultural communication, 46,
    112–14, 118–19, 121–28, 150, 186
Internet, 8–11, 23–24; advertising, 174,
    176; connections, 23; as economic
    engine, 23; e-learning, 143;
    governmental control, 10; growth,
    8, 143; portals, 28, 171; service
    provider, 4, 9, 10, 20, 28–29, 34, 133,
    166
investment, 49; categories, 89; forms,
    102, 154; in SOEs, 96; in the
    hinterland, 30; laws, 102, 154; risks,
    97, 130; strategies, 84. See also
    foreign direct investment
investments, 1–7, 20, 24–29, 89, 132,
    142, 154, 171; western provinces, 15
ISO certification, 147–51

Japan: automotive industry, 35;
    Chinese emigration to, 37; double
    taxation agreement, 115; foreign
    direct investment, 24, 89; kaizen,
    150; overseas Chinese, 116;
    recession, 21; telecommunications
    industry, 9; textile industry, 21
Japanese-Chinese War, 197
Jiang Qing, 195
Jiangsu, 180
Jiangsu Chunlan Refrigerating
    Equipment, 12
Jiang Zemin, 100, 105
Jing Dong Fang, 28
Jitong Communications, 30
joint venture, 101–2; contractual joint
    venture (CJV), 26–27, 102–3, 137;

equity joint venture (EJV), 26–27,
    102–3, 137; guidance catalogue,
    154; laws, 101; Sino-foreign
    investment law, 16

kaihui, 67
kaizen, 21, 147
karaoke, 202, 205
Kentucky Fried Chicken, 27, 177
keqi hua, 68
KingSoft, 29
knowledge management, 143
knowledge transfer, 6, 24, 41, 66, 71,
    85, 88–89
Kodak, 28, 141–43, 176; education of
    employees, 142; Express shops,
    142; market share, 142
Kohl, Helmut, 52
kolkhoz, 193
Konka Electronic Group, 12
Korea. See South Korea
Kunming Cigarette Factory, 13
Kuomintang Party, 193

labor cost, 108
labor market, 106
Lacoste, 157
Language, 50–51, 58–60; addressing,
    50–51, 54; body, 61–62; business
    cards, 59; company names, 172;
    conversation, 54–62, 68–71; pinyin,
    61; simplified Chinese, 59; titles,
    55; traditional Chinese, 59;
    translation mistakes, 177;
    translation of names, 165–67,
    172–73; Wade-Giles, 61
Lao Tzu, 210
laws: CCC certificate, 151;
    franchising, 27; intellectual
    property rights, 155; joint venture
    (CJV, EJV), 26–27, 99–103; patent,
    155; ROs, 101; Sino-foreign
    investment law, 16; trade, 153;
    trademark protection, 156; TRIPS,
    152, 155–57, 178; WFOEs, 101
Lawson, 170
Lee Kuan Yew, 42

Legend. *See* Lenovo
Lego, 157
leisure activities, 179, 200–202
Lenovo (Legend Group), 13, 28, 38, 165, 177
letter of intent, 104
lian, 43, 124, 169, 189
Liaoning, 180
Liebherr (Libohaier), 40, 172. *See also* Haier
Li Ka-shing, 116
Li Peng, 196
logistics, 14, 21, 34, 135–38, 146, 148, 151, 178–80
Lowe's, 38
loyalty, 113, 161–63; company, 120, 161–63; customer, 149
Lufthansa, 201
Luis Vuitton, 161
lunar year, 111
luo pan, 209

Macao, 192
macroeconomy, 89, 91, 100, 135
Made in China, 12, 21–22, 39
Made in Taiwan, 148
Maglev, 35
Mahatir Mohamad, 41
Malaysia, 41; Chinese exports to, 41; overseas Chinese in, 37, 116
managers, 106; expatriates, 21, 114, 116, 181, 199, 217; new generation, 118; old guard, 119; overseas, 115
Mandarin (putonghua), 58, 173, 186
Maoism, 50
Mao look, 194
Mao Zedong, 193–94
marketing, 164, 165, 177
market research, 166
market segmentation, 7
materialism, 119, 181
Matsushita, 178
McDonald's, 27, 168, 178
McKinsey, 36
media, 14, 89, 167, 174–76
mediation, 159

megacities, 8, 170, 174, 179, 196
Mercedes-Benz, 161, 165, 167, 173, 181; branding, 173
Metro, 170
mianzi, 43, 124, 169, 189
Microsoft, 28–29, 178
Ming dynasty (1368–1644), 203
Ministry of Foreign Trade and Economic Cooperation (MOFTEC), 101, 103
Minolta, 28
mission and vision, 140–41
mobile phone market, 9–11, 13, 23, 30, 37, 118, 178–79; penetration, 9, 30; standards, 30
monetary reform, 19, 58, 129, 131–33; devaluation, 58, 133
moral standards, 46, 123–28
motivation of employees, 120, 124–25
Motorola, 22, 30, 143, 178; e-learning, 143; Six Sigma, 143
Munich Re, 36

names and salutations, 50–54
naming of companies, 172
Nanjing, 33, 162, 192
nanotechnology, 33–34; patents, 34
NASDAQ, 9
NCPC Orchid Pharmaceuticals, 12
negotiations, 45–48, 66–77, 92–95, 186, 190, 208, 214; strategies, 76–78
Neo-Confucianism, 197
nepotism, 66, 112, 182
Nestle, 171, 176
NetEase, 28
networking, 7, 39, 57, 163, 182–84
New China, 196
new generation, 119
newly rich, 181
New York, 40, 131, 164
Nielsen/NetRatings, 167
Ningbo, 30, 178
Ningxia, 90
Nissan, 21, 165
Nokia, 30, 178
non-performing loans, 36, 87, 96, 129–31, 217

Office Depot, 38
old guard, 119
Olympic Games 2008, 36, 161, 164, 196
Olympus, 28
one-child policy, 28, 49, 53, 109
One Country, Two Systems, 193
Opium Wars, 123, 191, 193
Oracle, 29, 145, 173; naming, 173
overcapacity in manufacturing, 39
overseas Chinese, 37, 48–49, 115–18; Asian destinations, 116; associations, 117; foreign direct investment, 24; networks, 49, 117, 118, 152, 196; returnees, 199; in the United States, 116–18

partner: finding a, 92; selecting a, 95
patriarchy, 42, 43; in business, 120
Pearl River Pianos, 177
Peoplesoft, 146
People's Republic of China, 16, 49, 59, 61, 209; foundation, 193
Pepsi, 176; market share, 176
per capita income, 14, 86, 135
PetroChina, 41
pharmaceutical industry, 1, 12, 14–15, 89, 145, 150, 174, 177
Philippines: overseas Chinese, 24
Ping An Insurance, 36
pinyin, 60, 193
piracy, 29, 155–57, 178; laws, 155–56; software, 29; toys, 155
Pizza Hut, 27
planned economy, 16, 18–19, 49, 87, 100, 106, 163, 193
Politburo, 17, 19, 195
political reforms, 19, 217
population, 28, 96; changing demographics, 28; migrant workers, 18, 87; one-child family, 28, 96, 109
Portugal, 192
positioning, 165, 167–69, 177
presents, 63–64, 183–84
President Chain, 170
price war, 22, 148, 165
Procter & Gamble, 12

protocol, 75
purchasing power parity, 7, 14, 28, 83, 90, 160
putonghua (Mandarin), 58, 173

Qing dynasty (1644–1911), 118, 191, 193
Quality Management, 151
Quality Standards, 13, 147–51; CCC mark, 151; ISO, 147–51; Six Sigma, 142–43

rapid prototypers, 155
real estate market, 27, 32, 89, 161
recruitment, 106
Red Guards, 194
reengineering, 150
reform, 217; banking, 36–37, 131; economic, 17–18, 194; educational, 198; financial, 19, 36–37, 129; political, 17–19, 185, 193, 217; social, 128, 196; social security network, 18
regional differences, 105
relationships, 7–8, 47, 122; business, 66, 71–72, 94, 159, 183; social, 8, 204
religions, 169
renminbi (RMB) yuan, 131–32, 158, 174
representative office, 25, 27, 71, 102, 154
Republican Era (1911–1948), 118
retail industry, 38, 170
reverse brain drain, 116
reverse engineering, 150, 218
RichWin, 29
risks of China business, 16, 41, 83, 116, 129, 141, 178; avoidance of, 84, 97, 130; feasibility study, 104, 135; financial, 97, 130; management mistakes, 124, 145; political, 87; in SOE's, 87
Roche, 171
Rolex, 161
Rolls Royce, 167, 181
romanization, 61
Rongshida, 12
Russia, 163

safety standards, 13, 142, 150–52
salaries, 108–9, 117, 214–15
salutations, 51–54
SAP, 145
SARS, 3, 63
Schröder, Gerhard, 63
seating arrangements, 203, 208–9
semiconductor industry, 30, 31;
    American investment, 30;
    Taiwanese investment, 31
Semiconductor Manufacturing
    International, 31
seniority, 66–67; in marketing, 8
7–Eleven, 170
Shaanxi, 90, 199
Shandong, 95, 180
Shanghai, 37, 196, 214; high-speed
    train connection, 35; luxury
    markets, 40; per capita income, 2;
    real estate, 40; rent, 214
Shanghai Auto Industries, 146
Shanghai Automobile Group, 12
Shanghai Bailian Group, 170
Shanghai Bao Steel, 177
Shanghai Pudong Development Bank,
    36
Shanghai Zhenhua, 177
Shenzhen, 2, 36, 95, 161–62, 201
Shenzhen Development Bank, 36
Sichuan, 12, 34, 90–91, 95, 109, 202
Siemens, 30, 35, 40, 173, 178;
    branding, 173
Sina.com, 9, 28
Singapore, 39, 42–43, 59, 117, 209;
    Chinese emigration to, 37; foreign
    direct investment, 24, 38, 116;
    Lee Kuan Yew, 42; overseas
    Chinese, 116; traditional characters,
    59
Sino-foreign investment law, 16
Sinotrans, 35
site selection, 92, 95
Six Sigma, 139, 142–43, 147
socialist market economy, 17, 19, 42,
    49, 87–88, 98, 118, 129, 139, 165,
    195, 217
social market economy, 19
social reform, 196

Social Reform Era (1977–present),
    118
social security network, 107;
    restructuring of, 18, 19
social values, 127–29
software piracy, 29
Sohu.com, 9, 10, 28
Sony, 28, 165, 178
South Korea, 4, 20; foreign direct
    investment, 24; overseas Chinese,
    116
special economic zone (SEZ), 90, 95
standardization, 151
Starbucks, 27, 171; herbal tea, 171;
    market penetration, 171
State Administration for Foreign
    Exchange (SAFE), 132
State Development Bank. See China
    Development Bank
State Development Planning
    Commission (SDPC), 2, 29, 101, 104
State Economic and Trade
    Commission (SETC), 101, 223
state-owned enterprise (SOE), 17, 20,
    25, 37, 87, 101, 107, 129, 142, 148,
    167, 197; debt, 130; employees, 199;
    revitalization, 148; risks, 87
Stone Group, 29
strategies, 83–85; negotiation, 76–78
Sun Yat-sen, 193
Sunzi, 179
superrich, 7, 8, 202
supply chain management (SCM), 14,
    21, 34, 91, 145, 164, 179–80

table manners, 204
tai chi, 201
Tai Ji Group, 12
Taiwan, 4, 37, 87; brain drain, 32;
    investment in mainland, 24, 31, 38;
    Made in Taiwan, 148; overseas
    Chinese, 116; relations with the
    United States, 87; renegade
    province, 30; semiconductor
    industry, 30–31; students in the
    United States, 116; traditional
    characters, 59; workers in mainland
    China, 32

Taiwan Semiconductor
  Manufacturing Co. (TSMC), 31
TaKaRa, 32
Taoism, 210
Target, 38
tax regulations, 157–58, 213–14;
  corporate income, 157; double
  taxation, 115, 158, 214; exemptions,
  158; VAT, 158
TCL International Holdings, 12, 30,
  177
Technischer Überwachungsverein
  (TÜV), 151
technology drain, 32
technology transfer, 6, 24, 41, 66, 71,
  85, 88–89
telecommunications industry, 1, 9,
  20–22, 30, 37–39, 41, 118, 151, 165,
  178
textile industry, 1, 12, 15, 21, 27, 37,
  89, 133, 177
Thailand: Chinese exports to, 41;
  overseas Chinese in, 116
Thompson, 175, 177, 210
Three Gorges Dam, 34
Thyssen, 35
Tiananmen Square Massacre, 196
Tianjin, 33, 95, 157, 192
titles, 48, 50–54
Tong Ren Tang Pharmaceuticals, 12,
  177
tourism industry, 64, 154, 201
township and village enterprises, 18
toy industry, 1, 37, 150, 155
Toyota, 21, 133, 157, 165, 178
trade: deficit, 6, 133; dispute with the
  United States, 153; laws, 153
trademark protection, 155–56
Trade related intellectual property
  rights (TRIPS), 155–57
translation: mistakes, 177, 208; names,
  165–67, 172–73
translator, 60; selection of, 76
transportation industry. See logistics
Treaties, 192
Tsingtao, 192
Tsingtao Brewery, 12, 38, 40, 165, 177,
  192

unemployment, 3–4, 18–20, 83, 87,
  107, 109, 133, 217
unequal relationships, 42
Uniqlo, 21
United Microelectronics Corporation
  (UMC), 31
United Parcel Service, 35
United States: automobile industry,
  35, 133, 149, 171, 178; double
  taxation agreement, 115; foreign
  direct investment, 24, 29–30, 38, 89;
  foreign trade, 20–21; loss of jobs,
  133; overseas Chinese, 38, 116–18;
  returning overseas students, 117;
  telecommunications industry, 9;
  trade deficit, 6, 133
urbanization, 2, 18, 128

value-added marketing, 171
value-added tax, 158
ventures, 101
Vietnam, 37, 39, 41
Volkswagen, 12, 22; branding, 165;
  CRM, 147; financing models, 133
Volvo, 165

Wade-Giles system, 61
Wal-Mart, 38, 170
Wangxia, 192
Wangxiang Automotive Parts, 177
Western: advertising, 161; capitalism,
  194; company names, 172; cultural
  values, 114, 169; investments, 6–7,
  24–27, 29, 89, 142, 154;
  management, 97, 114–17, 121,
  138–40; management problems,
  116–17; mentality and values,
  113–14, 120, 138, 169
wholly foreign-owned enterprises
  (WFOE), 24–25, 101–3, 138, 154;
  preferred investment form, 27
World Bank, 2–4, 78, 83
World Trade Organization (WTO), 15,
  19–22, 30–34, 89, 151–57, 164;
  admission to, 19, 21, 29, 151; non-
  compliance, 153
Wu Jichuan, 28
wulun, 42, 44, 121

Xiamen, 142, 162

Yahoo!, 9, 28, 116
Yamaha, 157
Yanjing Brewery, Beijing, 12–13, 39, 40, 177

Yao Ming, 39, 40, 201
Yunnan, 90–91

Zhang Ruimin, 40
Zheijiang, 180
Zhu Rongji, 3

About the Author

DR. BIRGIT ZINZIUS is a native German and has lived and worked many years in Asia, Europe, and the United States. She is founder and managing director of the *Seminar for Intercultural Communication and International Management,* an international consulting company on business, economics, human resources, management, and politics in China, Europe, and the United States. She received her doctorate in American Studies, and has published many books: *Chinese America: Stereotype and Reality* (2004), *China Business* (2000), *China Entdecken* (1999), *Das Kleine China-Lexikon* (1999), *Der Schlüssel zum Chinesischen Markt* (1996), and *Sino-Amerika* (1996). Dr. Zinzius is currently living in Jakarta, Indonesia.